Pan Breakthrough Books

Pan Breakthrough Books open the door to successful self-education. The series provides essential knowledge using the most modern self-study techniques.

Expert authors have produced clear explanatory texts on business subjects to meet the particular needs of people at work and of those studying for relevant examinations.

A highly effective learning pattern, enabling readers to measure progress step by step, has been devised for Breakthrough books by the National Extension College, Britain's leading specialists in home study.

Geoffrey Knott is principal lecturer in Accounting, and head of the Accountancy Division, at Norwich City College of Further and Higher Education. On the examiners' panel of the Chartered Association of Certified Accountants and the Association of Accounting Technicians, he has been closely connected with the Business Education Council as a member of the B2 Finance Board, of working parties for development of accounting modules for BTEC courses, and of validation committees for BTEC Higher National and Post Experience accounting courses. He acts as a consultant management accountant to businesses in East Anglia.

Pan Breakthrough Books

Other books in the series

Pan Breakthrough Books

Practical Cost and Management Accounting

A Fresh Approach

Geoffrey Knott

A Pan Original
Pan Books London and Sydney

If you wish to study the subject matter of this book in more
depth, write to the National Extension College, 18
Brooklands Avenue, Cambridge, CB2 2HN, for a free copy
of the Breakthrough Business Courses leaflet. This gives
details of the extra exercises and professional postal tuition
which are available.

First published 1983 by Pan Books Ltd.
This new and revised edition published 1987
by Pan Books Ltd, Cavaye Place, London SW10 9PG
9 8 7 6 5 4 3 2 1
© Geoffrey Knott 1987
ISBN 0 330 29747 3
Printed and bound in Great Britain by
Cox & Wyman Ltd, Reading, Berkshire

Contents

Introduction

You do not necessarily have to be studying to qualify as a professional accountant to benefit from reading this book, for it is structured in such a way that others who may have an interest in management accounting, whether they be employed or self-employed, clerk or manager, will find it easy to work their way through its contents without any previous accounting knowledge or experience. This is not to imply that accountancy and business students will find the self-learning text shallow. The basic ideas implicit in the subject are adequately unpacked, and their applications illustrated in a practical context throughout the book.

Some knowledge of business organization and administration will obviously help, but you do not have to be a mathematical genius to cope with the numeric work. Ability to manipulate figures using the four basic rules of arithmetic, to construct and understand the application of simple graphs, and to solve the simplest of algebraic equations, should suffice.

What is management accounting?

We are probably more alive now than at any time in history to the knowledge that resources on this planet are not unlimited in quantity. A huge growth in population over recent centuries, together with ever-increasing personal, social and economic aspirations, has created an almost insatiable demand for some commodities that cannot be fully met by current production, and whose supply can be measured in decades rather than centuries. Witness oil!

There has to be, therefore, some kind of allocation system to ensure that scarce resources are not frittered away, but that the best use is made of them. Internationally, and inside some countries, this is accomplished through the pricing system, whereby supply and demand are brought into balance by appropriate price adjustments.

In other countries, the state assumes part, or the whole, of the role of resource allocation, according to social and economic priorities determined by their governments. Whatever the political or economic system, scarcity has to be recognized and best use made of finite resources.

On a smaller scale, organizations providing goods and services, whether profit motivated or not, are confronted with the same economic facts of life. At the moment of their formation they will have a limited availability of funds that will only be able to command a limited stock of the resources required to reach their objectives. They will need land upon which to erect buildings; they will need labour to make goods or to render services; they will need the output of other organizations, e.g. raw materials and machines, to convert into their own output; and they will need entrepreneurs and organizers to create the ideas and markets for their products, and to bring the factors of production together in the most effective way. It is the job of business managers to decide the appropriate mix of resources that will optimize the satisfaction of their customers and, if the organization is a profit-making one, will yield an acceptable profit on the total value of resources invested. In carrying out this aim they are aided in no small measure by management accounting.

Decision-making is essentially a process of choosing between alternatives. At the simplest level – to do, or not to do, a given thing. To charge this price or that; to purchase one machine or another; to make or to buy a product; to pay this price or that; and to quote a fairly recent example, to buy *The Times* newspaper business or not. No decision can be happily made without the help of guiding information – simple or sophisticated – and a lot of this intelligence, particularly as regards cost, is provided by the management accountant.

Once decisions are made, they are incorporated into the production and marketing plans of the organization, in the form of budgets for the whole firm, and appropriately subdivided budgets for each of the services contributing towards the master plan, e.g. for research and development, personnel, accounting, stock control and general management.

The management accountant is at the centre of this planning

activity, providing a lot of the facts and figures to the management team responsible for all these budgets, and then helping to determine and consolidate the whole budget for the organization.

As operations proceed, management accounting keeps managers informed, at all levels, of actual costs, sales, prices, productivity and measured variations from plan, to enable them to have full control of their areas of responsibility, and to indicate where corrective action or indeed changes to plans are necessary.

This book sets out clearly the concepts, systems and techniques employed to enable the management accountant to fulfil a valuable role in business planning and control.

Part 1
Management accounting concepts

1 | Setting the scene – the management process

Objectives

In order to operate effectively an organization must have a very clear idea of what it is aiming to achieve, otherwise it will be like a ship that is not being steered – probably going round in circles!

> *Activity*
>
> Assume that you have recently had a big win on the football pools, and instead of investing your money in a savings account to earn interest, you have decided to give up your job as a chef to open up a restaurant in a nearby town. When you eventually open your business, which of the following would be your *primary* objective?
>
> **(a)** to develop your enjoyment and talent of preparing food for other people; or
> **(b)** to provide employment for your family and friends; or
> **(c)** to be independent of working for someone else; or
> **(d)** to earn a reasonable profit.

SOLUTION

The alternative use for your money appears to be a savings account yielding an appropriate rate of interest. It is logical to presume therefore that you would not proceed with your plan unless you thought that the value of your original investment would grow by more than the interest that you could earn in a savings account, after paying all the restaurant operating costs, including an amount to recompense you for giving up your previous job. This hoped-for increase in your wealth is profit and it would have to be at a level sufficient to compensate you for the risks that you are taking. Your *primary* objective, therefore, is to make an acceptable profit, for without it you would probably not be motivated to continue, despite your other, quite laudable, *subsidiary* objectives.

Investors measure the success of a business by the profit it attains, therefore all businesses adopt profit as their primary long term objective. Other, subsidiary, business objectives exist, such as the maintenance and promotion of local employment, support for social and artistic projects, and the maintenance of good relationships with customers, employees, suppliers, and central and local government. These all prevent the *maximization* of profit, more especially short-term 'opportunist' gains, but despite such constraints a business must *optimize* its profit in the long term if it is to survive.

Other, non-business organizations that are patently not motivated by profit still have to determine their objectives. Charities such as Oxfam will have as their goals the improvement of the living standards of people in developing countries, and the alleviation of suffering caused by natural disasters. The Sports Council aims to extend the availability of sports facilities to all who wish to take part in sporting activities.

Strategy

Having determined their objectives, organizations must then decide and adopt policies or strategies that they consider offer the best means of achieving their objectives. This will invariably involve choosing between alternative courses of action.

For example, an airline company has to decide whether to carry freight as well as passengers, and in what proportions of each; which of alternative routes their aircraft will fly; the most effective and efficient network of maintenance and operating facilities for their aircraft; flight frequencies; and whether to carry standby, economy, normal tourist or first-class passengers.

These alternative strategies embrace two prime decisions:

- regarding *choice of product* – in this case, freight or passengers or both; and
- determining *the segment of the market* in which to operate; the airline being influenced by choice of routes and choices of fare-paying passengers.

Self-check

Let us return to your stroke of luck on the football pools, and to your decision to open a restaurant. In planning your strategy, what decisions would you have to make, bearing in mind the choices open to you?

ANSWERS

Foremost among your decisions would be:

(a) where the restaurant is to be sited to attract the type of customer that you have in mind;
(b) whether to be conservative and serve only English food, or be more adventurous and 'go' continental, Indian or Chinese;
(c) the hours during which you will be open;
(d) the range of food to be offered on the menu;
(e) whether to buy any prepared food from outside suppliers;
(f) the prices you intend to charge.

You will observe that the restaurant owner and the airline have to make the same two basic decisions:

- *what service or product to provide;*
- *what customer group to provide for.*

These are problems to which all organizations must address themselves.

Self-check

1 What do you consider to be the main objectives of (a) a hospital and (b) a coach-hire business?
2 Which of the following would be part of the strategy of the coach hire company?

   (a) to maintain its vehicles to a high standard;
   (b) to operate contract hire, excursion and tour services in the United Kingdom only;
   (c) to charge lower fares than all its competitors;
   (d) to advertise its services regularly in the local press.

ANSWERS

1 (a) The main objective of a hospital is to provide an adequate medical service for the sick, injured, disabled and aged in a particular locality.

  (b) A coach-hire company would have as its main objective the attainment of a reasonable profit on the money invested in the business by its owners.

2 (b) and **(c)** reveal the product and marketing strategy of the company by setting out the services to be offered, limiting operations to the United Kingdom, and planning to charge cut-price fares.

Organizing to implement the strategy

If you operated a one-man window-cleaning business you would be solely responsible for planning and carrying out your work. You would have to decide whether to aim for industrial contracts or domestic jobs or both; how much to charge; you would have to clean the windows; collect money from your customers; keep the accounts. You do the whole thing yourself, and you have only yourself to organize.

However, as organizations become larger and more complex, responsibility for decision-making and control has to be delegated to trained specialist managers because it becomes more and more difficult for the person who started the business to be directly involved with every aspect of its operations.

Young Simon Poacher set himself up in business to make and sell high-quality pies and pâté, with game pie a particular speciality. With only his wife to help him, he not only had to make his products using equipment installed in an extension to his house, but had also to travel far and wide in his van selling his wares. Eventually, his winning combination of quality products at fair prices, good service and effective selling techniques led to such a huge regular order-book that he had to acquire premises on a local authority trading estate, install a complete new range of ovens and other equipment and buy three new vans. Obviously, Simon could not be directly involved in every activity any longer. He had to hire production staff and delivery staff, with each of these functions headed by a manager reporting directly to him. Simon's wife provided the accounting and administrative services for the whole business.

Inevitably Poacher's Pies and Pâtés became household names, a limited company was formed and many more factory production units, delivery vans and staff were employed. Production was divided into separate pie and pâté departments, and the sales effort into sales administration, promotion and distribution departments, each one being the responsibility of a supervisor who had to report to either production or sales managers respectively. Specialist maintenance, general administrative and personnel, product research and development and accounting departments had to be created to provide supporting services for the main functions of production and selling. Each service department had a manager who, together with the production and selling managers, reported directly to a newly appointed managing director. Simon became the company chairman, but his wife concentrated her talents as the manager of the general administration and personnel department.

Figure 1. Organization chart – Poacher's Pies and Pâté Co. Ltd

The above can now be depicted as a hierarchy of responsibility in an organization chart (figure 1), with lines showing the responsibility relationships between managers.

The duties and responsibilities of each manager and supervisor would be clearly defined, and there should be no doubt as to whom each should report – as depicted by the lines on the chart. This diagram provides a clear organizational framework, that is created as part of the plan to achieve the company's objectives, and more will be heard about the decentralization of planning and controlling in later chapters.

It is important to realize that the chart cannot possibly reveal all the informal relationships existing between managers that are so vital a part of the day-to-day running of a business. The chief accountant, for example, reports directly to the managing director, but he will be in frequent contact with all departments regarding cost control.

Self-check

Norfolk Agrimek Ltd has a research and development department that has designed and developed a range of machinery and implements for the agricultural and horticultural industries. These the company manufactures and distributes using its own transport, through a network of dealers, who in turn supply farmers and smallholders. Production is completed through one or more of the machining, pressing, welding, and assembly and finishing departments, and the production division manager also controls the services provided by the production administration, maintenance, industrial engineering and stores departments.

Transport, finished goods warehousing, sales administration, sales promotion and field sales representation are the responsibility of the marketing division manager, whilst the chief accountant, who also doubles as the company secretary, deals with general administration, personnel and training, as well as all accounting matters.

The managing director has overall responsibility for the company's operations.

Without referring to the answer below, see if you can construct a chart showing the organization structure of the firm, and briefly show why it is so necessary to depict clearly the departmental lines of responsibility.

ANSWER

As businesses grow in size and complexity, the original founders and owners have to delegate responsibility to managers to control the production and selling departments, whether they are selling goods or services. The need for specialist expertise in supporting services has also to be recognized and met.

The above organization chart reveals how the responsibility

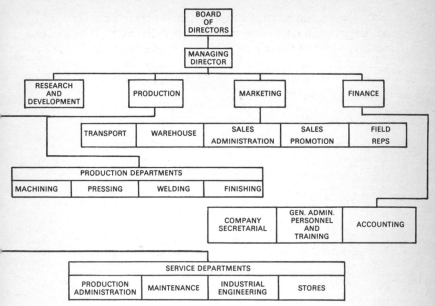

Figure 2. Organization chart – Norfolk Agrimek Ltd

for all the decentralized functions is delegated to departmental and subdepartmental managers.

Planning, controlling and the need for supporting information

Successful achievement of any goal requires careful planning, and then close control of subsequent operations. *Planning* is the process of deciding what action to take. *Controlling* involves putting plans into action, and then monitoring progress to ensure that they keep on course, or are changed if circumstances dictate.

You will already appreciate that determining strategy is planning at its highest level, providing the overall framework for the attainment of an organization's objectives. Within this framework, further *operational* planning is carried out, primarily concerned with the acquisition of resources necessary to carry out the strategic plan.

To illustrate the nature of the decisions that have to be made consider the case of John Jennings, who until recently was the tour manager for a large coach operating company. He had some savings, had recently come into a large legacy, and was able to borrow substantial additional funds from his bank, to invest in a newly formed coach operating company. His overall commercial objective was the realization of a 20% return on the total capital invested, and he planned to achieve this target profit by organizing and selling Jennings' Continental Tours. In the off-season he would offer cut-price tours particularly to attract 'senior citizens'.

Activity

Try to contact the owner of a local coach-operating company, and very tactfully ask him what would be the initial essential resources to operate continental tours. A travel agent could be a suitable alternative source of information.

You will not be surprised to learn that without adequate finance ,you will be unable to proceed. John appears to be well endowed in this respect, and can therefore make decisions to acquire the necessary premises, coaches, maintenance facilities and staff. In addition, he would have to negotiate contracts for hotel accommodation, appoint agents for ticket sales and plan publicity campaigns. In order to make all these very important decisions, he would of course require information regarding the alternatives in each case.

John would then reflect all these plans in a set of budgets prescribing the operating and financial targets for the coming year.

'It will all come together on the day' is a saying frequently heard among people who organize activities, whether it be a drama production or a football team training for a cup match. Such a philosophy can only be justified, however, if an organized management closely *control* the *implementation* of plans: firstly, by bringing together and *coordinating* the resources required for the particular activity and, secondly, by effectively *directing* the use of those resources from day to day. The success of John's tours will depend crucially upon the provision of comfortable, well-maintained vehicles, well-briefed crews and couriers, and accommodation and excursions abroad being available as timetabled; the whole of the operation should be adequately supported by well-timed publicity campaigns, thoughtfully sited ticket-selling agencies and effective direction of operations by an efficient management.

Control also implies good communication, in the sense that managers are better motivated to direct operations if they are adequately consulted and informed. An impending political disturbance in one of John's overseas touring areas can only be handled if information is swiftly to hand; and costs can be better controlled if information about actual costs is fed back to the responsible manager very quickly.

In every organization there has to be an adequate and efficient system to identify, collect, present and interpret information, which may come from internal or external sources, be based upon past experience or forecasts, and will be transmitted in documented, visual or verbal form.

Figure 3 summarizes the main elements of the management process that have been discussed in this section.

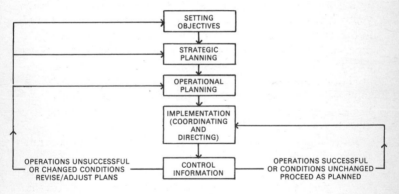

Figure 3. The management process

Review

1 Which of the following statements correctly describes the need for an organization to specify its objectives:

    (a) to ascertain the amount of finance required;
    (b) to agree the structure of its organization;
    (c) to recognize clearly what it is aiming to achieve;
    (d) to plan the coming year's activities?

2 (a) Explain the term 'strategic planning' in relation to an organization.

(b) Which of the following would be part of the strategic plan of a scrap-metal dealer:
   (i) employing men to work in the scrap yard;
   (ii) deciding to deal wholly in the collection of non-ferrous metals, e.g. copper and lead;
   (iii) seeking contracts with local engineering works for their scrap;
   (iv) planning the daily journey schedules for the lorries;
   (v) siting the scrap yard as near as possible to the sources of its scrap collections?

3 As a business grows its owner has to delegate responsibility. Which one of the following statements describes why?

(a) He can play more golf during the week.

(b) He is completely incompetent.

(c) He wishes to put the blame for errors of judgement on to other people.

(d) He has not the time, energy or expertise to be directly involved in all aspects of the growing business.

(e) He needs younger men to take over the reins of management.

4 You are the owner of a TV and radio shop. Given the stages in the management process depicted in figure 3, indicate the stages to which the following activities apply:

(a) Assigning jobs to TV repairmen.

(b) Analysing customers' outstanding orders.

(c) Planning to dovetail the repair shop and delivery activities.

(d) Deciding whether or not to purchase another shop.

(e) Deciding between alternative new delivery vans.

(f) Planning to make a return of 30% on capital invested.

ANSWERS

1 Statement **(c)**. Objectives set out the purpose for which the organization exists.

2 (a) Strategic planning is determined by the highest level of management in an organization, and is concerned with agreeing and adopting policies that are considered to offer the best means of achieving the objectives of the organization.

  (b) **(ii) (iii)** and **(v)** would be part of the scrap dealer's strategy. **(ii)** specifies the *type of product* to be dealt in; **(iii)** and **(v)** relate to the *segment of the market* with which the dealer plans to do business.

3 Statement **(d)**.

4 (a) Directing.
  (b) Control information.
  (c) Coordinating.
  (d) Strategic planning.
  (e) Operational planning.
  (f) Setting objectives.

2 | Management accounting as an aid to management

The all-purpose accounting system

Information to help managers be more effective comes from many sources, but in most business organizations a significant proportion of it is gleaned from the accounting system.

This system collects data generated by operations and records it in such a way that both detailed and summarized information can be extracted from it. Separate accounts are maintained to record sales; amounts owing by customers; the purchase of machinery and buildings; amounts owing to suppliers; hours worked by employees; hours worked on each job; wages paid; cash received and paid; stocks of raw materials, work in progress and finished products; finance provided by owners and lenders; taxation paid and payable; interest and dividends paid; materials bought; services received; and countless other transactions arising from day-to-day activity.

This collection of accounting data then forms a common source from which is drawn information relevant to the needs of two groups of people:

- individuals and bodies *external* to the business, such as shareholders, the taxation authorities, investment advisers and government departments;
- the *internal* managers who are directly responsible to owners for the achievement of business objectives.

The first category require financial information, whereas the second group are better served by management information, and although it is the purpose of this book to explain and illustrate the management accounting function, it will be useful at this stage to compare the two types of accounting information.

The basic similarity has already been noted – they both draw upon the same data base, although management information is considerably supplemented from outside the system, for example regarding forecast rates of inflation. A further parallel that can be drawn is that they both present *summarized* statements to their users. Shareholders of companies receive accounts that summarize trading results for a whole year, whilst departmental managers get operating statements periodically that summarize the performance of each of their areas of responsibility.

Differences arise because the purposes for which the information is required are at variance.

The following table summarizes the major differences:

Financial accounting	*Management accounting*
1 Most organizations have to produce financial accounts, at least once in every year, that show how well or badly their resources have been used and maintained.	Such compulsion does not apply. The development of management accounting varies from organization to organization.
2 Financial accounts present an essentially *historic* picture of *past* operations.	Concerned with decision-making for the *future* as well as reviewing past operations.
3 The statements presented are subject to a relatively high degree of accuracy.	Because decisions are about the future and cannot be delayed, the emphasis is upon the prompt production of relevant information.
4 Usually the statements present a *whole* picture of the financial state of the organization, and are an *end* in themselves.	The variety of decisions concerned with planning and controlling require different volumes of information, the intention of which is to aid the decision-making process rather than be an end product of the accounting system.
5 Financial accounts are prepared in accordance with generally acceptable accounting principles. For example, the measurement	Management accounting information may be guided by completely different principles. In judging the profitability of a proposed project, for example,

of past profit takes into account all goods sold in a period, whether these goods are paid for or not by the end of that period.

the *timing* of cash *receipts* is more important than when goods are actually sold.

6 Financial accounting statements are concerned almost wholly with monetary information.

Other types of quantitative information may be more relevant to the needs of management, for example tons of steel produced, miles run or hours worked.

Self-check

Which of the following are concerned with financial accounting and which with management accounting?

1 A copy of the annual accounts of a company submitted to the Inland Revenue authorities.
2 A report revealing the past costs of operating a department.
3 The cost budget for the transport department of a company.
4 The final accounts of a rugby club presented to them at their annual general meeting.
5 A summary of miles flown and passengers carried on each airline route.
6 A report urgently required by your managing director using figures expressed to the nearest £10.
7 A cash receipts and payments forecast.
8 A profit and loss account of a business prepared according to generally acceptable accounting principles.

ANSWERS

1 *Financial accounting*. Total accounts, accurately prepared for taxation purposes.
2 *Management accounting*. Control information to ensure that costs are on target.
3 *Management accounting*. A forecast of *future* costs.

4 *Financial accounting.* Total accounts presented to members in accordance with the rules of the club.

5 *Management accounting.* Non-monetary information, not usually required to any degree by financial accounts.

6 *Management accounting.* A report produced promptly, when called for by the director, fine accuracy not being called for in relation to the decision to be made.

7 *Management accounting.* A report about the future.

8 *Financial accounting.* A final account prepared in compliance with generally accepted accounting concepts.

The management process and accounting information

In the section in Chapter 1 discussing planning and controlling it was indicated that, at each stage of the management process (see figure 3), information is vital for monitoring progress of plans, changing plans or making new plans. This section describes how management accounting has evolved to service a large part of this requirement.

Imagine that you are a member of the Fiveways Community Centre. Once every year the treasurer presents a statement of receipts and payments of cash relating to the past year, to members of the centre at their annual general meeting. This is the only accounting information produced either for members or for the committee. Would you be satisfied with this lack of communication, bearing in mind that the centre organizes a comprehensive range of indoor and outdoor sporting activities, socials, drama, dinner dances, discos and many other events, as well as running a bar and a cafeteria? Considerable revenue and expenditure is involved in all this activity.

Activity

Reread the section on planning and controlling, then very tactfully approach the secretary of a local community or leisure centre and ask him what financial and other information you think the committee and others ought to have throughout the year, to run its affairs. You should be guided by figure 3 and put forward your suggestions covering each stage in the process.

Accepting that the objective of the centre is to provide cultural, recreational and sporting facilities for the benefit of the Fiveways community, your groups of items will include some of the following. Give yourself a pat on the back if you included at least half the information on my list.

- *Strategic planning*
  Long-term plans, but with on-going changes and additions as required.
      Knowledge of the existing or changing age-range mix in the local population.
      Information on activities requested by local people.
- *Operational planning*
  Towards the end of each year – for the following year
      A schedule of proposed activities and their organizers.
      An estimate of the expected receipts and payments for each activity.
      An estimate of the general costs of running the centre.
      A forecast of membership, and the proposed level of fees.
      A list from the equipment officer, with estimated costs of equipment, furniture and fittings that are proposed to be bought.
      A summary of total expected cash receipts and payments for the centre.
- *Implementation*
  Required throughout the year relating to this year's plans
      Changes envisaged in planned activities.
      Progress and financial reports from organizers of planned activities, including any personal or organizational difficulties being encountered.
      Requests for further spending on equipment, etc.
- *Control information*
  Reports required throughout the year relating to completed and continuing activities
      A periodic updated cash forecast for the twelve months ahead.
      Details of changes in membership.
      Information to organizers of receipts, payments, bookings, etc. related to each of their activities.
      Reports upon completed activities. Were they well sup-

ported? Were they popular? If not, why not? Did sports teams win? What were the financial results?

Reports on continuing activities, viz. the bar, cafeteria, sports teams, etc.

Comparisons of actual with planned overall costs of running the centre.

An equipment report.

Notice how the above list is arranged. The first group relates to the initiation and changes of strategy; the second to plans for next year; and the third and fourth groups to 'getting activities moving', and then controlling them, respectively. The Fiveways committee has overall responsibility for the way that the centre is operated, and therefore needs the kind of reports shown in the first and second groups for forward planning.

They will look at all the alternative proposals and estimates, and after carefully considering the *differences* between them as regards costs, receipts and the probability of success, choose the combination that they consider comes nearest to achieving the objectives of the centre for the coming year. Thus the plan for that year is born, and what were previously referred to as *forecasts* are now firm plans – or *budgets*.

These will comprise budgets for the whole centre, and more importantly for control purposes, a budget relevant to each activity, which will be the responsibility of the appropriate organizer. Quite clearly, if he is to be held responsible for results, the organizer should play a leading part in the compilation of his budget; for, if allowed to participate in this way, he will be more motivated to achieve the plan.

Throughout the year, information of actual costs, etc. will be communicated by the treasurer, to enable organizers to spot any deviations from plan such as overspending or lack of support, to enable them to take prompt corrective action either to bring the plans back on course or to modify or cancel them. In this respect, prompt information will be more valued than absolutely accurate but delayed information.

Business organizations go through much the same process of planning and controlling as that described in the Fiveways example, although possibly on a much larger scale. The major part of the quantitative information required in this process is the province of management accounting, which deals mainly in money measurements but not exclusively so. Most business activities can be ascribed a money value, e.g. sales, costs, wages paid and fuel used, but certain other operating results are more effectively expressed in alternative ways. Miles run, passengers carried, spectators attending, orders outstanding, complaints received, products sold and hours worked – all are vital expressions of business activity, telling stories that guide managers in their day-to-day directing of operations.

In some circumstances, non-monetary and monetary data can be combined to produce a vitally significant third measurement. For example, knowledge of the cost per mile operated by its vehicles enables a coach company to quote economic prices for private hire, and to help control future costs. Total operating costs divided by total miles run gives the information required.

It is probably considered by most people that management accounting is only concerned with cold figures, that people do not count in the harsh economic world. This is nowadays far from the truth. Accounting has a human face. The Fiveways committee want to know, for example, whether audiences enjoyed drama performances, that their football team won last Saturday; and they certainly have to be open to receiving complaints or plaudits about any activity. These indications of a behavioural or qualitative nature will play their part in influencing future decisions, and are of no less importance to business managers. Customers' complaints, delays in receiving raw materials and industrial disputes with employees must be taken seriously if a business is to retain the goodwill of its customers.

To sum up then, management accounting is mainly concerned with the provision of quantitative information to managers to aid them in:

- decision-making, as part of the strategic and operational planning processes, including the compilation of budgets;
- coordinating and directing operations;
- controlling operations by feeding performance reports to them at appropriate intervals.

At the same time, the management accountant cannot ignore non-quantitative influences, and will qualify the information he provides if he considers that behavioural matters are just as important to future decision-making.

Review

Given below are examples of accounting information relating to a restaurant. Indicate at which of the following stages each item would be required: **(a)** setting objectives, **(b)** strategic planning, **(c)** operational planning, **(d)** implementation, **(e)** control information.

1 Periodic summaries of past costs and receipts.
2 Forecast receipts for the coming year.
3 Reports of absenteeism among waiting staff.
4 An analysis of the varieties of meals served last month.
5 Information on the profit being earned by a competitor.
6 Costs of alternative replacement ovens.
7 The forecast effects upon sales and the number of customers of introducing Italian foods.
8 An increase in staff turnover.
9 The forecast effects of the recession upon future profits.
10 The probable effect of a proposed reduction in prices.

ANSWERS

1 Control information – to monitor past performance.
2 Operational planning – for use as the budget for next year.
3 Implementation – to consider the redirection of staff.
4 Control information – to consider changes in the menu.
5 Setting objectives – determining the target profit.
6 Operational planning – to replace equipment.
7 Strategic planning – to consider a change in the product.
8 Implementation – to investigate the reasons for staff leaving.
9 Setting objectives – determining the target profit.
10 Strategic planning – to encourage a change in customers.

3 | What do we mean by 'cost'?

Cost – the small word with the big meaning

Although business transactions involve both costs and revenues, cost generates the bulk of the data processed and accumulated in the management accounting system. Because of the importance of cost, therefore, this chapter aims to make clear to you the fundamental meaning of the word as used in management accounting, and introduce you to the basis of cost composition.

Ask anyone the meaning of the apparently simple little word 'cost' and the answer will almost certainly be – 'the price paid for something'. Now in certain limited circumstances this is perfectly true. If you pay a price of £30 for a coat, that is its cost to you; but not to the retailer. His total cost would be the price paid to the manufacturer for the coat plus a share of the costs of running his shop – something less than £30 – otherwise he would not make a profit. The manufacturer's cost will include the various materials used, wages paid and a share of the other costs incurred in operating his factory. Thus three values could be said to be the cost of the coat, one for each of the manufacturing, retailing and consuming stages, illustrating the need to be alive to the purpose for which the cost information is required.

Suppose that you always keep a gallon can of petrol in your garage for emergencies, and that you had paid £1.30 six months ago for the gallon you presently hold. The price of petrol is now £1.50 a gallon. One day your neighbour calls, asking if he can buy your can of petrol as all the garages are closed and he has to make an urgent car journey. How much would you charge him? Because he is a good friend you might feel obliged to ask him to pay the £1.30 paid by you, that is, its original, *historic* cost. However, you have to replenish your emergency supply, and as the *replacement* cost is £1.50, that is how much you should charge, otherwise your stock will be less than planned. Furthermore, your neighbour will have gained at your expense, for he would have had to pay £1.50 at the garage.

Taking the car analogy a little further, assume that you are planning your holiday for next year – a continental car tour.

Petrol would be one of your largest expenses, and as it would almost certainly increase in price next year, your *budgeted* total cost for the trip will have to be calculated using the future expected price, not the current one. Should you wish to know the budgeted cost per mile (the *unit cost*), it could be calculated by dividing total cost by planned mileage.

Having had a wonderful holiday, you return home in the best of health, but driving a car not in the least healthy. It probably climbed one Alpine pass too many, and your kindly local second-hand car dealer says that it is worth only a scrap value of about £50. As you paid him £1,000 for it twelve months previously, you could be excused for feeling that you had been 'taken for a ride'. However, 'enter your friendly neighbour' who, noticing that your car is for sale, asks how much you are prepared to take for it. What *minimum* price would you charge him? Would it be £1,000 – the price you paid – less some reasonable figure for your usage during the past year?

To answer this question, you have to ask yourself what is the best alternative opportunity open to you. At the moment this appears to be the scrap value of £50, so this would be the lowest selling price acceptable to you, and can be referred to as the *opportunity cost*.

You can see, therefore, that very like the chameleon, the value attributable to the word 'cost' changes with circumstance, and that we have to be very clear about our cost purpose to determine the appropriate value to use. That is to say:

- the past or current price paid for a resource is not applicable in every circumstance;
- 'cost' may relate to a particular stage reached in the production/selling/consuming process of goods and services;
- we could be reporting upon a completed or planned activity;
- total cost may more meaningfully be broken down into units, e.g. cost per mile or cost per department.

To summarize, *cost is the relevant value of resources used or planned to be used for a particular purpose.*

Self-check

1 You own a boat which cost you £500 to build two years ago. You could sell it to a dealer today for £750. What is the minimum price you would ask in your newspaper advertisement to sell it privately, and why this price?

2 Your wife makes embroidered wall-hangings at home. The material for each costs £2, and each one takes four hours to complete. If she worked for an employer doing similar work she would receive £2 per hour. Other costs amount to £1 for each wall-hanging.

   You sell these articles on your stall in the market, and the total costs of transport and stall hire for each is estimated at £1. You charge customers a price equal to total production and selling costs, plus 25%. In respect of each wall-hanging, calculate:

   (a) total production cost;
   (b) its total cost to you and your wife before sale;
   (c) its cost to the customer.

ANSWERS

1 The original cost is irrelevant here, for you have the opportunity to sell the boat for £750, which is the minimum price to use in your advertisement.

2 This is how your workings should appear:

	£
Material	2
Labour	8
Other expenses of making	1
	—
Total production cost	11
Transport and rent	1
	—
Total selling cost	12
add Profit 25%	3
	—
Cost to consumer	15
	—

Note particularly that labour is shown at the opportunity cost of £8 – the amount that your wife could earn elsewhere.

Direct and indirect cost

Having recognized that cost is a relative term – that we are concerned to discover the value appropriate to a particular objective – we now turn our attention to the 'nitty-gritty'. What are the constituents of cost?

Consider the book that you are currently reading. What resources do you think were combined to produce it? Paper, ink, cardboard and binding materials are obviously recognizable materials in the finished product, and they can easily be *traced directly* as costs in the book right through the production process. Likewise wages paid to printing machine operators and book binders can quite readily be identified directly with the production of a particular edition of a book. Costs specifically and easily related to a particular cost objective, in this case the cost of producing books, are termed 'direct costs'.

This is not the full story, however, for the conversion of various materials by skilled labour into the finished article calls for the use of various other resources. There has to be a building to house the printing and other machinery; buildings and machinery have to be repaired and serviced – using labour and materials; rates and insurance have to be paid on buildings, and they have to be heated by electricity or gas; electricity, oil and perhaps water are needed to operate machinery; administrators and clerks using stationery and other office costs are also required to ensure that the whole operation runs smoothly and to plan. All of these items are called 'indirect costs', because it is difficult or impracticable to trace the specific portion of them used up in the production of a particular article. For example, which publication should bear the cost of repairing a printing machine?

This difficulty is solved by *averaging* indirect costs over different products in some logical, predetermined way; for example, in proportion to the number of hours worked on each product – but more of this later.

In summary then, the total production cost of an article or a service is comprised of its direct costs, plus a share of indirect costs, as shown in figure 4.

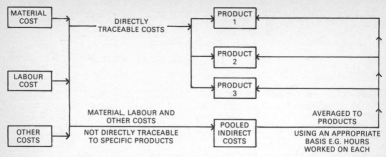

Figure 4. Composition of product cost

Self-check

Norfolk Agrimek Ltd incur the following costs in the manufacture of their small cultivator:

Insurance on machinery	Sheet steel
Finishing paint	Labourers' wages
Foreman's salary	Employer's National Insurance
Electricity	Gas
Electric motors	Fitters' wages
Telephone calls	Rent
Maintenance materials	Water
Stationery	Small nuts and bolts
Machine operators' wages	Oil
Rates	Machine parts
Maintenance wages	Administration salaries

Required

Rearrange this list into three columns headed Material, Labour and Other costs, and indicate by the side of each whether you think it is a direct or an indirect cost of the cultivator.

ANSWER

Material		*Labour*		*Other costs*	
Finishing paint	D	Foreman's salary	I	Insurance on	
Electric motors	D	Machine operators'		machinery	I
Maintenance		wages	D	Electricity	I
materials	I	Maintenance		Telephone calls	I
Stationery	I	wages	I	Rates	I

Sheet steel	D	Labourers' wages	I	Employer's NHI	I
Oil	I	Fitters' wages	D	Gas	I
Small nuts and bolts	I	Administration		Rent	I
Machine parts	D	salaries	I	Water	I

D = direct.   I = indirect.

Review

Bright and Red are in business as painters and decorators. They carry approximately two months' stock of a range of gloss paints, as far as possible in the colours currently demanded by their customers, and they replenish their stocks from the local wholesale paint dealers at the end of each month.

They had paid £4 per gallon for the gloss paint in stock at 30 June year 1, but during the next six months they would have to pay £4.50 per gallon to replace their stock. The wholesaler has also advised them that the price was expected to rise to £5.00 per gallon from the beginning of year 2.

Some of the brown paint presently held by Bright and Red had completely lost favour with their customers, and could be sold for only £1 per gallon if not used in their business.

It is anticipated that they will paint 250 houses in year 2, each of them requiring four gallons of paint.

1 What cost per gallon should Bright and Red include in their estimate for paint for a house to be painted blue in July year 1?

2 At what cost will paint held at 30 June year 1 be shown in the stock records?

3 What minimum value should be ascribed to the brown paint to persuade a customer to specify that colour?

4 What will be the forecast total cost of paint for the whole of year 2?

5 What will be the cost of paint used on each house during year 2?

6 Would you classify the paint used as a direct or an indirect cost and why?

7 Give an example of an indirect cost appropriate to Bright and Red's business.

ANSWERS

1 £4.50. The temptation will be to apply £4.00 because that is the original cost of the paint in stock. It has to be recognized, however, that it will cost £4.50 to *replace* the paint used, and that this amount will have to be recovered from the customer in the price charged for the job. In this instance, we are using the *replacement cost*.

2 £4.00 per gallon, that is, the original price paid which will be recorded in the stock records. This is the *historic cost*.

3 Should the original cost of £4.00 per gallon be quoted, the potential customer would be inclined to reject it, as he is looking for a bargain knowing that brown is not 'the colour of the month'. As £1 per gallon is the value of the best alternative opportunity open to Bright and Red, it is the minimum amount that could be charged, i.e. it is the *opportunity cost*.

4 £5 × 4 × 250 = £5,000. This is the total *budgeted cost* based upon the forecast price per gallon for year 2.

5 £5 × 4 = £20. This is the cost of paint for one house, that is, the *unit cost*.

6 The paint is a *direct* cost because it can be specifically and easily related to the cost of redecorating a particular house.

7 Indirect costs are those that can be related to more than one cost purpose, and in respect of which it is either difficult or impracticable to trace to a particular job. Bright and Red's indirect costs would include supervising foreman's wages, store-keeping costs, advertising, administration salaries, stationery.

4 | Cost as a function of volume and timing

How changes in volume of production affect cost

In your studies of the previous chapter you found that the manufacturing cost of an article can be expressed as:

direct materials + direct labour + a share of indirect costs.

By definition, direct costs are those that can easily be identified as part of the finished article. Given different levels of output, therefore, one can for the sake of simplicity assume that the total direct costs will vary directly with production level. They are, as a consequence, termed 'variable costs'. For example, one finished article will use up £20 of material, whilst 100 articles will consume £2,000.

However, the major problem of compiling cost does not lie with direct costs, but in ascertaining what share of indirect costs to add to those direct costs. To do this we have to decide:

- the basis for averaging indirect costs to the items produced, e.g. the number of hours taken to produce each item; and
- what the total indirect costs will be.

Both decisions will be discussed in later chapters in greater depth, but the second is so fundamental to the whole subject of management accounting that a brief introduction to the concepts that apply will be helpful at this stage.

If you refer to the answer to the self-check question at the end of the previous section on direct and indirect costs, you will recall that items were labelled 'direct' or 'indirect'. Which of the items classified as 'indirect' would not change their values whatever the volume of production?

You will most likely have noted down some or all of the following: foreman's salary, maintenance wages, administration salaries, insurance, rates and rent. Given the present size of production facilities, all these services continue at all output levels, that is to say, they are 'fixed costs'.

The remainder of the indirect costs will vary in value to some extent with output changes, and can therefore be classified as 'variable indirect costs'. The amount of stationery used, for example, will fall with decreasing volumes of production, and increase as output rises.

Consider a factory producing one type of electric heater, with fixed costs totalling £100,000. Should only 100 heaters be made, then fixed costs per heater would be £100; but with sales of 100,000 heaters, this cost reduces dramatically to £1 a heater. On the other hand, the total variable costs at the two levels of production would vary directly with the number of heaters produced. We have, then, the paradox that fixed cost *per unit* varies with volume of output, whereas variable cost *per unit* is fixed whatever the volume. This knowledge of the cost/volume relationship will be seen to be at the very heart of all the aspects covered in this book.

Self-check

Referring to the electrical heater example in this section, where fixed costs totalled £100,000. Assuming that variable costs per heater are £20, draw up a schedule to show the cost per heater at output levels of 20,000, 40,000, 60,000, 80,000 and 100,000. Why does total unit cost vary?

ANSWER

	£100,000	£100,000	£100,000	£100,000	£100,000
Fixed costs	£100,000	£100,000	£100,000	£100,000	£100,000
Total units	20,000	40,000	60,000	80,000	100,000
Fixed costs per	£	£	£	£	£
unit	5.00	2.50	1.67	1.25	1.00
Variable cost					
per unit	20.00	20.00	20.00	20.00	20.00
Total unit cost	25.00	22.50	21.67	21.25	21.00

The cost per heater reduces with increased volume, entirely due to the fixed nature of some costs at all levels of output.

You may have produced your answer in total cost form. This is acceptable, as long as your cost per unit is the same as that shown in the above schedule.

When does a resource acquired become a cost?

Before you read further, you should be clear that you understand the concept discussed in the first section of Chapter 3, that cost is the value of resources used for a particular purpose. This section considers the word 'used' in the context of time.

When is a resource used? To consider this let us examine figure 5, which shows in very simple form the flow of resources through a manufacturing business from acquisition to sale of finished products.

Resources may be used but not paid for at the time (see figure 5, stages A and C).

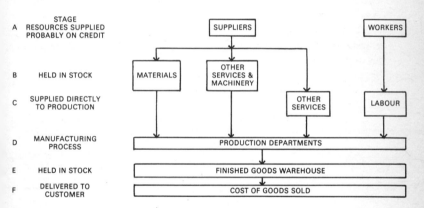

Figure 5. The resource flow in manufacturing

The process commences with the purchase of materials, labour, machinery and services, but these need not be paid for immediately. In the same way that you and I can buy goods on credit, suppliers allow businesses time to pay, the time varying from industry to industry, but anything from four to six weeks would not be unusual. Similarly, production workers may not be paid for a particular week's work until the end of the following week; and electricity is supplied well in advance of being charged to the consumer.

In each case, any material bought and used, work carried out and electricity consumed become costs of production immediately they are *acquired*, even though they may not have been paid for at the time.

Resources are acquired but not necessarily used immediately (see figure 5, stage B).

Most manufacturers hold stocks of raw materials, partly to cover the possibility of delays in replenishment by suppliers, and very often to take advantage of bulk buying discounts. Whatever the reason, raw materials could be held in stock for some time before being issued to the production department – only then being 'used' and becoming part of the cost of production. A parallel case arises when services are paid for in advance, such as rent and rates. Only that part of such services relevant to the current production period is charged as costs, the remainder being 'held in stock' to be charged into following periods.

Likewise, prepayment for resources arises in connection with buildings and machinery, technically referred to as 'fixed assets' because they are purchased to be retained in the business, to be employed over a period equal to their useful lives. The problem is, what proportion of the costs of these assets do we charge to each of the years in which they are used?

There are various methods employed, and these are discussed further in Chapter 10, but the simplest and most used is to make an equal annual instalment of their costs over their lives to production, this annual charge being known as 'depreciation'. For example, a machine costing £1,000 and estimated to last five years would be costed at £200 per year. The balance of the value remaining on these fixed assets each year is 'held in stock', to be charged against future production.

Goods are produced or purchased, but not necessarily sold immediately (see figure 5, stages D and E).

Supposing that your local supermarket declared that, as an economic measure, it would not in future hold stocks of goods in its warehouse behind the store. Instead, shelves would be replenished direct from lorries by weekly deliveries. There is little doubt that this policy would create shortages on shelves from time to time, as transport can be delayed and supplies held up at the central warehouse or suppliers' factories. Frustrated shoppers would soon transfer their custom elsewhere.

Stocks are held on shelves to ensure that a full range of goods is always available to meet normal demands, and to tempt customers to buy more. The back-up store in the warehouse is there to make sure that shelves can be replenished at a moment's notice, and to act as a buffer in case deliveries from the central warehouse or suppliers are delayed.

Further back in the chain of supply, manufacturers or the central warehouse will hold stocks of finished products, awaiting orders from supermarkets. They have to be sure that they can always fulfil orders, despite possible delays in production or delivery to them. This inventory policy also assists manufacturers to plan a smooth production programme.

Thus cost of goods manufactured or cost of goods purchased do not become cost of goods sold until customers take delivery of them (see figure 5, stage F). This distinction is of crucial importance in the measurement of business profit and emphasizes once again the importance of stating our objective in the ascertainment of cost.

Self-check

Norfolk Agrimek Ltd manufacture motor mowers. During January they took delivery of 100 electric motors at a price of £15 each, but had not paid the supplier for them by the end of the month. 50 motors were fitted to mowers completed during January, the remainder being held in store.

Ten of the completed mowers remained in stock at the end of the month, but would probably be sold in February.

(a) Should the motors be excluded from the cost of production because they are not paid for? Explain.
(b) If you consider that they should be included, what would be the value charged to cost of production?
(c) The management accounts at the end of January show *cost of sales* of 50 mowers. Is this correct?

ANSWER

(a) The fact that motors have not been paid for at the time they are used in production does not exclude them as production costs. They are owned by Norfolk Agrimek when they are received from the supplier, and immediately they are fitted to mowers they become costs.
(b) 50 motors at £15 each, i.e. £750, should be incorporated in the

cost of mowers produced during January. The remainder are still in stock and cannot be considered as costs until they are used.

(c) No, this is not correct! Although 50 mowers have been produced, ten are unsold and remain as stock at the month end. Cost of sales for January would be related to 40 machines, the other ten probably featuring with February sales.

Review

1 Define (a) fixed cost and (b) variable cost, and give two examples of each that might apply to an airline company.

2 Joe Sculptor makes and sells pottery, aided by one part-time assistant who makes one type of vase and is paid £2 for each of the 15 hours that he works. The cost of clay and other materials used in each vase is £1, and the electricity and other indirect variable costs are estimated at 20 pence per vase. The fixed costs associated with vase-making amount to £60 per week, and a vase can be finished in 15 minutes. Calculate (a) the total cost of each vase presently made; (b) the total cost of each vase if the part-time worker extends his working time by 10 hours.

3 Gas consumed in your business in the March quarter is paid for in April. Should you charge the amount consumed to cost of production in the month in which the bill is paid?

4 A machine costing £500 is bought in January 1981. Explain why you would not charge the whole machine cost to production for 1981.

ANSWERS

1 (a) A fixed cost is one that does not change with variations in in volume of activity, during a certain time period.

Examples: aircrew salaries (would still be paid whether aircraft flew or not); rates on airport buildings (fixed costs charged by a local authority cover a one year period, and have to be borne even if all aircraft are grounded).

(b) Variable costs are those that change directly and in proportion to fluctuations in operating activity.

Examples: fuel for aircraft (would only be used if aircraft

flew); in-flight meals (would not be consumed if planes were grounded).

2

Cost of making one vase

	Hours worked	
	15	25
Fixed costs	£60	£60
Number produced:		
in 15 hours	60	
in 25 hours		100

	per vase	per vase
Fixed cost	1.00	0.60
Variable costs:		
Material	1.00	1.00
Labour	0.50	0.50
Indirect	0.20	0.20
Total cost	2.70	2.30

Note that the cost per vase is reduced when output is increased, due to fixed cost being averaged over a greater output.

3 No! Gas used in production during January, February and March should be counted as costs of producing during those months, even though it had not been paid for at the time.

4 A machine is usually bought to be used in a business over a longer period of time than a year. The amount paid for it in January 1981 is in essence a prepayment of service to be rendered by the machine in future years as well as the current one. We therefore calculate the *depreciation* to charge into 1981, as that proportion of the value of the machine used in 1981. The remainder of its value is held over to be charged against future years' output.

Part 2
Costing systems

5 | Presenting the 'big picture'

Introduction

When you put a coin into a slot machine, you do so with the expectation that the coin will 'trigger' a process which eventually yields a promised output – perhaps coffee, music, space invaders or, with a little bit of luck, a fruit-machine 'jackpot'.

You fill the petrol tank of your car with similar intention. Your engine fires, and you have output in the form of motive power and thus transport. These three basic elements – input, processing and output – are present in all systems and certainly apply to business operations organized to supply goods and services.

As you have already seen, inputs into manufacturing operations normally include materials, labour, machines and services. A planned conversion process then takes place, and when it is completed the planned output in the form of a finished product emerges, ready to satisfy a customer's needs.

Parallel with the physical process of a manufacturing operation, and rather like a camera filming the story of production as it unfolds, the accounting system records this flow of resources through the various stages of manufacture, in monetary terms.

Inputs into business operations all have different physical or service characteristics, but they all lend themselves to being represented in the accounts in the one common unit of measurement – money. This is of great help to management, as it would be difficult to measure and monitor progress if the records simply recorded quantities and descriptions of each resource. It also follows the logic of investment in the sense that the people who initially provide the finance, which in turn is converted into the resources required to achieve business aims, will look for a reasonable return on their investment – expressed in terms of money.

Thus the accounting records will reveal a dynamic picture of the values of resources – unprocessed, partly processed, finished and ultimately sold – at any time. The updated value shown in the work-in-process account at any time, for example, is the monetary equivalent of the unfinished work still being processed through the production department.

A well-designed accounting system should provide much more than stock valuations, however. It will at least provide the information from which can be prepared a *total* picture of producing and selling goods and services during a particular period. We could call this 'the big picture', and although the remainder of this book shows how this total information is broken down into smaller segments for control and planning purposes, this chapter concentrates upon the production of the 'big picture'.

Recording the flow of resources

The physical flow of resources through a manufacturing operation was depicted in figure 5 and, as stated earlier in this chapter, this flow is matched by appropriate entries in the accounting records.

Figure 5 shows how the cycle commences with the acquisition of resources, and ends when manufactured goods are supplied to customers. The payment and receipt of cash is, of course, implicit in the cycle. Suppliers of materials, services, machines and labour will receive cash in payment, and customers will ultimately pay for the goods sold to them.

The summary shown below describes each stage of the resource flow sequence, together with the accounting records affected by the transfers of value. Note particularly that just as each transfer involves the giving of value out of one stage, and the receiving of that value into another, so also does the accounting system show the giving and receiving of value in two appropriate accounting records.

Value transfer sequence	*Accounts affected*	
	Receiving value	*Giving value*
1 Materials are acquired and held in stock for future use.	Materials stock	Suppliers
2 Machines are acquired for use over a long period of time.	Machinery	Suppliers

Value transfer sequence	*Accounts affected*	
	Receiving value	*Giving value*
3 Materials and services are acquired for immediate use in production (including gas, electricity, etc.).	Work-in-process	Suppliers
4 Suppliers are paid.	Suppliers	Cash
5 Employees supply labour and skill to to production.	Work-in-process	Employees' wages
6 Employees are paid for services rendered.	Employees' wages	Cash
7 Materials are issued from stock to production.	Work-in-process	Materials stock
8 Part of the value of machinery is used up in production – the value consumed is known as 'depreciation'.	Work-in-process	Machinery
9 Completely finished goods are transferred from production to finished goods warehouse.	Finished goods stock	Work-in-process
10 Goods sold and transported from the finished goods warehouse to the customer.	Cost of goods sold	Finished goods stock
11 The customer is sent an invoice for the goods supplied.	Customers' accounts (debtors)	Sales
12 Cash payments received from customers.	Cash	Customers' accounts
13 Selling and general services rendered.	Selling and general expenses	Suppliers
14 Cash paid to suppliers for selling and general services received.	Suppliers	Cash
15 The sales, cost of sales and selling and general expenses are summarized in the trading and profit-and-loss account	Sales T&P&L	T&P&L Cost of goods sold Selling and general expenses

From the value transfer summary given above can be constructed a block diagram in which the blocks represent records in the accounting system to coincide with those scheduled against each transaction. This is shown in figure 6 in which the sequence of transactions broadly flows from left to right.

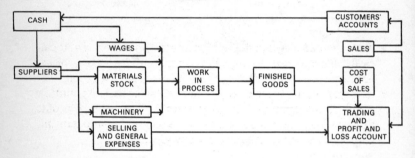

Figure 6. The flow of resource values through the accounting system of a manufacturing concern

From figure 6 it can be inferred that:

- The cycle of operations and accounting entries begins and ends with cash; the natural business expectation being that there ought to be more cash or its equivalent at the end of the operations than at the beginning, if the business has been trading successfully. Of course, the actual cash held at any time may not evidence an increase, because debts may be owing to and from suppliers and customers respectively, and cash may have been invested in machinery and other resources for further expansion.
- A considerable volume of finance is constantly tied up in various stock accounts, including materials, work-in-progress and finished goods, as well as machinery and customers' accounts; even though there is a continuous movement of value through those accounts.
- The trading and profit and loss account summarizes the result of selling goods to customers during a stated period as follows:

	£
Sales	XXX
less Cost of sales	XXX
Gross profit	XXX
less Selling and general expenses	XXX
Net profit	XXX

- Although the diagram depicts a manufacturing concern, it can easily be modified to one that simply trades in *purchased* finished goods, by extracting the work-in-process account.
- It should be possible to draw far more management information from the accounting system than simply a statement of profit. For example, a detailed summary of the costs of manufacturing goods over a period of time can be produced.

Activity

Try your hand at preparing a trading and profit and loss account from the following information:

	£
Costs transferred into work-in-process account	19,000
Unfinished work at month end	2,000
Stock of finished goods at the beginning of the month	1,500
Stock of finished goods at the end of the month	2,000
Sales invoices sent to customers	25,000
Selling and general expenses paid	1,000

SOLUTION

	£
Sales	25,000
less Cost of goods sold (see working below)	16,500
Gross profit	8,500
less Selling and general expenses	1,000
Net profit	7,500

Working:	£
Costs input into work-in-process account	19,000
less Unfinished work at month end	2,000
Goods completed during the month	17,000
add Opening stock of finished goods	1,500
	18,500
less Closing stock of finished goods	2,000
Cost of goods sold	16,500

Self-check

1 Below are given the names of some accounting records to be found in a manufacturing concern, followed by descriptions of some value transfers through the system of accounting. Name the two accounts affected by each of the transfers.

Cost of goods sold	Materials stock
Cash	Finished goods
Wages	Suppliers
Work-in-process	Customers
	Machinery

Value transfers
(a) Materials purchased on credit for immediate use.
(b) Cash received from customers.
(c) Employees supply labour to production.
(d) Materials acquired on credit for stock.
(e) Machinery is used in production.
(f) Completed goods are transferred from production.

2 'The trading and profit and loss account is a statement showing the detailed costs of goods manufactured during a period.' Is this statement (a) true or (b) false? Explain.

ANSWERS

1 (a) Work-in-process/Suppliers.
  (b) Cash/Customers (debtors).
  (c) Work-in-process/Wages.
  (d) Materials stock/Suppliers.

(e) Work-in-process/Machinery (depreciation).
(f) Finished goods/Work-in-process.
2 (b) False – the trading and profit and loss account is a summary of sales of goods during a period, less the cost of producing and selling those goods. Detailed costs of manufacturing are dealt with in a separate manufacturing account.

The accounting system at work

Accounting records can be maintained in a variety of forms whether recorded manually or by computer, but for our purposes what is referred to as a T-account is quite adequate. The account has two sides: the left showing transfers into the account, and the right, transfers out, as shown below:

Value transferred *in* or simply + (plus)	Value transferred *out* or simply − (minus)

Taking this as our model, we could for example enter the purchase of material for stock £1,000 as follows:

Material stock		*Supplier*	
Supplier 1,000			Material stock 1,000

Activity

The following transactions of the Scott Engineering Company relate to their first month of trading.

Enter them into relevant accounts – two entries for each transfer of value. Cash at commencement was £50,000.

		£
1	Materials purchased on credit from suppliers	15,000
2	Machinery purchased from suppliers on credit	20,000
3	Suppliers provide services for production on credit	2,000
4	Wages paid	4,000
5	Material issued to production from stock	5,000
6	Selling and General Expenses supplied on credit	1,000
7	Labour used in production (£3,000 direct, £1,000 indirect)	4,000

		£
8	Machinery depreciated at £200 per month	200
9	Cash paid to suppliers	38,000
10	Cost of goods sold	9,000
11	Goods sold to customers for	15,000
12	Cash received from customers	13,000
13	Goods finished during the month	10,000

SOLUTION

Cash

Opening	50,000	Suppliers	38,000
Customers	13,000	Wages	4,000

Wages

Cash	4,000	Work-in-process	4,000

Suppliers

Cash	38,000	Materials	15,000
		Machinery	20,000
		Selling and general	1,000
		Services	2,000

Work-in-process

Services	2,000	Finished goods	10,000
Wages	4,000		
Materials	5,000		
Depreciation	200		

Materials stock

Suppliers	15,000	Work-in-process	5,000

Finished goods

Work-in-process	10,000	Cost of goods sold	9,000

Machinery

Suppliers	20,000	Work-in-process (depreciation)	200

Cost of goods sold

Finished goods	9,000		

Selling & general exps

Suppliers	1,000		

Sales

		Customers	15,000

Customers

Sales	15,000	Cash	13,000

Manufacturing accounts

It was stated at the end of the previous section that a summary of the cost of goods manufactured during a period ought to be able to be drawn from the accounting system. The manufacturing account, as it is known, can be prepared to compare the actual costs for a period with the expected costs for that period, as well as to indicate the cost per unit of output produced. Quite obviously, very large manufacturing companies, with a diversity of products, will further subdivide this account into its various activities for control purposes.

Using the accounts produced in the previous activity, the

following manufacturing account is produced for the Scott Engineering Company. Note that most of the information is gleaned from the work-in-process account.

Scott Engineering Company
Manufacturing account for the month of January 19XX

	£	£
Direct materials		5,000
Direct labour		3,000
Total direct (or prime) cost		8,000
Production indirect costs:	£	
Indirect labour	1,000	
Services	2,000	
Depreciation of machinery	200	3,200
Total production cost		11,200
less Closing incompleted work		1,200
Cost of finished goods manufactured		10,000

Activity

Now complete a trading and profit and loss account for the Scott Engineering Company by extracting information from the relevant accounts. It will probably be of help if you refer to the first activity in this chapter to remind yourself of the contents and form of this summary.

SOLUTION

Scott Engineering Company
Trading and profit and loss account for the month of January 19XX

	£
Sales	15,000
less Cost of sales	9,000
Gross profit	6,000
less Selling and general expenses	1,000
Net profit	5,000

Self-check

Two years later, the accounts of the Scott Engineering Company showed the following figures at the commencement of the year:

	£
Direct material stock	2,000
Work-in-process	500
Finished goods stock	2,500

During the month that followed, manufacturing and selling operations involved the transactions listed below:

		£
1	Direct materials purchased	3,000
2	Direct materials issued to production	2,500
3	Direct labour paid	2,000
4	Production indirect labour paid	500
5	Selling and general expenses paid	700
6	Indirect material purchased for immediate use in production	700
7	Paid for other indirect services	600
8	Depreciation on machinery was	200
9	Goods sold during the month	9,200
10	Work-in-process at the month end	1,000
11	Finished goods stock at month end	2,000

Required

Draw up a manufacturing account and a trading and profit and loss account for the month.

ANSWER

Manufacturing account for the month of ......

		£
Direct materials used		2,500
Direct labour		2,000
		———
Prime cost		4,500
Production indirect expenses:	£	
Indirect materials	700	
Indirect labour	500	
Other services	600	
Depreciation	200	2,000
	———	———

		£
Total production cost		6,500
add Work-in-process – opening	500	
less Work-in-process – closing	1,000	500
Cost of finished goods manufactured		6,000

Trading and profit and loss account for the month of ......

	£
Sales	9,200
Cost of sales (see note below)	6,500
Gross profit	2,700
Selling and general expenses	700
Net profit	2,000

Note: cost of sales is calculated as follows:

	£
Opening stock of finished goods	2,500
Cost of finished goods manufactured during the month (see manufacturing account)	6,000
	8,500
Closing stock of finished goods	2,000
	6,500

Review

1 Referring to the previous self-check question, if direct materials purchased had been £3,500, what would the closing stock of direct materials have been?

2 Why do we not transfer the whole of the cost of a machine to work-in-process at the time it is purchased?

3 Why is the total manufacturing cost adjusted for work-in-process?

4 Why is the cost of finished goods produced not deducted directly from sales?

ANSWERS

1 Assuming that the same value of material is used in production,

an increased purchases figure of £3,500 would result in a closing stock value of £3,000.

2 As explained in Chapter 4, the use of a machine will extend over a long period of time. Therefore current production is only charged with that proportion of the value of the machine *estimated* to have been consumed (or depreciated) in the period that has just ended. The remainder is carried forward for use in future production.

3 An increase in work-in-process over the period means that some of the production cost, represented by this increase, cannot be included as finished work, but must be carried forward into the following period.

4 We can only deduct the quantity and cost of *goods sold* from the sales figure, and this might not necessarily coincide with the quantity and cost of *goods manufactured* if stocks have been allowed to increase or decrease.

6 | Breaking down the 'big picture'

Introduction

'England, First Innings 650 for 1 declared; West Indies, First Innings 89 all out, Second Innings 102.' Truly an historic result! Some would greet it with great joy, whilst the sceptics would take some convincing of its truth. Yet others would be completely uninterested. The real cricket 'buff', however, would search hungrily for more information. He would wish to know the individual batsmen's scores, how each was dismissed, and the bowling averages achieved by each side. This breakdown of the 'big picture' information would give far more insight into individual performances, and analyse the circumstances leading to England's victory. To selectors of future teams, this more detailed information of how players have performed is central to their deliberations, which are aimed at choosing that combination of men who are most likely to achieve their objective of winning the next Test Match.

This search for more than just 'big picture' information is true for most organizations, and particularly for businesses. Summaries of total manufacturing costs and of the profit made during a period are very useful, but neither throws light upon the efficiency of the different processes and services combining to produce the finished product, nor reveals the detailed cost make-up of each unit of output. An effective management accounting system will therefore incorporate the following three features:

- the accumulation and grouping of costs into areas that are the responsibility of a particular supervisor – commonly referred to as 'cost centres';
- the measurement of production or services expressed as units of output, e.g. tons of coal;

● a system designed to ascertain the cost per unit of output.

This chapter examines each of these features a little more closely.

Cost centre control

If you refer back to figure 6 (Chapter 5), you will recall that the production process is represented by a single work-in-process account. Now this may represent the situation, say, in a very small bakery, but not in one of the larger regional baking businesses, where each of the processes involved will be on a much larger scale and require a full-time supervisor to overlook the operation in terms of output and costs.

The concept of cost centre control is a consequence of management's recognition that centralized control cannot effectively supervise every unit of a business from afar, and that delegation of responsibility for cost control to managers who are directly able to influence the level of those costs will motivate them to manage resources under their command more effectively and give them a greater sense of purpose. Reference to the section in Chapter 1 entitled 'Organizing to implement the strategy', and particularly to the organization chart (figure 1) in that section, illustrates how businesses are organized into responsibility centres, each of them in the charge of a manager or a supervisor.

A cost centre can therefore be described as an area of responsibility whose costs are separately analysed to facilitate their control. A centre need not be a whole department, it could for example be a *section* of machines in the sewing department of a garment producer, when that department is too large to be in the charge of one person. It could be one machine – a huge three-colour two-sided printer, whose costs can easily be segregated; it could be a production service department, e.g. maintenance; or it could be the sales promotion department.

Figure 7 below illustrates the basic operations in the growing and production of mushrooms, and is a good example of how a production department is very often subdivided into many distinct and separately controlled sub-departments.

Each of the production and service centres shown has its own supervisor who would receive a periodic operating statement relating to his department, primarily showing a comparison between

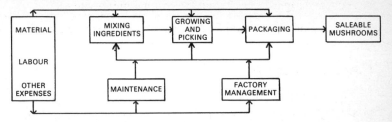

Figure 7. Mushroom production and service departments

planned and actual production and costs. The objective in this feeding-back of information is to highlight major deviations from planned operations, and to put the responsibility for remedial action squarely on the shoulders of the people most able to recognize the problem.

Self-check

By reference to the following statement of output and costs, explain how cost centre control is more effective than overall control. Assume that all costs are variable, that output of department 1 is transferred to, and becomes the input of, department 2, and that normally there is no wastage.

	Planned output		Actual output	
	Units	Cost £	Units	Cost £
Department 1	1,000	1,000	1,100	900
Department 2	1,000	500	1,000	600
Total final output and cost	1,000	£1,500	1,000	£1,500

ANSWER

If a summary of results were given merely showing the last line of information, management might be lured into believing that all was well – for actual and plan are in line! However, we would be hiding the fact that department 1 output was higher than planned by 100 units, and its cost, which should have been £1,100 (on a variable cost basis), was effectively reduced by £200. In addition, whilst department 2 output was on target, this overlooks the 100 units more than planned transferred from department

1 that appear to have 'gone missing'. Further, costs are £100 more than they ought to be.

What is a unit of output?

The measurement of the output of manufacturing or service activity will naturally vary according to the activity being pursued. Builders, civil and general engineers work on *jobs* or *contracts* to erect buildings, bridges or machines respectively. Sometimes a single product is continuously output. For example, steelworks produce *tons* of steel; bus companies operate *miles* of service; electricity is produced in *kilowatt-hours*; educational institutions express their activity in *student-hours*; and some hospital departments recognize *patient-days* as being a suitable measure of their endeavours.

A great number of manufacturers produce a diverse range of products, albeit in the same industry. Cosmetic, pharmaceutical and food producers are good examples, where different parts of a factory will be devoted to different products within their product ranges. In these cases, orders will be given to the production department for a *batch* of a certain type of product, say 100,000 tubes of sun-tan lotion, but with a standard measuring unit of *1,000* tubes.

It is necessary to recognize the appropriate unit of output in order to ascertain the cost per unit, the purpose of which is discussed later in this chapter, but for the moment let us just define a unit of output as the most appropriate and useful measure of the results of productive or service activity, in respect of which costs can be meaningfully ascertained.

> *Self-check*
>
> 1 What do you consider to be the most appropriate cost unit for Harrods store in London?
> 2 Which of the following expresses the most appropriate unit in respect of which costs should be ascertained in a solicitor's office?
>
> (a) By partner in the firm.
> (b) By individual employee.

(c) By hour.
(d) By client.

ANSWERS

1 Costs are most usefully expressed by department in a departmentmental store such as Harrods, although supplementary statistics are very often produced to indicate, for example, the cost per unit of selling floor space in each department.

2 **(d)** By client. Charges have ultimately to be made to the client or perhaps to another solicitor in respect of a client. However, **(c)** provides part of the answer, for in most professional offices a cost per hour is determined for the different grades of employee engaged on clients' work, and this will be the rate used in the accumulation of client costs.

A choice of two basic systems

It will be apparent from the last section that the measured unit of output is a direct function of (a) the operations or technical functions involved, and (b) the need to ascertain the costs of each production order.

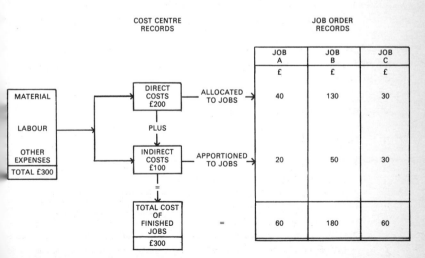

Figure 8. A job-order costing system

In circumstances where the latter information is required, a *job-order costing system* is adopted whereby all the costs attributable to a particular customer's order, or identifiable production order (see sun-tan lotion example above), are accumulated on additional job-order records; additional, that is, to the accounting records maintained for total or cost-centre reporting (see figure 8).

In all other circumstances, where *like* units are produced through a *continuous* series of processes or operations, a system of *process or operating costs* applies. As units proceed through their various processes, the *total* costs of each process during a particular period are divided by the output during the same period to arrive at the cost per unit at each stage. The finished output of one process becomes the input for the next, accompanied by its cost to date, until, upon completion of the production cycle of operations, final cost per unit is ascertained (figure 9).

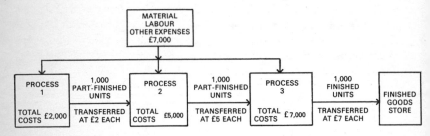

Figure 9. A process costing system

Job-order and process costing are the basic cost ascertainment systems, but both can apply to non-manufacturing as well as manufacturing organizations. For example, job-order costing is used by accountants to accumulate client costs; whilst bus companies use an adaptation of process costing referred to as operating costing to calculate costs per mile run.

Some businesses use a mixture of both systems. For example, certain components that are common to different models of lawn-mower may be manufactured continuously for stock using process costing, and then assembled along with other components to satisfy a production order for a specified quantity of a particular model of mower.

Self-check

Which of the following statements are correct?

1 In both job and process costing, the cost per unit includes a mixture of fixed and variable costs.
2 A separate cost record is maintained for each customer's order in process costing.
3 Process costing is usually adopted when like units are produced through a continuous series of processes.
4 Cost centre records are only maintained when a process costing system is in operation.

ANSWERS

1 Correct – fixed costs are charged to each production cost centre whether job or process costing is in operation. In job costing each job order is charged with an appropriate apportionment of indirect costs which include fixed costs. In process costing, the total costs of a process, including fixed costs, are divided by the output to give cost per unit in that process.
2 Incorrect – a separate record is maintained in a job order system but not in process costing.
3 Correct – the emphasis here being upon the word 'like'.
4 Incorrect – cost centre records are kept in both job and process systems, the difference being that additional job order records are created in job costing to record the value of work carried out on each order in each cost centre.

Why do we need to know unit cost?

The additional cost involved in calculating the cost per unit of output, especially in job-order costing where a record is maintained for each order, has to be justified, in the same way that the use of any resource has to be justified by the benefits it produces.

When it is agreed between a buyer and a seller that the selling price of goods or services is to be based upon total cost plus a stated profit margin, then a job-order costing system is called for. Even when selling prices are predetermined, it would probably be desirable to check actual costs and profit against planned figures for control purposes. Cost control might also be a good reason for applying a job-order system to batch production, that is, when production is not earmarked for any specific customer, but is processed in a predetermined quantity.

Other good reasons for ascertaining unit cost include:

- the valuation of stocks – to be used in the measurement of overall profit, and for inclusion in the balance sheet as an asset;
- measuring the profitability of each product line or department;
- the provision of cost information to facilitate future cost control (to be dealt with in more detail later);
- providing a breakdown of cost into fixed and variable elements – valuable information, when decisions may rest upon knowing which costs will actually be changed because of some proposed action.

Self-check

Costs per unit are ascertained for five of the following reasons. Which is the 'odd man out'?

1 Providing information for decision-making purposes.
2 To inform shareholders.
3 To help to fix selling prices.
4 Measuring the profitability of each product line.
5 To value stocks.
6 Providing information for future cost control.

ANSWER

2 Shareholders as a whole do not require such detailed information. Management do.

Review

Poacher's Pies and Pâté Co. Ltd, referred to in Chapter 1, have gone from strength to strength. Both the pie and pâté production departments have added production facilities to meet a rising and continuous demand for each of their regular lines. In addition, a further department, with its own supervisor, has been added to deal with special pie orders – demands from customers to meet their own specifications as to weight, content and quantity required.

1 Referring to figure 1 (Chapter 1), to what extent has the organization chart altered, and why?

2 What unit(s) do you think the company uses to express its output? (Note particularly the different mode of operation in the new department.)

3 Do you consider that the company uses a job-order or process costing system?

4 Why does the company need to know the cost per unit of its output?

ANSWERS

1 An additional department will be added, responsible to the production manager, and alongside the existing pie and pâté departments. This is necessary because the operations of the new department are not standard, unlike its two brother departments, and will require a separate analysis of its costs and output to report back to the new cost centre supervisor.

2 In the old pie and pâté departments the continuous output will be expressed in terms of weight, per kilo or 100 kilos, as the products are sold by weight. In the new department the cost unit will be the job order created for each customer.

3 In the old departments, process costing systems will be used; total costs for each process on each production line period (say each month) being divided by total weight of output on each line. In the new department, a job-order system will operate to collect the costs relevant to each customer's order.

4 To value its stocks; to measure the profit on each line; to provide information for future cost control; to provide relevant information for decision-making.

Part 3
Resource flow control

7 | Controlling direct materials

Introduction

In the last chapter we identified two fundamental features of an accounting system designed to satisfy the information needs of managers:

- the collection of costs by function or department – referred to as 'cost centres'; and
- the allocation and apportionment of those costs to products.

Part 3 of this book probes more deeply into how control is exercised over the acquisition and use of resources, and reveals how the problems associated with the ascertainment of cost can be dealt with.

Chapters 7 and 8 focus their attention specifically on direct materials.

What, when and how much to order

Shopping is a mixture of pleasurable window-gazing and more objective searches for goods and services to satisfy our many needs. The weekly grocery expedition falls into the latter category, and housewives have to be particularly well organized to squeeze the best value out of their precious housekeeping-money. They will compile lists of the items they wish to buy, influenced partly by price, partly by the amounts already held in the larder and the quantities required.

The 'housewife' of a business firm is the purchasing manager, or buyer, who adopts similar principles of 'good housekeeping' in the function of acquiring the materials and supplies needed for the business. Decisions are made upon what to order and from whom, when to order and how much to order; and like the housewife, the efficiency with which the job is carried out can make or break the firm.

What to order

> *Activity*
>
> Examine the range of cosmetics on a lady's dressing table, then make a list of the packaging parts and probable ingredients that are contained in the items.

The length of the list could shock you! It may possibly indicate something about the personality of the user, but that is not the present purpose of your investigation.

Each cosmetic product is comprised of many materials. A bottle of perfume, for example, will include a carton, a carton label, a protective corrugated packing piece inside the carton, a 'how to use it' instructional leaflet, a bottle, a label, a bottle cap, a packing piece inside the cap and the ingredients in the perfume itself. These might include perfume oil, alcohol and water. If you have discovered ten cosmetics on the dressing table, your list of materials could be 100 items long. Given that the cosmetic manufacturer sells 300 items – of different shades, perfumes and sizes – you begin to understand that the company's buyer has quite a responsibility in having to ensure that the right materials are available in the right quantities, at the right price, at the right time.

Specifications of new products, design drawings with lists of parts required, formulas and recipes will provide the breakdown of materials required initially. Suppliers will then be approached for quotations for the various materials, and the buyer will be careful to compare quality, prices, delivery dates and assurances of continuity of supply, before choosing a particular supplier. Thereafter replenishment of material stocks will be put on a routine basis, subject to determining when and how much to order and to a continuing review by the buyer of alternative materials and suppliers.

> *Self-check*
>
> **1** Who is responsible for the procurement of supplies in a business?

2 What original source of information will indicate what materials are required in the production of **(a)** cakes; **(b)** medicines; **(c)** farm machinery?

ANSWERS

1 The buyer.
2 **(a)** recipes; **(b)** formulas; **(c)** drawings and parts lists.

When to order

If you are lucky enough to have a centrally heated house, your stock of fuel oil will require replenishment from time to time, but when should you call the supplier? Certainly not when you run out of stock completely. You will most likely order another delivery when your stock has reached a level that you know will cover your needs up to the time when you expect delivery to take place; that is, your average daily consumption of oil multiplied by the number of days you expect to have to wait for delivery.

Businesses use the same approach; for if they did not set an appropriate reorder level, production and customers' orders would be disrupted. As an example, an orange cordial manufacturer filling 10,000 bottles a week, and having to wait two weeks from the date of sending an order to the bottle supplier before receiving them, should order new supplies of bottles each time the stock level falls to 20,000 bottles. Figure 10 illustrates this example.

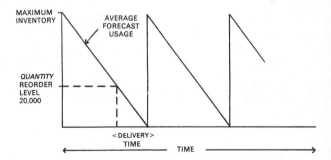

Figure 10. Stock levels when usage and replenishment times are known

Self-check

Poacher's Pies and Pâté Co. Ltd use large quantities of flour in making their pies, and they currently reorder further flour supplies when their stock reaches 500 kg. The supplier indicates that he is now in a position to reduce delivery time from 10 to 6 days. What is the new reorder level?

ANSWER

Daily flour consumption $\dfrac{500}{10} = 50$ kg.

New reorder level (daily usage × 6) = $50 \times 6 = 300$ kg.

The above calculations assume that delivery times and usage remain stable, but this is a little unreal as delivery may be slower and usage higher from time to time. Such uncertainty calls for the prudent addition of safety stocks, to prevent production delays and consequent loss of customers. Calculations of how much safety stock to carry can be a little involved, as they include the mathematics of probability theory; but in simple terms the optimal amount will be that which minimizes the total of the cost of holding safety stocks, and the profit from lost customers. If too much safety is built in, to the extent that no customers are lost, the cost of stockholding could well exceed the total of holding lower stocks and losing a few orders. Figure 11 shows how the stock held and reorder levels change with the addition of safety stocks.

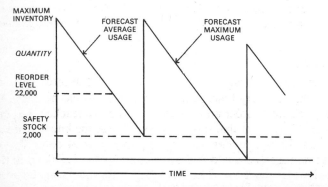

Figure 11. Stock levels when usage and replenishment are uncertain

Self-check

Norfolk Agrimek Ltd install a certain type of electric motor in a number of their small agricultural machines. Information regarding this motor is as follows:

Average daily usage: 30 motors
Normal delivery time from supplier: 10 days
Maximum stock level: 1,020 motors
Standard quantity usually ordered: 900 motors

Calculate **(a)** the safety stock level, **(b)** the reorder level.

ANSWER

(a) Safety stock level = maximum stock level *less* the standard quantity ordered:

= 1,020 − 900 = 120.

(b) Reorder level = (average daily usage × delivery time) plus safety stock:
= (30 × 10) + 120 = 420 motors.

How much to order

Activity

Joe Crowe, a boatbuilder, uses 5,000 of a certain boat-fitting fairly evenly throughout each year. He knows precisely how long he has to wait for further deliveries from his suppliers, and he places only one order each year. What is his maximum stock of this fitting? What would be the average stock?

ANSWER

Given an even rate of consumption and complete certainty regarding delivery time, his *maximum stock* would be 5,000, for he would not reorder until he knew that he had reached the point where his stock at that time would just cover the known delivery period. Then assuming a continuing even rate of consumption, his average stock would be 5,000 divided by 2 = 2,500; i.e. half of the time his stock would be more than 2,500 and during the other half it would be less.

Obviously, the costs of *holding* such a large stock would be quite high, viz. building-related costs such as rates, heating, maintenance, insurance of both building and stocks, interest on the capital tied up in stock, deterioration of stocks. On the other hand, *ordering* costs, such as clerical salaries, costs of receiving and handling deliveries, would be relatively low – being restricted to one order and one delivery.

Developing this theme further, you can see that placing two orders a year would increase total ordering costs, but would considerably diminish stock holding costs. Two orders a year would result in an average stock of 2,500 ÷ 2, i.e. 1,250 – which would probably halve the holding costs.

It will be apparent that ordering cost grows as more orders are placed, but conversely that stock holding costs diminish, until a point is reached at which the *total* of the ordering and stock-holding costs are at a minimum. This point will indicate the most *economic order quantity* and can be expressed as follows:

Holding cost

$$\left(\frac{\text{quantity ordered}}{2} \times \text{holding cost per unit} \right) +$$

Ordering cost

$$\left(\frac{\text{annual demand}}{\text{quantity ordered}} \times \text{cost of placing an order} \right)$$

or in short $\left(\dfrac{Q}{2} \times H \right) + \left(\dfrac{A}{Q} \times C \right)$.

Self-check

Assuming an annual demand of 5,000 of the boat-fitting described in this section, an annual holding cost of 4 pence per fitting and an order cost of £2 per order, draw up a schedule showing the total cost of holding and ordering fittings, given that the number of orders placed are as follows: 1, 2, 4, 5, 7, 10, 25, 50.

What is the economic order quantity?

ANSWER

No. of orders placed	1	2	4	5	7	10	25	50
Size of order	5,000	2,500	1,250	1,000	700	500	200	100

Average stock	2,500	1,250	625	500	350	250	100	50
Annual holding cost @ £0.04 per fitting	£100	50	25	20	14	10	4	2
Annual order cost @ £2 per order	£2	4	8	10	14	20	50	100
Total annual cost	£102	54	33	30	28	30	54	102

The economic order quantity is 700 fittings, because at this level total holding and ordering cost is minimized. Note that holding and ordering cost are the same at the EOQ level.

Figure 12 shows graphically how ordering, holding and total cost change relative to quantity ordered.

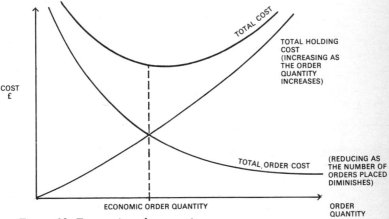

Figure 12. Economic order quantity

You will observe that the carrying costs and ordering costs are the same at the EOQ cross-over point, thus:

$$\frac{Q}{2} \times H = \frac{A}{Q} \times C$$

and after cross-multiplying

$$Q^2 H = 2AC$$

and

$$Q^2 = \frac{2AC}{H}$$

and finally

$$Q = \sqrt{\frac{2AC}{H}}$$

which is the well-known EOQ formula.

Self-check

Now check the answer in the previous self-check question by applying the EOQ formula.

ANSWER

$$Q = \sqrt{\frac{2AC}{H}}$$

$$Q = \sqrt{\frac{2 \times 5,000 \times 2}{.04}}$$

$$Q = \sqrt{500,000}$$

$$Q = 700 \text{ (approx.)}.$$

Of course, the cost of this level of sophistication in calculating the amount of every stock item to order – or to produce internally – might not be justified, but if applied to the high cost items, which attract the highest storage costs, it may well be worth considering.

8 | The material control system and valuation

Introduction

Direct materials comprise a very high proportion of the cost of manufactured goods, and if one adds to this other supplies and materials categorized as indirect materials, you can appreciate the need for very close monitoring of the ordering, receipt, storage and usage of materials. The last chapter emphasized the importance of making optimal decisions about what, when and how much to order. In this chapter we take the story on from there and reveal the procedures and practices that control the storage, flow and efficient use of direct materials, together with some of the problems arising out of frequent changes in price levels and their effects upon valuation for cost and stock purposes.

Tracing the flow of materials

Many people live deep in the country, away from the hustle and bustle of town, and many others dream from time to time of living in such idyllic surroundings. One of the problems of this kind of existence, however, is the difficulty of obtaining food and other necessities. If you lived in a remote area, subject to being cut off by snowdrifts in the winter, you would have to carry a considerable stock of foodstuffs and dry goods to 'tide you over' the snowed-up periods. Whether you replenish your stocks by using a delivery service or use your own transport, your trips to the nearest town would tend to be infrequent, or deliveries relatively few, because of the high cost of transport. It would obviously be the sensible thing to carry sufficient stock of necessities to cover the period between deliveries. You certainly would not calculate reorder levels or economic order quantities, but your subjective judgements in these matters would be aimed at minimizing the total cost of holding goods and having them delivered.

Your order to the supplier would then be made up of items that you normally stock and those that you do not.

Along would come the delivery van, winding its way down the valley, and after a chat and a cup of tea with the driver you would check the goods received against your order to ensure that he has delivered what you ordered, in the right quantity, and then restock your larder.

This homely procedure has its parallel in business, where purchase requisitions are passed to the buyer from the store-keeper, or from the production planning department for new materials. After appropriate technical inquiries, the buyer will send a purchase order to the selected supplier, following this up with reminders to urge delivery when necessary.

Delivery will eventually be made, and the goods received are checked to ensure that they are as ordered, both as regards quality and quantity, and a goods received note is created to record the precise nature and quantity of the goods received. Two copies of this document might be raised and be sent to:

- the accounting department, to match against a copy of the purchase order held there, and against the supplier's invoice for the goods, before payment is made; and
- to the stores department with the goods, to ensure that the amount put into stock is in agreement with the amount received, and to update the stores record relating to these items (see figure 13).

Of course, that is not the end of the story, for the direct materials bide for only a while in store before being withdrawn by a production department for conversion into the planned product. A 'material requisition', authorized by the manager of the appropriate production department (see figure 14), is used for this purpose, and after the material has been issued, an entry is made into the relevant stock record, to record the issue and update the figure shown as the current stock.

The material requisition is then priced and passed to the accounting department for incorporating into the costing records.

Yet another document that may be completed is the 'materials transfer note', which records the transfer of part-completed

MATERIAL DESCRIPTION:
MATERIAL CODE NO.:

DATE	VOUCHER NO.	RECEIVED			ISSUED			BALANCE IN STOCK		
		QUANTITY	UNIT PRICE	VALUE	QUANTITY	UNIT PRICE	VALUE	QUANTITY	UNIT PRICE	VALUE

Figure 13. Stores record card

MATERIAL REQUISITION				
COST CENTRE:			JOB NO.:	
ITEM DESCRIPTION	ITEM CODE	QUANTITY	UNIT COST	VALUE
AUTHORISED BY:			DATE:	

Figure 14. Material requisition

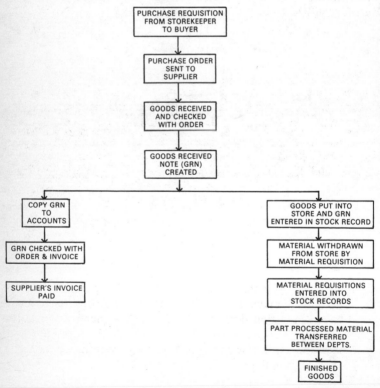

Figure 15. Tracing the flow of direct materials

manufactured goods from one production department to the next, and completed goods to the finished goods warehouse. Both the production planning department and the accounting department are interested in this document, as it signals the exact stage in the production process that has been reached by the particular item, which information helps update the work progress plan, and the work-in-progress account and finished goods account in the accounting records.

Figure 15 summarizes the procedure described above, governing the flow of direct materials.

Self-check

Which of the following statements are correct?

1 A 'material requisition' is the document sent to the buyer by the storekeeper to request that an order be placed with a supplier.
2 Notification of goods received is only sent to the storekeeper along with the goods.
3 A 'materials transfer note' notifies production planning and accounting departments of the current progress of part- and fully completed work through a factory. This information is entered into the progress record and work-in-process accounts respectively.
4 Suppliers' invoices are only checked with the purchase orders before payment.
5 A 'goods received note' is a receipt sent to the storekeeper by a production department to acknowledge that it has received direct materials.

ANSWERS

1 Incorrect – the appropriate document is the 'purchase requisition'. The 'material requisition' is passed to the storekeeper by a production department to withdraw materials for processing.
2 Incorrect – a further copy is sent to the accounting department to check with the supplier's invoice.
3 Correct.
4 Incorrect – as stated in 2 above, suppliers' invoices will also

be checked against a 'goods received note' to ensure that what is being charged by the supplier is exactly what has been received.

5 Incorrect – a 'goods received note' is the document raised by the goods inwards department, detailing materials received after they have been checked as to quantity and quality.

Valuing the flow of direct materials

Management accounting information is largely expressed in monetary terms, even though, in appropriate circumstances, other units of measurement such as tons, miles or hours may be more meaningful. Thus direct materials will be ordered, received, stored, recorded and issued in non-monetary units, e.g. kilos, but at the same time will have to be valued. In this section we examine closely the problem of what cost to attribute to goods sold, material used in production, and stock.

There would be no difficulty if prices remained stable, for each unit of material would have its unchanging supply price. With continuing inflation, however, what is dubbed 'cost' today may well be out of date tomorrow, with consequent effects upon selling prices, total costs and profit measurement. At any one time stocks of items held could have been purchased at different prices, and this poses the problem of what price to use when charging issues to cost of sales, or to cost of production, and to apply to the stock held at the end of any trading period.

Let us suppose that Joe Crowe, our boatbuilder, has the following stock record of a boat fitting sold in his chandlery shop at a price of £5 each:

Date	Receipts	Issues	Purchase price	Stock
	Units	Units	£	Units
1 January			2	200
9 February	300		3	500
31 March		200		300

Note: current replacement price at 31 March, £3.50.

If we assume that the fittings are issued physically on a 'first to be received – first to be issued' basis (known as FIFO), which invariably will not be the case when all the fittings are identical, then a trading statement for the three months to 31 March will show:

		£
Sales	200 @ £5	1,000
	£	
Opening stock	400	
add Purchases	900	
	1,300	
Closing stock 300 @ £3	900	
Cost of sales	400	400
Profit		600

This calculation of profit appears to be quite sensible, based as it is on the 'actual cost' to Joe of the fittings sold, and he might be excused for believing that he had done very well on the sale. However, presuming that he continues in business, and that he replaces the 200 fittings previously sold, at the current replacement price of £3.50 each, the actual amount of cash surplus from the previous sale would be £1,000 − £700 = £300, and not the £600 reported. You can see that this has arisen because it has cost £3.50 − £2.00 = £1.50 more to replace each of the fittings sold. Thus Joe has only got £300 more wealth than he previously possessed.

In times of rapidly rising prices, therefore, it would appear to be more realistic to apply replacement cost rather than FIFO cost to the *measurement of profit*, although it must be said in defence of FIFO that it does at least result in the valuation of stock being reasonably realistic, as the items still held at any time are valued at the most recently paid prices.

A partial solution to this problem can be effected by assuming that each item sold or issued to production has been drawn from the most recently received batch, that is, 'last item in − first item out' (or LIFO), not only in physical terms but also as regards value. Thus the 200 boat-fittings sold on 31 March will be deemed to have been sold out of the batch received on 9 February, that is, at £3.00 each, with the result that the closing stock will now include the 200 held on 1 January at £2.00 each, together with the remaining 100 out of the 9 February batch at £3.00 each.

Self-check

Using the information in the previous paragraph, construct a trading statement in similar form to the one shown on page 87, but this time adopting the LIFO approach.

ANSWER

		£
Sales	200 @ £5	1,000
	£	
Opening stock	400	
add Purchases	900	
	———	
	1,300	
less Closing stock		
200 @ £2		
100 @ £3	700	
	———	
Cost of sales	600	600
	———	———
Profit		400
		———

The resultant profit is certainly more realistic than that using FIFO, but because it still does not provide for the complete replacement of the resources used in the transaction, it still overstates the profit by £100.

Furthermore stock held at any time is valued at earlier, unrealistic prices, resulting in a misleading undervaluation of this asset. LIFO is not much used in practice.

Another method used is average pricing, which involves the calculation of a new average price of stock held each time a new consignment is received from suppliers. In our example, the average price per unit at 1 January is £2, but this changes to £2.60 at the time of the next delivery, as shown below:

	Units	Price	Value
		£	£
1 Jan. In stock	200	2	400
9 Feb. Delivery	300	3	900
	———		———
	500		1,300

New average price £1,300 divided by 500 = £2.60.

Applying this average price in the production of a trading statement for Joe Crowe results as follows:

		£
Sales	200 @ £5	1,000
	£	
Opening stock	400	
add Purchases	900	
	1,300	
less Closing stock		
300 @ £2.60	780	
Cost of sales	520	520
Profit		480

Note that profit is still overstated in terms of replacement prices, average pricing being somewhere in between the results obtained under FIFO and LIFO. It has the administrative advantage over the other two approaches, however, of specifying only one value for each unit in stock, the other two being more unwieldy in requiring stock held at any time to be recorded at the different prices paid for it. Because of its relative simplicity, average pricing is much used, and is highly practicable when prices do not change too rapidly.

Perhaps the most sophisticated method developed to tackle the valuation problem is the use of *standard prices* as part of a larger, comprehensive control system known as 'standard costing' which we will be studying in later chapters.

The standard for each item in stock is the price that is expected to apply during the coming accounting period, which might be a year or even a shorter period. Standard prices are set by the buyer of the firm because he is the person who will be responsible for explaining differences between actual and planned prices.

These differences or 'variances' are separated when suppliers' invoices are authorized for payment, the price variances going into one account and the standard cost of the material received into another, the latter being the total stock account representing the standard value of all items in stock at any time. Because the price variances are extracted separately, the individual stock records need not be valued, as each item has a *standard* price. This saves much clerical work in both the stock recording and in pricing material requisitions to record the transfer of material from stores to work-in-progress.

Let us say that the standard price of the boat-fitting in our previous example was set at £3. The trading statement would then read:

		£
Sales 200 @ £5		1,000
less Standard cost of sales 200 @ £3		600
Profit		400

This is the same profit as that under LIFO, and suggests that the use of standard prices does not automatically provide for replacement unless the standard coincides with replacement cost.

The one thread that runs through all these valuation differences arising from the use of different methods is the fact of *changing prices*. If these changes are low and infrequent, little difference in profit measurement arises whichever method is used, as long as one method is used consistently.

In conditions of spiralling inflation, however, profit and stock valuation are considerably distorted. The best solution appears to be the use of standard prices, with revisions at suitable intervals, because it facilitates cost control through variance reporting, saves clerical cost in administration and uses relatively up-to-date values.

With regard to the external financial reporting required of limited companies, the problem of inflation has been recognized, and companies, who largely still report their trading results without adjusting them to current replacement cost, may produce an *additional* 'current cost' set of statements to show the overall effect of changing prices on their historically based figures.

Quite obviously, the management accountant must always be aware of the effect of changing price levels upon such decisions as setting prices and investment in new products.

Self-check

1 In times of rapidly rising prices, the method of pricing stores issues that results in the lowest profit is: **(a)** FIFO,

(b) averaging pricing, **(c)** LIFO, **(d)** replacement, **(e)** standard. Indicate which alternative is correct.

2 The stock record of a certain model of radio held by an electrical wholesaler showed the following entries:

	Received	Issued	Stock balance	Price per item £
1 April Stock held			200	15
8 April Issues		30	170	
12 April Purchased	100		270	20
20 April Issues		60	210	
28 April Issues		50	160	

Value the stock held at 28 April using the FIFO, LIFO, standard, average and replacement approaches. Standard price is £18. Replacement price at 28 April is £21.

ANSWERS

1 **(d)** Replacement – because in times of rapidly rising prices replacement cost results in the highest value being deducted from sales. Standard pricing could give the same result if the same standard is set at current prices.

	£
2 FIFO – (60 @ £15) + (100 @ £20)	= 2,900
LIFO – (200 – 40) @ £15	= 2,400
Standard – 160 @ £18	= 2,880

$$\text{Average} - \frac{(170 @ £15) + (100 @ £20)}{270} \times 160 = 2,696$$

Replacement – 160 × £21 = 3,360

Notes:
1 LIFO gives the lowest value as stock is valued at older prices.
2 Replacement gives highest value because of the recent price increase.
3 Standard is lower than FIFO and replacement because the *planned* price was predetermined at too low a figure.

'Waste not – want not'

In Chapter 7 the function of the buyer was described as being concerned with applying principles of good housekeeping to the purchase of goods or materials. The first section of the current chapter then outlined the kind of information system that keeps an eye on the flow of materials from acquisition to sale. In this section we extend the good housekeeping analogy to illustrate that businesses as well as individuals strive to reduce expenditure on goods and material purchased by constantly attacking waste and extravagance.

If you have ever been hiking you will appreciate the importance of keeping the weight of your backpack to a minimum. Certainly, Chris Bonnington and other leaders of mountaineering expeditions plan to the last detail to carry only what is vitally necessary for their purposes; not only to reduce the *burden* of individual loads, but also to keep investment in stores and equipment, and expenditure on the services of porters, within the constraints of limited expedition funds.

Considerable research and testing is carried out before equipment is purchased. Each item carried has to fulfil a necessary function, and materials and designs will be chosen that meet the most rigorous specifications. Tents have to be strong, easily erected, light, afford maximum shelter and warmth, and be able to withstand the worst of Arctic storms. Ladders to scale ice cliffs and to negotiate crevasses, oxygen equipment for climbing at altitude and personal clothing and equipment are designed to do their jobs efficiently but yet to leave a reasonable margin for safety.

Likewise, efficient business organizations are for ever seeking to discover *substitute* materials of improved design and quality at lower cost, to replace those presently used. In this respect, a now well-established and accepted technique known as 'value analysis' is of particular value. The technique involves an analysis of products, either at the design stage or at any time during their saleable lives, to determine their 'value' characteristics. These are the attributes that the customer is thought to look for and to be prepared to pay for, in the article, and include its *use value* (an assessment of its functional qualities), its *appeal value* (good looks, chromium plating, colour scheme, etc.), *second-hand value* (its trade-in price) and last but not least its *cost value* (to be as low as possible – consistent with maintaining or increasing the first three values).

The object of value analysis, then, is to build into a product the optimum of desired value at minimum cost, by using the most up-to-date appropriate designs, materials and methods of manufacture. No more value need be built into a product than is desired by the customer. For example, a bicycle frame would be very strong indeed if made of solid stainless steel, but because this degree of strength is not required, and because tubular steel or aluminium does the same job quite adequately, and at far less cost, it is chosen instead.

What other good housekeeping would be practised by an expedition storekeeper? Firstly, he would cut down on the number of items taken, for to satisfy all tastes and needs would be impossible and unnecessary. Records of past trips will reveal items for which there had been little call and highlight those that would be currently obsolete. A narrower, *standardized* range of supplies sufficient to cover all needs would cost less and probably weigh less, as well as being more easily packed and stored.

The principles of standardization, and the elimination of obsolete and slow-moving items, are also well-practised in industry, where firms take great care to limit the variety of sizes, quality and designs of materials used in their different products. This reduces the volume of stock held and therefore the investment in this asset.

Secondly, the use of the best storage and handling techniques is a major area for potential savings in material costs. Effective packaging, to reduce storage space requirements, will also help to preserve stores – particularly in the case of food. Ease of access to stored items and a good system for controlling issues will minimize waste, as will the support of an effective stores record system. All these practices apply equally to expeditions and business organizations.

Thirdly, expedition leaders have to make decisions regarding the siting of central and sub-stores. A fallback supply of most things would be held at base camp, but in addition the strategic siting of food, oxygen and other essentials in camps at progressively higher altitudes is vital to ensure the success of the mission. Whether to have centralized or decentralized stores is a familiar business problem. Centralized stores will be too distant from the work people, resulting in production delays. On the other hand, too many sub-stores carrying like items can be uneconomic. A good compromise is to have a central store, with sub-stores in strategic places carrying only those items used most frequently.

Other measures that can be adopted in industry that might not find their exact parallel in expeditions include:

- better training for workers, improved working methods and machines, to help to reduce wastage, especially by cutting down on faulty work;
- methodical inspection of part-finished and finished products to ensure quality standards;
- an efficient system of reporting the scrapping, rejection and over-use of materials.

Self-check

1 Differentiate between *standardization* and *substitution* of materials used in a manufacturing business.

2 Indicate which of the following, **(a)**, **(b)** or **(c)**, is correct. Value analysis is a technique aimed at:

   (a) valuing items in stock, so that their true value is shown in the balance sheet;
   (b) analysing the cost of producing an article;
   (c) maintaining or improving the value characteristics of a product, at the lowest possible cost.

3 Indicate which of the following could help to reduce the cost of materials used in production:

   (a) shorten the working week;
   (b) efficient inspection of production;
   (c) better training of workers;
   (d) economizing on fuel;
   (e) better machines and working methods;
   (f) good storekeeping;
   (g) better siting of stores;
   (h) increase the labour force;
   (i) regular material usage reports;
   (j) increase the annual holidays.

ANSWERS

1 *Standardization* refers to a reduction in the variety of materials

held usually in terms of quality and size. Will have the effect of reducing the total value of stock held.

Substitution is when an existing material is replaced by a superior material.

2 **(c)**.

3 **(b), (c), (e), (f), (g), (i)**.

Review

Top Garments is a small firm manufacturing ladies' dresses. On 1 January it had in store 200 metres of Shimmer material costing £3 per metre. On 1 February 400 metres were received from the supplier at a price of £3.50 a metre, and a month later 300 metres were issued to production.

With regard to the above information:

(a) Which of the following documents recorded the receipt of the material from the supplier – **(i)** 'goods received note'; or **(ii)** 'material transfer note'?

(b) Into which records would entries be made from the document evidencing the issue of material to production?

(c) Using FIFO and LIFO methods, calculate the value of stock at 31 March.

(d) How could value analysis be used by Top Garments to improve its products?

ANSWERS

(a) (i) 'goods received note'.

(b) (i) The stock record for the particular material.

  (ii) The relevant job-costing record.

  (iii) The work-in-progress account.

(c) *FIFO*: this method implies that issues are valued at the earliest prices of stock held, therefore stock will be valued at the most recent prices, i.e. 300 metres at £3.50 = £1,050

LIFO: each issue is made at the price of the most recently received batches, therefore stock will tend to be valued at earlier prices. In this case, the issue at 1 March is valued at the recent £3.50 price. Therefore stock will have a value of 200 @ £3 plus 100 @ £3.50 = £950.

(d) Value analysis would introduce a formalized procedure that might lead to the adoption of new designs, machines, methods of work and substitution of materials, with a view to maintaining or improving the attributes in its products most valued by its customers, at lower cost than at present.

9 | Controlling direct labour

Introduction

The Apex-Micro Co. Ltd was formed to manufacture the XF microcomputer. Sales in each of the first three years were forecast to be 2,000 units, and suitable rented factory space, hired machinery, direct and indirect employees and other production facilities were acquired to meet this demand. Further facilities could be obtained for any expansion beyond this three-year period.

In the first year only 1,000 computers were produced and sold whilst capacity remained at the planned level of 2,000. What effect would this disappointing first year's trading have on cost per unit?

If direct materials have been efficiently controlled, and purchases cover production of computers sold, and no more, then material cost per computer should be as planned. However, given that the company did not shed, or hire, any labour or other facilities during the year, the conversion cost (i.e. direct labour plus indirect expenses) per computer will have doubled, as 1,000 units had to bear the costs incurred to produce 2,000. Plainly, in the fiercely competitive microcomputer market, the Apex company will not survive for long with substantially higher unit costs than its competitors, unless its computer has features that are not supplied by others.

In this chapter we look at the way in which the management accountant can help to control direct labour cost, in conjunction with production managers, the personnel manager and the work study engineer. The *personnel manager* is responsible for hiring, training and negotiating the pay and conditions of employees, whilst the *work study engineer* is concerned with improving work methods and processes.

We look firstly at the calculation of direct labour requirements, then examine the nature of productivity and how to improve it, thirdly at the system of accounting for labour, and finally at labour control information.

How much direct labour do we require?

Activity

The Tempest Toy Yacht Co. Ltd has been set up to produce three models of plastic yachts – small, medium and large.

The small model is on average built in 2 hours, the medium in 4 hours and the large one in 6 hours. The demand in the coming year is forecast to be: small 7,500, medium 8,000 and large 6,000. Each direct employee works 35 hours per week, for 48 weeks in each year. The total number of suitable potential employees in the area is 40. As the management accountant for the company you are asked the following questions:

(a) Calculate the number of employees required for the coming year.

(b) How many employees will actually be hired?

(c) Specify the three main factors that govern the number of direct labour employees required by any manufacturer.

ANSWER

Your calculation of **(a)** will no doubt look something like the following:

Model	Forecast demand	×	Hours to build each model	=	Number of hours required
Small	7,500		2		15,000
Medium	8,000		4		32,000
Large	6,000		6		36,000

Total direct hours required   83,000

$$\text{Number of direct workers required} = \frac{\text{total hours required}}{\text{annual hours worked per employee}}$$

$$= \frac{83,000}{35 \times 48} = 50.$$

However, although you require 50 employees, there are only 40 available. Thus your answer to **(b)** is 40, this being the factor limiting your ability to meet the forecast demand for toy yachts.

The above example illustrates the three main factors that govern the forecast labour requirement of any manufacturer, viz:

(i) forecast sales (or activity) during the coming year;
(ii) the number of direct hours required for each product;
(iii) known factors limiting the ability to produce.

Self-check

Norfolk Agrimek Ltd produced 1,000 type MMK 301 motor mowers during 1980. It was then forecast that 1981 sales would be 10% more than in 1980. Each man normally works 36 hours per week for 50 weeks in a year, the standard assembly time for each mower is 18 hours and the number of assembly workers employed in 1981 was based upon this time.

Sales and production in 1981 turned out to be 1,500 and the average time taken to assemble one machine was 15 hours.

(a) What was the mower production forecast for 1981?
(b) How many assembly workers were employed based on this forecast?
(c) Given that no more assembly workers than planned were employed in 1981, how many mowers should they have completed during their *normal* working hours, bearing in mind the actual average time taken to assemble one machine?
(d) How do you account for the difference between your answer in **(c)** and the number of mowers actually completed?

ANSWERS

(a) Mower forecast for 1981: $1,000 + (10\% \times 1,000) = 1,100$.

(b) Assembly workers employed:

$$\frac{1,100 \times 18}{1,800} = 11.$$

(c) Number of mowers that should have been completed:

$$\frac{19,800}{15} = 1,320.$$

(d) With no further workers engaged in 1981, and the average production time being 15 hours, the additional production of 1,500 − 1,320, i.e. 180, must have been produced in hours worked more than the normal 36 per week, that is in overtime; unless the 180 were supplied by a subcontractor.

What is productivity and how can it be improved?

In year 1, Poacher's Pies and Pâté Company produced and sold 30,000 kilograms of pâté, followed by 36,000 in year 2, with no increase in production facilities, nor in the number of hours worked by the 5 employees in the pâté department.

Production obviously increased by 6,000 kg (or 20%) over year 1, each worker having produced 1,200 kg more than expected. The volume of output or activity per worker or per hour worked over a period of time is referred to as *productivity*, and when the productivity of a period is compared with that of a previous period or with some planned figure, the resultant percentage is a measure of the *efficiency* of productivity.

Simon's pâté productivity was 6,000 per worker last year and 7,200 in year 2. Efficiency in year 2 was therefore

$$\frac{7,200}{6,000} \times 100\%, \text{ or } 120\% \text{ over year 1.}$$

However, if we suppose that an additional worker was hired in year 2, together with proportionately increased production facilities, the productivity at

$$\frac{36,000}{6} = 6,000 \text{ kg per worker}$$

is the same as last year, even though total production has increased, and the efficiency of productivity would of course be 100% compared with year 1.

The importance of productivity is the effect it has upon the cost of each unit of output. For example, if Simon's cost of direct labour in year 1 was £20,000, and production overhead £52,000, the conversion cost per kg of pâté would have been

$$\frac{£72,000}{30,000} = £2.40.$$

In year 2, assuming unchanged costs, but with the higher productivity, the cost per kg was reduced to

$$\frac{£72,000}{36,000} = £2.00.$$

Should an additional worker have been engaged in year 2, together with proportionately increased production facilities required by him including fixed costs, then total costs would have amounted to £72,000 plus $\frac{1}{5} \times £72,000$,

resulting in a cost per kg for that year of $\dfrac{£86,400}{36,000} = £2.40$

– the same as in year 1.

Thus increased production without increased productivity will not reduce the cost of a unit of output. If productivity reduces the cost per unit produced, then selling prices can be held at competitive levels, a reasonable profit results and even in times of recession a business can survive.

Self-check

The number of lipsticks produced by the Glamour Cosmetic Co. last year was 240,000 in a total of 12,000 hours, with the direct labour and overhead cost totalling £60,000. In the year that followed 300,000 lipsticks were output in the same number of hours and at the same conversion cost as last year.

(a) Calculate the productivity for each year, and the efficiency of the second compared with the first year.
(b) Calculate the conversion cost per lipstick for each year, and explain the difference.
(c) If the cost of a lipstick this year had been the same as last year, what would the total conversion cost be for this year and the total hours worked for this year? Assume production at 300,000 lipsticks.

ANSWERS

(a) Productivity last year: $\dfrac{240,000 \text{ lipsticks}}{12,000 \text{ hours}} = 20$ per hour.

Productivity this year: $\dfrac{300,000 \text{ lipsticks}}{12,000 \text{ hours}} = 25$ per hour.

Year 2 efficiency: $\dfrac{25}{20} \times 100\% = 125\%$.

(b) Cost per lipstick last year: $\dfrac{£60,000}{240,000} = 25$ pence.

Cost per lipstick this year: $\dfrac{£60,000}{300,000} = 20$ pence.

The cost per unit is less because higher productivity was attained at no increased total cost.

(c) $\dfrac{X}{300,000} = 25$ pence, therefore total cost = £75,000.

And $\dfrac{75,000}{60,000} \times 12,000 =$ total hours worked $= 15,000$.

Activity

Assume that, in the second year, Simon Poacher's pâté productivity increased by 20% over the previous year without working additional hours, and without any further expenditure. Jot down how you think they achieved this.

You will probably have included some or all of the following in your list:

1 The employees hired last year became more expert this year.
2 Work was better supervised in the second year.
3 Improved working methods, at no additional cost, were introduced this year.
4 There was less wastage in production this year, for any or all of the above three reasons.
5 Production stoppages last year, perhaps due to machine breakdowns or electricity cuts, were not repeated this year.

Of course, if stoppages are a regular occurrence, then it might be advisable to change the basis for measuring productivity from the number of workers to the *number of direct working hours*, supported by a report explaining how production hours were lost. After all, production can continue only so long as facilities are fully operable, and workers' productivity should not be biased by including hours lost for reasons beyond their control.

> *Activity*
>
> Supposing that Simon Poacher's 20% increase in productivity was accompanied by no additional working hours, but that there was some additional expenditure. How could the additional spending have improved productivity?

This could have happened in one, or both, of the following ways:

1 Additional or improved machinery or equipment, and/or improved working environment, could enable employees to be more effective and thus increase their output per hour worked.
2 Additional payments to workers, over and above their normal rates of pay, for beating a specified target of output over an agreed period. Most workers will respond favourably to such agreements, generally referred to as incentive schemes.

The essential feature of any expenditure, whether on improved working conditions or incentive schemes, is that *it must reduce unit cost*, after taking into account any necessary additional expenditure. Moreover, as regards incentive schemes, there are also certain other conditions that have to be met, if they are to be successful:

• Targets of efficiency prescribed to earn additional payment should be reasonably attainable by the average worker, otherwise frustration will set in and the scheme will collapse.
• They must be easily understood.
• There should be relatively few production hold-ups, and time allowances should be made when stoppages are not the fault of the employee.
• The schemes should not be allowed to fall into disrepute because of delays in settling complaints or disputes.
• The schemes should match the working conditions. For example, work calling for a high degree of skill, or quality output, might not be suitably rewarded by applying a scheme based upon a high rate of output per hour.

The different schemes upon which the management accountant might be called upon to give his advice can be grouped under four main headings:

- Payment of higher basic wage rates.
- Piecework plans.
- Individual bonus schemes.
- Group bonus schemes.

High wage rate schemes

These simply involve the offering of a higher than normal basic rate per hour, in return for an agreed higher than normal level of efficiency. For example, if Christmas-cracker workers each produced 1,000 crackers per 40-hour week at a normal hourly rate of £1.75 an hour, they may respond to an increased rate of £2.10 per hour by each producing 1,400 crackers each week. By offering this increased rate the labour cost of each cracker

is reduced from $\dfrac{£70}{1,000} = 7$ pence to $\dfrac{£84}{1,400} = 6$ pence.

Activity

Still following the Christmas-cracker example, but using slightly different figures, assume that the output of each worker was 2,000 per week at £1.75 per hour, but that this increased to 2,200 crackers at the higher rate of £2.00 per hour. Overhead costs are £3 per hour.

Under both the old and the new schemes, calculate the following:

(a) the labour cost of each cracker; and
(b) the conversion cost of each cracker.

ANSWER

	Previously	*Under new scheme*
Labour cost per cracker	$\dfrac{£1.75 \times 40}{2,000} = 3.50p$	$\dfrac{£2.00 \times 40}{2,200} = 3.63p$
Conversion cost per cracker	$\dfrac{£4.75 \times 40}{2,000} = 9.50p$	$\dfrac{£5.00 \times 40}{2,200} = 9.09p$

Note that in this example the additional wages paid have worsened the labour cost by .13p per cracker, but that the position is more than retrieved when we take overheads into account, and conversion cost is reduced by .41p per cracker. Can you spot how this has happened? It is because the unchanged overhead cost for the week is spread over a higher production.

This result would obviously please both employee and employer, the former receiving a higher return for each cracker produced, and the employer achieving an overall lowering of cost per unit. One of the drawbacks of high wage rate plans is that employees are not motivated to work any harder than a specified rate of efficiency, and management have to monitor production rate closely to ensure that the required target is being met.

Piecework plans

These reward *individual* effort more effectively than the high wage rate scheme, because employees are paid a price *for each unit they produce*. The more efficient a worker is, the more he will earn. For example, if machinists in a shirt factory working a 40-hour week are paid at the rate of 60 pence for each completed shirt, an employee finishing 100 shirts in a week would be paid 100 × 60 pence = £60, whilst another completing 120 shirts would be paid 120 × 60 pence = £72.

Some piecework schemes incorporate a guaranteed minimum wage to protect employees' earnings when production is low for reasons beyond their control. Other schemes include an increase in the amount paid per unit at higher levels of efficiency.

Two objections frequently levelled at piecework are that it may increase the volume of shoddy work because of a rushed rate of working and that piecework plans call for a relatively high cost of recording work completed.

Individual bonus schemes

There are many schemes that combine the security of a guaranteed basic wage with an additional payment – a bonus – when a task is completed in less than a predetermined target time. One such scheme, the Halsey premium bonus scheme, carrying the name of its originator, provides for a bonus of half the time saved on each job, paid at normal wage rate.

For example, if John, a skilled fitter, completes an assembly job with a target time of 12 hours in 8 hours, he would be paid 8 hours plus $\frac{1}{2}(12 - 8) = 10$ hours at his basic rate.

Other similar schemes vary only in the proportion of bonus time paid, some handing over all the time saved to the employee, but still being justified because higher productivity leads to a reduction in the cost per unit.

However, the high administrative cost of detailed job recording, and the resentment of employees against having to share the time saved with the employer, have led to the development of a more simplified system called 'measured day work'. Standard or target hours are scientifically predetermined for each job, and at the end of an agreed period, say every four weeks, the efficiency of workers is calculated by relating their total hours worked over this period to the total allowed time for all jobs completed in the same period. Reference is then made to a schedule containing increasing rates per hour for higher levels of efficiency, and the appropriate rate is then used as the hourly rate of pay for the following four-weekly period.

For example, John worked 160 hours in four weeks, and during that time had completed jobs with a total 'standard' time of 180 hours. His efficiency during the period was $\frac{180}{160} \times 100 = 112\frac{1}{2}\%$, therefore he would be paid during the following four weeks at £2.30 per hour by reference to the following table:

Efficiency	Rate per hour
%	£
Up to 95	2.00
96 to 100	2.10
101 to 110	2.20
111 to 120	2.30

Group incentive schemes

These are designed for situations where production is a team effort, where individual performance is difficult to measure or is governed by an assembly line. Each member of the team is paid the same bonus, and this might also include the supervisor. The basis for calculating the bonus might be piecework or time saved.

Though group schemes would appear to penalize the more efficient worker, they can do much to improve morale and bring out the best in the whole group.

Self-check

1 The higher rate paid under a high wage rate incentive scheme is the reward for higher productivity. Is this statement true or false? Explain.

2 What type of incentive scheme is more suited to car assembly lines and why?

3 Why is measured day work simpler to administer than premium bonus systems?

4 A machine operator, who is paid a basic rate of £2 an hour, produces a component that is planned to be completed in one hour. He completes 60 components during a 40-hour working week. Under the terms of his individual bonus scheme he is to be paid for the hours he works plus 50% of the hours he saves. How much will he receive for his week's work?

5 If a piecework system were operated, how much per component would the operator have to be paid to receive the same total wage as that under the individual bonus scheme described in 4 above?

ANSWERS

1 *True.* Workers understand that the high rate paid is in return for a higher than normal level of efficiency. The scheme would be abandoned if this target level was not achieved. However, it does not reward any effort beyond the stated 'norm'.

2 Because the output from a car assembly line is dependent upon a *team* of workers where individual effort is governed by the speed of the line, a group incentive scheme is the most suitable for this kind of work.

3 Measured day work is simpler to administer than premium bonus systems, because it cuts out the calculation of the bonus on *each job*, and then applies one predetermined rate of pay to all the hours worked in the following working period – usually about four weeks.

4 He saves 60 – 40 hours, therefore he will be paid 50% of this

20 hours plus his normal 40 hours at his basic rate of £2. He will receive 50 × £2 = £100.

5 In order to earn the same wage as in **4** above, under a piecework plan the operator would have to be paid $\frac{£100}{60}$ per piece, i.e. £1.67.

The need for an effective control system

Earlier in this chapter we stressed the importance of forecasting the direct labour requirements of a business. In the last section the keynote was productivity, its link with unit cost and the use of improved methods and incentive schemes to increase the productivity of labour. Much of this effort may be wasted, however, unless management ensures that the labour force it directs is being fully utilized; and although other departments are concerned in this matter, it is to the management accountant that they look for an effective system of recording and reporting upon the use of labour.

Activity

Imagine that you are a drill operator in an engineering factory, where you are responsible for drilling holes in a variety of metal components. You can well appreciate that the firm will have to operate a well-defined system of recording, not only of your attendance time, but also of the time spent on each job; the value of which will be paid to you in wages, and ultimately find its way as part of the cost of finished goods.

List the various stages that you think will have to be provided for in the recording system, from the time that you first set foot in the factory to the point where your wages cost is included in the total cost of a finished item.

You may not think of everything, but figure 16 below shows the various stages that should be in your list, in chronological order:
The procedure at each referenced stage is expanded upon below:

1 *Daily attendance time recorded.* Usually by time-recording clocks, into which time cards are inserted daily by each worker

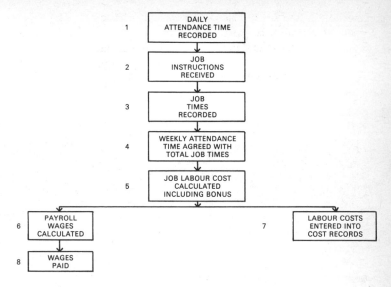

Figure 16. The various stages in a labour recording system

to stamp the start and finishing times. Absenteeism and lateness
are analysed from these cards.

2 *Job instructions received,* from the production planning department via the foreman, including material requisitions and job
time cards.

3 *Job times records.* Usually by time clock stamping the commencing and finishing times of each job. Alternatively, daily
or weekly time sheets may be used to summarize jobs completed
each day or week.

4 *Weekly attendance time agreed.* At the end of the week, total
hours on the weekly attendance time card are agreed with the
total of all the job times. Any time unaccounted for has to
be investigated, but in most cases can be attributed to 'idle'
– non-productive – time, for which a special time card is created
to show not only the lost time, but also the reason for the loss.
This could be due, for example, to waiting for materials or
a machine breakdown. These are later analysed for control
purposes.

5 *Job labour costs calculated* by the wages department.

6 *Wages calculated.* This is done in the accounting department by reference to the weekly clock card of each employee which shows total hours worked and payable at the appropriate basic wage rate, plus total bonus extracted from job cards and any overtime. For each employee, the payroll shows the gross wages payable, deductions for taxation, etc. and the net amount payable.

7 *Labour costs entered into costing records.* Individual job cost records are entered with the time and cost recorded on job cards, the total labour is charged to the work-in-process account, and when each job is completed, the total accumulated costs are transferred to a finished goods record.

8 *Wages paid.* Wages packets are made up by the wages office by reference to the payroll, and a wages slip in each packet indicates to each employee the make-up of his wages. It is essential that employees are identified as they collect their packets, and that any uncollected wages are carefully recorded and safeguarded, until they are eventually collected.

Labour control reports

If you had recently been appointed managing director of a small company building and selling small boats, what main kinds of information would you look for to control direct labour cost?

You would need two kinds of report:

1 showing the measurement of labour activity and performance;
2 information explaining the results calculated in 1 above.

Supposing that each of the boats built in your yard takes 100 hours to build, and that production over a 25-week period was 170 instead of the 200 boats planned. Each of your workers works a 40-hour week.

There could be two basic reasons for the shortfall in expected production. Firstly, there may have been fewer hours worked than planned, and secondly, the efficiency with which the employees worked was perhaps more or less than expected. Assuming that the direct labour hours taken to produce the 170 boats were 19,000, then activity would be reported as follows:

Efficiency	$\times$	*Capacity*	$=$	*Activity*
$\dfrac{\text{hours allowed for production attained}}{\text{actual hours worked}}$	$\times$	$\dfrac{\text{actual hours worked}}{\text{planned hours}}$	$=$	$\dfrac{\text{hours allowed for production attained}}{\text{planned hours}}$

$$\frac{17,000}{19,000} \quad \times \quad \frac{19,000}{20,000} \quad = \quad \frac{17,000}{20,000}$$

$$89.5\% \quad \times \quad 95\% \quad = \quad 85\%$$

This shows that although direct labour hours available were little short of full capacity, the efficiency during that time was 89.5% of expectations, resulting in 85% of planned activity.

> *Activity*
>
> Suggest reasons that could have caused the above production (17,000 hours) and hours worked (19,000) figures.

Management needs systematic reports of production and time lost and gained, otherwise they are working in the dark. The following are some of the more critical ones produced, and some of the reasons suggested by you in the previous activity will be included in them:

- *Lost production time*. Probably due to waiting for material, tools or instructions, or because of machine breakdown.
- *Overtime*. This represents hours worked beyond an agreed daily or weekly maximum figure, and is usually paid for at normal rate plus a premium. For example, if 8 hours is a normal day's work, £2 the basic rate per hour and a premium of $\frac{1}{4}$ the basic rate is paid for overtime, then someone who works 10 hours would receive 10 × £2 plus 2 × £.50 = £21. Premiums for overtime are usually treated as an indirect expense rather than part of direct cost. The overtime report might indicate that jobs are taking longer to complete than expected, or that overtime has had to be worked to cover the lost production time indicated in the first report.
- *Labour turnover* report relates total number of employees leaving over a period to the average number employed. A high rate would obviously be a cause for concern, and could explain current inefficiency because new employees need time to attain expected high efficiency levels. This report would detail the major causes of labour turnover so that remedial action can be taken.
- *Lateness/absenteeism*. An indication of poor morale and cer-

tainly bad management. Would explain the lower available capacity in the above example.

- *Extra time allowance report*. Where difficulties are encountered by workers, due perhaps to substandard materials or when some special modification is required to a regular product, additional time is allowed, otherwise bonus payments to workers would be affected.

Self-check

1 Why is it necessary to reconcile attendance hours with job hours? Why could differences arise?
2 Employees are not necessarily paid an amount that only equals the hours they work times their basic rate. Explain.
3 Why are direct labour costs entered into individual job records?

ANSWERS

1 Reconciliation of hours is necessary to ensure that all hours paid are accounted for, by either production or authorized 'lost' time. Differences can arise if no record has been made of 'lost' time, or if attendance time has been recorded fraudulently by someone other than the employee involved, when job hours would not exist to support them.
2 An employee may sometimes earn more than hours worked at his basic rate, by (a) working overtime or (b) being paid a bonus. Overtime is time worked in excess of normal daily or weekly hours, and such time attracts an additional payment of a fraction, perhaps $\frac{1}{2}$, of the extra time worked at the basic rate. This premium payment is usually treated as an indirect expense rather than as part of direct labour cost.
3 Direct labour cost is added to individual job records as part of the accumulating costs on each job. This might be needed for: (a) control purposes – to check against estimated costs; or (b) for setting prices, where these are based upon total cost.

Review

Electronic Educational Aids Ltd have been in business for one year assembling and selling a unique electronic mathematical teaching aid. They began to market their product following the award of a cash prize from a leading newspaper in a competition designed to encourage small businesses with promising products.

After the first year's operations, however, Tom Dawnet was extremely disappointed when sales for that year did not come up to budgeted expectations.

The expected assembly time for each aid is 2 hours, and the planned production for the first year was 4,500 aids.

Given that activity was 80% of plan in year 1, and that actual direct hours worked totalled 8,100, calculate the efficiency and capacity ratios of the company, and suggest what reports would contain the information to explain the disappointing first year's performance.

ANSWER

We have to explain two things: (a) why hours available were only 8,100 instead of 9,000, and (b) why only 3,600 aids (7,200 hours of work) were produced in 8,100 hours worked.

Calculation of efficiency and capacity ratios shows:

$$\text{efficiency} \times \text{capacity} = \text{activity}$$

$$\frac{7,200}{8,100} \times \frac{8,100}{9,000} = \frac{7,200}{9,000}$$

$$88.9\% \times 90\% = 80\%$$

The answer to (a) might be found in the lost time, labour turnover or lateness/absenteeism reports, which between them will explain why budgeted hours were not attained. With regard to (b) – the poor efficiency – the overtime report, extra time allowance or labour turnover reports contain the answer.

10 | Controlling overheads

The difficulty of sharing overheads fairly

You are now well aware that total product cost is a combination of direct and indirect costs, the former being those that can easily be traced to a specific product, such as the material that is a major part of the product, and those that cannot be so readily identified.

Direct costs are, therefore, relatively simple to tie a product cost label on; but what of indirect costs, also known as overheads? How much of such costs can be attributed to the process of converting raw materials into a finished product – these are termed production overheads – and how much to ensuring that the product ultimately reaches a customer – selling and general overheads? It was earlier suggested that some kind of averaging process would seem to be the logical solution. By dividing the total overhead cost for any month by the output for that month, we have an overhead cost for each unit produced. For example, if total overheads of a business for April were £18,000, and 3,000 units had been produced, the overhead cost per unit would have been £18,000 ÷ 3000 = £6.00.

Activity

Costs and output for the Cubic Rude Co. Ltd, a recently formed manufacturer of educational toys, for the months March to June inclusive are as follows:

Direct materials £5 per unit
Direct labour   £4 per unit
Indirect costs   assumed all fixed £1,500 per month excepting March, when there was an additional heating bill of £200

	March	*April*	*May*	*June*
Output units	500	600	450	700

Prepare a schedule showing the cost per unit for each month, and explain any differences that may arise between the monthly figures.

ANSWER

You may not present your calculations in quite the same way as the following, but the end result should be the same.

	March	*April*	*May*	*June*
Indirect costs	£1,700	£1,500	£1,500	£1,500
Output (units)	500	600	450	700
Indirect cost per unit	£3.40	£2.50	£3.33	£2.14
Direct material	£5.00	£5.00	£5.00	£5.00
Direct labour	£4.00	£4.00	£4.00	£4.00
Cost per unit	£12.40	£11.50	£12.33	£11.14

The differences in the monthly unit costs arise mainly because output has varied from period to period, whilst the major part of indirect costs in each month is relatively fixed. In consequence unit cost is lower as output increases, because the same overhead is averaged over a greater number of units produced. A further reason for the variations is the seasonal or irregular nature of certain expenditure – in this case, fuel cost in March, needed to heat the premises at the end of a cold winter.

Activity

Assuming the same information given in the last activity, what cost per unit would you use:

(a) to charge a customer for goods delivered in mid April, given that invoices are always sent to customers on the day that goods are delivered; and

(b) in respect of the first deliveries in May of a second toy to be added to the product range? This toy differs from the first in that its components are almost wholly purchased from a subcontractor, Cubic Rude adding a minor internally manufactured component during assembly, and spray-painting to finish the product. The first toy was wholly manufactured by the company.

Your answer to **(a)** might suggest that you use the March cost per unit, or perhaps some average of previous costs, or wait until the end of April to ascertain that month's cost per unit. Each of these figures would be different, so which do we use? Which is correct? If you delay your invoicing until the end of April you also delay receiving payment for the delivery. You have a problem!

As regards **(b)**, your problem is even more complicated, because not only will the overhead cost per unit have to be re-calculated – output having increased with no apparent increase in indirect cost – but this second toy does not go through the same processing as the first, which rather implies that it should not attract the same overall rate of overhead. The direct costs of this second toy would of course be known, but if we add an amount of overhead based upon 'wrong' assumptions, then our selling price might not be competitive.

To summarize, the ascertainment of an appropriate overhead unit cost faces four main problems:

- *Output may vary from period to period, whilst a large proportion of indirect costs remain the same.*
- *Overhead costs may vary seasonally, or because of infrequent periodic expenditure, causing fluctuations in the total costs applying to the same products.*
- *Using end-of-period rates, cost ascertainment is delayed.*
- *Products may be completely dissimilar in design, or kinds of processing required.*

The first three problems can be overcome by using *predetermined* overhead cost rates, calculated by estimating the total overhead cost for the year ahead and dividing that cost by the estimated production for the same period. For example, if overhead cost is £10,000 and production 1,000 units, the overhead rate will be £10 per unit for the whole of that period.

The fourth problem can be dealt with by expressing forecast output in terms of a common unit such as direct labour hours. For example, if a business produced two products A and B taking 2 hours and 1 hour to complete respectively, and output forecast for A is 3,000 and for B 4,000 units, with forecast total overhead at £10,000, the number of labour hours to be produced is:

A: 3,000 X 2 = 6,000
B: 4,000 X 1 = 4,000
              _____

              10,000
              _____

and the overhead rate would be £10,000 ÷ 10,000 = £1 per direct labour hour. Product A (2 hours @ £1) thus has twice as much overhead charged to it as to B (1 hour @ £1), because of the longer processing time.

This is an admirably simple solution, but poses the following questions:

1 What should the overhead cost be?
2 How is this total overhead cost distributed between cost centres?
3 How does overhead attach itself to products given that there is more than one cost centre?
4 What happens if the overhead incurred is different to the total amount charged to output?

Questions 1 and 2 are covered in the remainder of this chapter, whilst 3 and 4 are dealt with in the following chapter.

Self-check

In each of the following questions choose the most appropriate answer, briefly explaining the reason for your choice.

1 If production overhead remains the same in each of three succeeding months, and cost per unit decreases successively, would production in months 2 and 3 have (i) increased, or (ii) decreased?
2 If production is even in each month and overhead is normally the same, would the addition to overhead in one month of an unusually high building repair cost (i) increase or (ii) decrease the overhead cost per unit in that month?
3 Which of the following is used to calculate predetermined overhead cost rates?

   (i) Last year's overhead cost divided by this year's actual output.

(ii) Last year's output divided into forecast overhead cost for the coming year.

(iii) The coming year's forecast overhead cost divided by that year's forecast output.

(iv) The actual output of the coming year divided into that year's actual overhead cost.

ANSWERS

1 (i) Increased – because a higher output divided into an unchanging indirect cost decreases cost per unit.

2 (ii) Increase – because there is more overhead cost to spread over the same output.

3 (iii) – because we have to *forecast* the coming year's cost and output in order to calculate *predetermined* overhead rates.

Overhead costs identified and quantified

Assume that you are a director of the Cubic Rude Co. Ltd, manufacturer and supplier of educational toys. What combination and volume of resources will be currently employed by the company?

Direct material and the direct labour needed to convert that material into saleable products, and to speed them on their way to expectant customers, immediately spring to mind; but it will be obvious that labour cannot perform its tasks without factory space, machinery, tools, electrical power, gas heating, insurance, transport and a whole host of other vital resources that nowadays may be greater in total value than direct material and direct labour together.

Figure 17 tabulates some of the more common costs included under the umbrella term of 'overheads'.

Indirect materials	*Indirect expenses*
Tools	Rent
Nuts, bolts and nails*	Rates
Production glue*	Insurance – buildings and
Lubricating oil	machinery
Cleaning materials	Insurance – stocks
Maintenance material	Electricity – power
Coal for boilers	Electricity – lighting
Drawing office material	Gas
Office stationery	Water
Advertising material	National insurance

Indirect labour
Managers
Supervisors
Labourers
Cleaners
Quality control
  inspectors
Office staff – administration
            – production
            – sales
Stores clerks
Idle time
Overtime premium
Shift premium
Holiday pay
Salesmen
Market researchers
Transport drivers
Security
Research staff
Designers

Indirect expenses (cont.)
Depreciation – machinery
Depreciation – buildings
Vehicle and machinery hire
Repairs to vehicles
Repairs to buildings
Repairs to machines
Sales commission
Travelling and entertainment
Staff cafeteria subsidy
Transport – internal
Transport – external
Advertising
Telephones – external
Telephones – internal
Postages
Audit and accountancy fees
Consultancy fees

Figure 17. A list of the more common indirect costs

Notes:
1 The costs that do not group naturally into materials or labour
  are given the generic heading of 'indirect expenses'.
2 No attempt has been made at this stage to relate items to cost
  centres.
3 The costs starred (*) under indirect materials refer to items of
  small value that are basically *direct* materials, but are categorized as indirect to save the disproportionate administrative
  effort that would be needed to allocate them as direct.

Because the relationship between indirect costs and products is
more obscure than that of direct costs, the exact amount of each
required for production is more difficult to assess.

   However, we know from Chapter 4 that we can make some
distinction between those indirect costs that vary to a greater or

lesser degree with changes in output or sales and those that are relatively fixed in relation to output or sales.

Obviously, no cost can remain fixed for ever. All costs are variable in the sense that large changes in production capacity will increase them. Doubling factory capacity, for example, will double rent, rates and machinery cost, but over this new range of output those costs become fixed, unless of course economic forces change prices. Variable costs will include electric power used by production machinery and commission on sales paid to salesmen.

It follows that sales forecasts will broadly determine maximum production capacity requirements, and thus the level of indirect costs.

One factor that needs special mention is that expenditure upon resources such as machinery, buildings and leases, all of which are used over a period longer than one year, will of necessity have to be spread over their estimated or known lives. If this were not done, the year in which they are paid would have to bear a disproportionately high charge, with consequent effects upon the measurement of profit in that year.

The amount charged into each year's costs for machinery is called 'depreciation', and is largely calculated in one of two ways. One method takes the initial purchase cost less anticipated end-of-life sale value, and spreads it *evenly* over the expected productive life of the machine. This is called the *fixed instalment* method, because the same amount is written off the machine in each year. Another approach is the *reducing balance* method, which applies the same percentage to the reducing balance in each year to calculate depreciation. An example of each method is given below, relating to a machine purchased for £4,000, having a three-year life and an end-of-service value of £500.

	Fixed instalment £	Reducing balance £
Cost	4,000	4,000
Year 1 depreciation	1,167	2,000
Value at end of year 1	2,833	2,000
Year 2 depreciation	1,167	1,000

Value at end of year 2	1,666	1,000
Year 3 depreciation	1,166	500
	——	——
Value at end of year 3	500	500
	——	——

Notice that the depreciation charge under the instalment method is the same in each year; that the depreciation reduces annually under the 50% reducing balance method; but that both methods reduce the machine to its sale value at the end of its useful life.

Self-check

1 (a) What is the difference between direct and indirect costs?

   (b) Which of the following are indirect costs, all of them being incurred by a beer-bottling plant?

     (i) Rent
     (ii) Bottles
     (iii) Gum for the bottle labels
     (iv) Depreciation of machines
     (v) Workers on the bottling line
     (vi) Heating
     (vii) Factory manager's salary
     (viii) Caps for bottles

2 (a) Differentiate between variable and fixed indirect expenses.

   (b) Which of the following are variable, and which fixed, indirect expenses?

     (i) Factory heating
     (ii) Employer's national insurance costs
     (iii) Building insurance
     (iv) Gas used in production
     (v) Internal telephones
     (vi) Vehicle depreciation
     (vii) Rates
     (viii) Salesmen's commission

3 A machine costing £4,000 has an estimated operational life of six years, and an estimated residual value at the end of that time of £400. At the end of three years, the written-down value of the machine is £2,200. Which depreciation method has been applied?

ANSWERS

1 (a) Direct costs are those that are easily traced to jobs or products; indirect costs are not so readily traced, either because they represent the value of services or supplies that spread across more than one job or product, or because they are so small in value that the administrative effort in tracing them would not be worthwhile.

(b) Indirect: **(i), (iii), (iv), (vi), (vii)**. Direct: **(ii), (v), (viii)**.

2 (a) Variable expenses are those that vary with changes in volume of output; fixed expenses do not change as volume of output varies.

(b) Variable: **(ii), (iv), (viii)**. Fixed: **(i), (iii), (v), (vi), (vii)**.

3 The fixed instalment method. As £1,800 has been written off in three years, with £1,800 remaining to be charged to output over the next three years, it is obvious that the amount of depreciation in each period is the same.

Dividing overheads between cost centres

At the end of the first section of this chapter four questions were posed. 'How much overhead?' was dealt with in the last section. We now look at the second question and discuss how overhead costs may be assigned to cost centres, both for control purposes and as intermediate 'stopping-off places', prior to their being absorbed into the cost of finished output.

The discussion in the last section will have helped you to identify the kinds of costs classified as indirect material, labour and expenses, and to understand the factors that influence the volume of each cost, but how do we marshal these costs into appropriate cost centres?

In assigning indirect costs to cost centres, two basic rules apply:

- *If a cost is incurred by a specific cost centre, ALLOCATE it to that centre,* e.g. indirect material issued to one cost centre.
- *If a cost is incurred for the benefit of two or more cost centres, APPORTION it between the centres,* e.g. insurance on buildings.

Self-check

Which of the following costs would you **(a)** allocate or **(b)** apportion?

1 The maintenance manager's salary.
2 Total office and factory rental.
3 Depreciation of all factory buildings.
4 Long-distance telephone calls separately analysed into user centres.
5 Office and factory rates.
6 Depreciation of machinery in one production centre.
7 Loss on employees' cafeteria.
8 Lubricating oil issued to the machining department.
9 Telephone rentals.
10 Security costs.

ANSWER

1 Allocate – can be directly linked to the maintenance centre.
2 Apportion – rental applying to the premises as a whole.
3 Apportion – applies to all cost centres.
4 Allocate – if separately analysed, charge to user centres.
5 Apportion – applies to the whole premises.
6 Allocate – the value of this particular machine will be known.
7 Apportion – incurred for the benefit of all employees.
8 Allocate – specifically traceable to one cost centre.
9 Apportion – applies to the whole network of telephones.
10 Apportion – relates to a comprehensive buildings coverage.

Allocation of an indirect cost causes no problems, because the exact amount and the user centre are both known. When dealing with costs that have to be *apportioned*, however, an arbitrary element is introduced, and one must choose the most sensible and equitable bases for sharing the costs. Logically, one should try to determine the causal relationship between each cost and its origination, which is not necessarily volume of output. For example, telephone rentals can be related to the number of telephones, and depreciation of machinery to the *value* of machinery in each cost centre.

Other common bases for dealing with apportionment are:

	Type of cost
... of a building	Occupancy costs
... of a building	Heating
...er of employees	Personnel costs
...ue	Insurance, depreciation
...abour hours worked	Supervisor's salary
Technical estimates	Electric power, gas, water

Note: technical estimates are calculated by reference to the rating, size, capacity, etc. of the consuming unit, e.g. a machine that uses electric power will be known to have an electric motor and control gear of a certain size.

Self-check

Cubic Rude Ltd have two production departments and two service departments, with information regarding each as follows:

	Service depts A	Service depts B	Production depts X	Production depts Y
No. of employees	10	20	40	30
Floor area (sq. metres)	1,000	500	2,000	2,500
Machinery value	£20,000	£10,000	£100,000	£200,000
Volume (cu. metres)	2,000	8,000	15,000	25,000
Technical estimate – power	10%	5%	30%	55%

Apportion the following estimated costs between all four cost centres, using the most appropriate basis in each case.

Factory rent	£60,000	Building insurance	£9,000
Loss on cafeteria	£5,000	Heating	£6,000
Factory rates	£15,000	Lighting	£4,500
Machinery insurance	£3,300	Power	£12,000
Security	£7,500	Machinery deprecia- tion	£33,000

ANSWER

	Service depts A	Service depts B	Production depts X	Production depts Y
	£	£	£	£
Factory rent (floor area)	10,000	5,000	20,000	25,000
Loss on cafeteria (employees)	500	1,000	2,000	1,500
Factory rates (floor area)	2,500	1,250	5,000	6,250

Machinery insurance (value)	200	100	1,000	2,000
Security (floor area)	1,250	625	2,500	3,125
Building insurance (floor area)	1,500	750	3,000	3,750
Heating (volume)	240	960	1,800	3,000
Lighting (floor area)	750	375	1,500	1,875
Power (technical estimate)	1,200	600	3,600	6,600
Machinery depreciation (value)	2,000	1,000	10,000	20,000
	20,140	11,660	50,400	73,100

You are probably not surprised to learn that the most commonly apportioned costs are concerned with occupancy. This is specifically recognized in many large businesses by the creation of a nominal cost centre called 'occupancy costs' or 'buildings and grounds', into which are collected all the costs to be apportioned on an area basis.

Figure 18 now summarizes the stages covered so far in the process of attaching indirect costs to product cost:

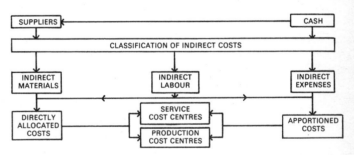

Figure 18. Classification and assignment of overheads to cost centres

Dividing service centre costs between production centres

What are service cost centres? The word 'service' implies the carrying out of some necessary supportive function on behalf of another person or cost centre. Hospitals, for example, require the services of laundries, kitchens, radiography, maintenance, etc. to service inpatients and outpatients. Companies manufacturing food products require personnel specialists, maintenance, steam and factory administrative services to ensure the smooth running of their main food-processing departments.

Service centres do not directly take part in production. It is only from production centres that the finished product emerges, hence the need to transfer the service centre costs to the producing centres that have benefited from them.

The assignment of service costs follows the same two basic rules enunciated at the beginning of the previous section. In short, if it is possible to *allocate* the costs to particular centres, perhaps by keeping records of the service provided to each, then this should be done. Machine maintenance costs, where substantial, are very often dealt with in this way, by keeping tag on the costs of each job executed. Steam-generating plant may be operated wholly for the benefit of the baby-food production centre of a food-processing factory, and its accumulated costs will be allocated to that one centre.

The service costs that cannot be allocated have to be *apportioned* in such a way as to reflect the value of the benefit received by each of the centres served. The bases should be consistently applied, and will probably represent a compromise between using an expensive approach to ensure 'accuracy' and a more simple but less costly one that yields a result not very different from the complicated one.

Figure 19 depicts the service costs transfer process:

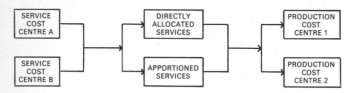

Figure 19. Transferring service costs to production centres

The factors chosen to apportion services are the ones that are considered to provide the best measure of the value of the benefits received from each service, and in most manufacturing firms would include:

In each production centre
The number of employees
The number of material requisitions issued

Machine hours operated
Labour hours worked
Area
Technical estimate

Activity

Scheduled below are two lists – one of service centres and the other of different apportionment bases. See if you can match each service with the most appropriate apportionment basis, giving reasons for your choice.

Service centres		*Apportionment bases*
1 Personnel and welfare	**A**	Technical estimate
2 Factory administration	**B**	Building value
3 Machine maintenance	**C**	Number of material requisitions
4 Electricity generating	**D**	Machine value
5 Stores	**E**	Labour hours worked
6 Steam	**F**	Area
7 Occupancy costs	**G**	Number of employees
	H	Machine hours worked

ANSWER

Full marks if you have correctly linked the service with the basis as follows. Pay particular attention to the explanations.

1 – G Costs incurred are relevant to people rather than production.

2 – E Administrative effort is closely related to hours worked.

3 – H Need arises mainly out of *using* machines.

4 – A Unless separately metered, this is the most accurate way.

5 – C Rather arbitrary if one considers the costs of storage, particularly of large items; but probably measures the administrative effort reasonably closely.

6 – A Same comments as electricity.

7 – F All of these costs are proportionate to the area owned or rented.

Note that building and machine values were irrelevant.

Self-check

Using the following information, distribute the service costs between the production centres.

Service costs	£
Personnel and welfare	20,000
Stores	30,000
Machine maintenance	24,000
Factory administration	16,000
	90,000

Production centre information	Centre 1	Centre 2
Number of employees	200	300
Number of material requisitions	1,200	2,400
Machine hours	800	400
Labour hours worked	7,000	9,000

Your distribution schedule should appear as follows:

	ratio	Centre 1 £	Centre 2 £
Personnel and welfare	2 : 3	8,000	12,000
Stores	1 : 2	10,000	20,000
Machine maintenance	2 : 1	16,000	8,000
Factory administration	7 : 9	7,000	9,000
		41,000	49,000

It is interesting to see that each service cost is apportioned on a different basis, showing that the use of a single method, for example labour hours worked, would considerably distort the resultant charge to products.

This simple example illustrates the 'direct' method of apportionment, and assumes that there are no inter-service transactions, which is probably unrealistic. However, the method is widely used for its simplicity; a more sophisticated approach would probably not add any more credibility to the already approximate apportionment bases.

Review

1 In respect of each of the following indirect costs, state and explain whether you consider that it should be **(i)** allocated, or **(ii)** apportioned, to cost centres.

(a) Depreciation of buildings
(b) Indirect materials
(c) Water
(d) Loss on sports club
(e) Works manager's salary
(f) Local telephone calls
(g) Stationery
(h) Overtime premium
(i) Coal for boilers
(j) Vehicle hire

2 What bases would you use to assign each of the costs you have chosen to *apportion* in question **1**, to cost centres?

3 Indicate whether each of the statements given below is true or false, and briefly explain your decision:

(a) Service cost centres exist only in manufacturing businesses.
(b) Service cost centres are allocated directly to products.
(c) Service costs are best apportioned to production cost centres, relative to the number of employees working in each of those centres.

ANSWERS

1 (a) Apportioned – the cost covers many cost centres.
  (b) Allocated – directly used by one cost centre.
  (c) Apportioned – unless metered, there is no method of perfect measurement.
  (d) Apportioned – has to be borne by all centres.
  (e) Allocated – to the factory administration cost centre.
  (f) Apportioned – too costly to attempt to allocate all calls.
  (g) Allocated – if high cost only – otherwise apportioned.
  (h) Allocated – this is the additional penalty payment to an employee for working in excess of his normal hours. Traceable to a particular centre.
  (i) Allocated – to the boiler cost centre.
  (j) Allocated – to user department; unless it serves more than one centre – in which case, apportioned.

2 (a) Area – as long as there is no difference between the costs of different buildings in use – in which case, specific value might be used first, then area to break down into centres.
  (c) Technical estimate – based upon normal usage by different processes.
  (d) Employees – facilities are provided for use by all.

  (f) Labour hours – telephone usage would be closely allied to working activity.

3 (a) False – all organizations have functions that are supportive to the main activity. For example, whether a firm manufactures goods or buys them for resale, there will be a selling and distribution department in both cases.

  (b) False – products are not processed through service centres – only production centres; therefore the value of services to be added to each product can only be charged indirectly, that is after the service costs have been assigned to production centres.

  (c) False – the number of employees in each production centre is not necessarily the best measure of the services received by those centres. For example, more electric power is consumed by a machine-based department than a labour-intensive one. It would be misleading to charge more power to the department employing most people.

Part 4
How much is the cost of each unit?

11 | Putting job costs together

Introduction

We now link together the discussions in the last three chapters, to show how the costs of individual jobs are compiled, and how the details entered in job cost records are exactly paralleled by a succession of entries in the main accounting system recording the total values of materials, labour and overheads flowing through production.

The first section of this chapter is essentially a continuation of the process described in the last chapter – that of trying to ensure an equitable apportionment of indirect expenses to jobs. After dealing with the procedure for recording job costs, we will then look at the problem of over- or under-applied overhead that usually stems from the use of predetermined overhead rates.

Averaging overheads over jobs

The difficulty of sharing overheads fairly was discussed at length in the first section of the previous chapter, and it was suggested that the use of overhead rates calculated in advance of production could best overcome this difficulty. This involves choosing an appropriate output level, and a forecast of the costs associated with that output. Choice of output level is developed further in the penultimate section of this chapter, but for our immediate purpose we will use for illustration a firm – the ABC Co. – that is expecting to produce 16,200 hours of work next year.

Simple overall rate

Activity

Assuming the 16,200 output level, calculate the production overhead rate for the ABC Co., given that its total indirect fixed costs are estimated at £100,000, and its indirect variable cost is £2 per direct labour hour for next year.

ANSWER

Overhead rate $= \dfrac{\text{fixed costs}}{\text{expected hours}} +$ variable rate per hour

$= \dfrac{100,000}{16,200} + £2$

$= £6.17 + £2$

$= £8.17$ per direct labour hour.

This same 'blanket' rate will be applied to the hours worked on *every* job regardless of any variations in the operations carried out on different jobs, and ignoring the fact that these operations are carried out in separate cost centres with widely differing costs.

Cost centre rates

Activity

ABC Co. has three production departments – A, B and C, and the division of fixed overhead costs and output between these three cost centres is as follows:

	A	B	C	Total
Fixed overheads	£55,000	£25,000	£20,000	£100,000
Hours	4,000	9,200	3,000	16,200

Using £2 per hour as the variable rate applying to all cost centres, calculate the total overhead rate per hour for each centre.

Now check your answer with the following:

	A	B	C	Total
Fixed overhead	£55,000	£25,000	£20,000	£100,000
Hours	4,000	9,200	3,000	16,200
Fixed overhead rate	£13.75	£2.72	£6.67	£6.17
Variable overhead rate	2.00	2.00	2.00	2.00
	£15.75	£4.72	£8.67	£8.17

Note the wide differences between the rates for the A and B departments and the overall rate. A's low labour hours but high fixed costs suggest that it is essentially a mechanized production centre, and this would appear to justify the determination of *separate* cost centre overhead rates, to differentiate between the activities of different centres. This is pointedly illustrated in the next activity.

Activity

The ABC Co. has just completed two jobs – BP and TD, each of which took 200 hours to finish. 100 of these hours were spent in production centre C in both cases, whilst the other 100 were worked in centres A and B respectively. Using the rates calculated in the previous activity, compare the overhead cost of each job, applying the cost centre rates, with the cost of them using the overall 'blanket' rate of £8.17.

Would you continue to use the overall rate?

ANSWER

Using cost centre rates

	£	£	£
Job BP A – 100 hours @ 15.75 =	1,575		
C – 100 hours @ 8.67 =	867		2,442
		———	
Job TD B – 100 hours @ 4.72 =	472		
C – 100 hours @ 8.67 =	867		1,339
Overall rate		———	
in each case 200 hours @ 8.17 =			1,634

This shows that the BP and TD job costs, using cost centre rates, differ widely from the £1,634 overall rate approach. A selling price for BP based upon the overall rate would be grossly understated, and conversely for TD. When jobs take different paths through several production processes, or differ in the number of hours that they spend in each cost centre, then the use of cost centre rates is justified. On the other hand, if units produced do not vary in processing methods, an overall rate will be justified and certainly a lot simpler than having to calculate and account for cost centre rates.

Machine hour rate

Let us assume that A is a predominately machining department, that overhead cost in that department is incurred largely when machines are operating, and that the estimated machine hours in a year are 3,000. If machine hours are used as the basis for calculating the overhead rate, this would be £63,000 ÷ 3,000 = £21 per machine hour.

> *Self check*
>
> Two jobs X and Y each take 10 labour hours to complete in production centre A, but X uses three machine hours, and Y eight machine hours.
>   Calculate the overhead costs chargeable to X and Y through centre A, using (i) machine hours, and (ii) labour hours, as the basis for your calculations.

ANSWER

Now check your figures with the following:

Machine hours	Labour hours
£	£
X – 3 @ £21 = 63	10 @ 15.75 = 157.50
Y – 8 @ £21 = 168	10 @ 15.75 = 157.50

The much lower cost of X using machine hours compared with labour hours leads us to the conclusion that when machines are the main influence on overheads, machine hours rather than labour hours should be the basis for charging. Both labour and machine hours are, of course, time-related, and as most overhead costs are largely influenced by time, either one of these bases can be found to be commonly used to apply overhead to job costs, depending upon which is the most influential factor.

Other bases that might be used in job costing are related to material or labour *cost*, but although these are administratively simple approaches, they can only be applied when the material content and labour processes are the same for all products.

To summarize this section, in order to charge overhead as fairly as possible to jobs, we have to:

- Calculate a *predetermined* overhead rate, by reference to a chosen expected level of output and the forecast overhead cost at this level.
- Use separate *cost centre* rates where processing differs between jobs.
- Choose the most appropriate basis for charging overheads to jobs – usually labour or machine hours.

Recording job costs

Tom Rogers has built up a thriving little foundry and wrought-iron business in the heart of Norfolk Broadland, giving welcome employment to fifty people who live in nearby villages. All orders placed by customers are treated as unique, because the firm does not produce articles of standard design. Customers specify their particular requirements, and quotations based upon estimated costs are sent to the inquirers. Tom Rogers likes to compare original estimates with actual job costs, and the latter can be built up because individual jobs can be easily identified as they proceed through the workshops. It is these three conditions of (a) uniqueness, (b) need to monitor actual with estimated costs and (c) traceability of jobs through production that generally justify the maintenance of a job order system in any firm.

About three months ago, a builders' merchant inquired whether Tom could supply 200 pairs of wrought-iron gates of a special design in batches of 50 each week. Being anxious to do business with this new customer, Tom asked his cost clerk to prepare an estimate of costs for the job, to which Tom added an appropriate margin of profit and dispatched the quotation to the merchant.

An order for the gates as specified was duly received, and it was entered into the customers' order record. An internal job order number – 203/G – was allocated to it, and the necessary work was included in the production programme, scheduled for an early start.

On the scheduled production start date a job order, together with drawings and specifications of processing and materials requirements, was passed to the production manager by the production control supervisor; a copy of the order going to the cost office to advise them that work was about to commence. In preparation for this the cost clerk opened a job cost record

JOB COST RECORD						

Customer: Apex Building Supplies.
Description: 200 pairs Gates.
Quotation: 5 February 19..

Job Order No. 203/G
Promised Delivery
   Date: 31.3.19..
Date Started: 1.3.19..
Actual Delivery
   Date: 28.3.19..

Direct Material		Direct Labour			Overhead	
Reqn Summary Date	Amount	Date	Hrs	Amount	Hrs × Rate	Amount
19..		19..			£	
1 March	200.00	5 March	300	600.00	300 × 4	1200.00
8 March	200.00	12 March	320	640.00	320 × 4	1280.00
15 March	200.00	19 March	280	560.00	280 × 4	1120.00
22 March	200.00	26 March	300	600.00	300 × 4	1200.00
	£800.00			2,400.00		4,800.00

        Cost Summary: £
        Direct Materials   800.00
        Direct Labour   2,400.00
        Direct Expenses
        Overhead   4.800.00

        Factory Cost   8,000.00

Figure 20. Job cost record

in the form shown in figure 20, on to which all costs incurred in respect of job 203/G would be recorded.

The four processes involved in the manufacture of the gates are cutting bars of steel to various lengths, bending and forming the different lengths, joining them by welding and brazing and finishing including spray-painting. Bar steel for each batch of 50 is withdrawn from stores by material requisition, at the commencement of each week's production, whilst handles, hinges and decorations are added at the finishing stage.

The material requisitions are initially passed to the stores record clerk who records the issues on the individual stock cards, and then passes them to the cost clerk who values them and enters them on to the job cost record cards in detail (see figure 20).

As part of the main accounting system, a stores control account and a work-in-progress account are maintained. The former represents the total value of all items held in stock at any time and entered on the individual stock cards kept by the stores record clerk. The latter is the control account for the job cost records, and at any time it should equal the total of the value of unfinished work accumulated on individual job cost records. Periodically, the total value of material issued to jobs, summarized from material requisitions, is transferred from the stores control account to the work-in-progress account (see figure 21).

Production employees record their daily attendance times on clock cards, and also complete a weekly time sheet showing the breakdown of total time worked into hours spent on different jobs. This weekly time sheet is the document used to calculate the wages payable to each employee, and is also the source of information for individual labour cost entries into job cost records (see figure 20). Each week, the total direct labour cost is transferred from the wages control account to the work-in-progress account (see figure 21).

Tom Rogers applies overhead to jobs at the rate of £4 per direct labour hour. He uses a single factory rate because the size of his operations does not warrant the use of separate cost centre rates. The addition of the overhead cost to the record now completes the cost recording for job number 203/G (see figure 20), and the costs are summarized at the bottom of the record card. In support of all the overhead charged to jobs, there will be a transfer from the overhead absorbed account (see last section of this chapter) to work-in-progress account each month. Thus the work-in-progress account now holds the total of the costs accumulated on all the job cost records (see figure 21).

Because job 203/G is now complete, its £8,000 total cost will be transferred from the work-in-progress account to a finished goods account, prior to delivery to the customer. When that takes place, the value of the gates will be taken out of finished goods and into cost of goods sold. Likewise, the job cost record is closed, and a finished stock card entered with the details of the gates and the cost of £8,000.

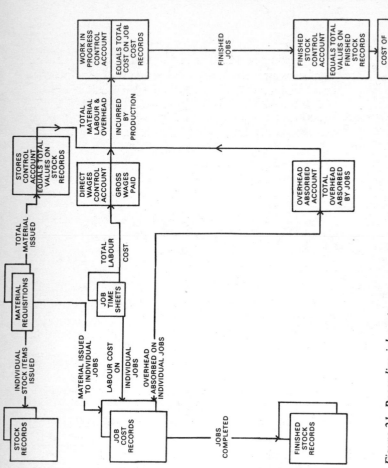

Figure 21. Recording job costs

Finally, the customer is invoiced at the quoted price, and the gates taken out of the finished stock records.

Self-check

1 A job costing system is generally used when **(a)** only one product is produced, **(b)** when a batch of work can be readily identified as it proceeds through production.
Indicate which of the alternative answers is correct.

2 Materials issued to jobs are entered in **(a)** the stock records, **(b)** the job cost records, **(c)** the work in progress account and **(d)** .... Fill in the missing account.

3 What account represents the total costs accumulated on job cost records at any time?

4 For what purposes can the information on a job cost record be used?

ANSWERS

1 **(b)** When only one product is manufactured, a process costing system is used.

2 The stores control account, to record the material withdrawn and transferred to work-in-progress account.

3 The work-in-progress account is the total record representing individual cost entries on job cost records.

4 Three purposes basically: (i) stock valuation, (ii) pricing, (iii) assessing product profitability.

Choosing activity level in calculating overhead rates

'The best laid schemes o' mice and men/Gang aft agley' – so wrote poet Robert Burns, an apt quotation indeed to apply to businessmen continually called upon to forecast the future. Even with the clearest of 'crystal balls' things very rarely turn out as planned, although modern techniques of risk analysis can smooth out some of the uncertainties attached to forecasting.

Ascertainment of *predetermined* overhead cost rates concerns an uncertain future, and it would be a rash management accountant indeed who would claim that he could predict future levels of output and their attendant costs exactly. Patently, this task is easier in industries where demand and supply are fairly stable, but not so in more volatile areas.

Relating back to the ABC Co. example cited earlier in this chapter, you will recall that a forecast level of activity of 16,200 hours was assumed in the calculation of the company's overhead cost rate, with no explanation as to why this figure was chosen. Supposing that the company could employ a maximum of 10 direct workers, who normally work a 40 hour week, for 50 weeks a year.

Taking fixed overhead as £100,000 and variable overhead at £2 per direct labour hour as before, the company's overhead rate would be:

$$\frac{\text{fixed overhead}}{\text{hours available}} + \text{£2 per direct labour hour}$$

$$= \frac{100,000}{20,000} + \text{£2 per direct labour hour}$$

$$= \text{£7 per direct labour hour.}$$

However, this rate is based upon the assumption of employing to maximum capacity, and upon expectations that workers will be 100% efficient and productively employed during their 40-hour working week. Rather unrealistic assumptions!

Past records may probably reveal that direct employees are productively engaged for only 90% of their working week. Past experience may also show that the average number of workers employed over, say, the last five years has been 9, whilst it is anticipated that only 8 direct workers will be required next year.

> *Activity*
>
> Using the above information, calculate the overhead rates per hour at each of the activity levels mentioned. That is, for 10 (practical activity), 9 (normal activity) and 8 (expected activity) employee levels.

ANSWER

First of all you had to work out the practical, normal and expected activity levels in direct labour hours:

Practical 10 employees × 50 × 40 × 90% = 18,000 hours
Normal 9 employees × 50 × 40 × 90% = 16,200 hours
Expected 8 employees × 50 × 40 × 90% = 14,400 hours

The following schedule summarizes the calculation of the over-head rates at the various activities:

Level of activity hours	Fixed overhead £	Fixed overhead rate £	Variable overhead rate £	Total overhead rate £
18,000	100,000	5.5556	2.0000	7.5556
16,200	100,000	6.1728	2.0000	8.1728
14,400	100,000	6.9444	2.0000	8.9444

Observe that the overhead rate increases as output decreases, this being the result of spreading fixed overhead over fewer hours. But which level of output should be used? To answer the question we have to recapitulate the reasons for calculating overhead cost rates. We do so in order to add an equitable proportion of over-head to the cost of each product, the latter being required for stock valuation, profit measurement and possibly for setting selling prices.

If we consider that the management of a business commits itself to providing capacity sufficient to satisfy *maximum* demand for its products in the foreseeable future, then if this maximum is always achieved, *practical capacity* is the basis to use. In these circumstances, as long as the actual costs are as predicted, all the overhead incurred will be charged to output. Using the information scheduled above, if actual activity is 18,000 direct labour hours, the total overhead cost of £136,000 will be absorbed by output by using the £7.5556 rate.

Next year's *expected activity* is 14,400 hours, considerably less than maximum output, implying that output volumes are subject to considerable variations. Should output fluctuate considerably from year to year, so too will the overhead rates calculated at the different activities. It could be argued that if there is never much difference between actual and expected activity, high or low, then expected activity should be the basis for calculating overhead rates. The weakness of this argument, however, is that changing rates would cause misleading variations both in stock valuation and in product costs used for pricing purposes.

To get over this problem of fluctuating overhead rates, *normal level* is chosen by many firms. This rate is based upon long-term expectations of being able to make and sell, and is the *average* of foreseeable annual activity. By using the same rate each year the effects of trade cycles are smoothed out. Stock is valued using the same annual rate, and selling price quotations can benefit from the stability of the normal rate.

Activity

In the year just ended, the ABC Co. charged 15,000 hours to various jobs, and the actual overhead costs were: fixed £120,000 and variable £31,500.

Using the normal activity overhead rate of £8.1728 shown above, calculate:

(a) the total overhead charged to jobs in the year;
(b) the difference between the amount calculated in (a) and the actual overhead cost;
(c) the amount of overhead under-absorbed because activity was at a different level from normal; and
(d) the amount of overhead under-absorbed because actual overhead cost was not as planned.

Check your answers with the following:

(a) Overhead charged to jobs = 15,000 × £8.1728 = £122,592.
(b)

	Fixed £	Variable £	Total £
The actual overhead cost is	120,000	31,500	151,500
The overhead absorbed is	92,592	30,000	122,592
Difference	27,408	1,500	28,908

(c) The amount of overhead under-absorbed because ABC's output was less than normal refers to fixed overhead only as variable overhead should change directly with activity. Thus:

Normal activity 16,200 hours
Actual activity 15,000 hours

1,200 @ £6.1728 = £7,408

	£
(d) Note that the fixed overhead absorbed is	92,592
and the fixed overhead under-absorbed is	7,408
Planned overhead	100,000
Actual overhead	120,000
Additional fixed overhead cost	20,000

In the case of variable overhead the whole difference shown in **(b)** of £1,500 is due to overspending against plan.

Dealing with under-/over-absorbed overhead

Differences between actual and absorbed overhead cost are therefore due to:

- activity being different to plan;
- overhead cost being higher or lower than anticipated; or
- something of both.

In figure 21 overhead is added to job cost records, and also transferred from overhead control account to work-in-progress account. In practice, most firms do not enter the amount transferred from the overhead control account into that account. Instead, they create an additional overhead absorbed account, which accumulates by periodic additions. If, by the end of the year, the actual and planned activity are the same, and overhead no more than planned, then, although there may be monthly over- or under-differences compared with the overhead actually incurred, the total overhead cost in the overhead control account should be matched exactly by the amount in the overhead absorbed account.

This is a rare event, however, as illustrated in the last activity, it being more usual for there to be an amount of over- or under-absorbed overhead. If there is, it is usually transferred to cost of goods sold at the end of the year. Figure 22 illustrates the accounting entries, using the figures from the last activity. Note that the overhead absorbed account equals the amount in the overhead control account after the final adjustment for under-absorbed cost.

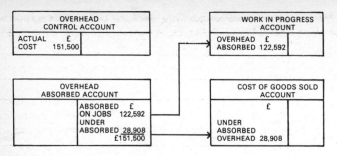

Figure 22. Absorbing overhead

Self-check

Indicate and explain which of the alternatives in each of the following questions is correct:

1 If practical activity is used for calculating overhead cost rates, it results in rates **(a)** higher, **(b)** lower than if normal activity were used.
2 If normal activity was used in the calculation of overhead rates, then a period of higher than normal activity would result in an **(a)** over-, **(b)** under-absorption of overhead.
3 Differences between actual and absorbed overhead are due solely to activity being different to planned activity. **(a)** True or **(b)** false?
4 Overhead absorbed and transferred to work-in-progress account is transferred out of the overhead control account. **(a)** True or **(b)** false?
5 Under- or over-absorbed overhead cost is transferred to the finished goods account at the end of the accounting year. **(a)** True or **(b)** false?

ANSWERS

1 **(b)** Lower – because *more* hours are divided into the same fixed overhead.
2 **(a)** Over- – because the cost rate was calculated on a lower figure of activity.
3 **(b)** False – could also be due to overhead cost being different from expected.

4 (b) False – a separate overhead absorbed account is used.
5 (b) False – the transfer is to the cost of goods sold account.

Review

Acme Pressings have two production departments – machining and finishing – and the following operational forecasts relate to the year 19.1:

	Machining	*Finishing*
Normal activity	30,000 machine hours	120,000 labour hours
Manufacturing overhead	£150,000	£240,000

The following data relate to job number 87 which was completed during 19.1:

	Machining	*Finishing*
Materials used	£269	£43
Direct labour hours worked	37	60
Direct labour rate payable	£3.00	£2.50
Machine hours worked	60	—

Actual *total* costs and activities for the year 19.1 were:

	Machining	*Finishing*
Cost	£170,000	£200,000
Activity	32,000 machine hours	110,000 labour hours

Required

1 Calculate the overhead cost rate for each of the departments.
2 Compile the costs of job number 87.
3 Specify which accounts in the main accounting system are affected by each of the elements of cost in **2**.
4 Calculate the overhead absorbed by both departments in year 19.1.
5 Calculate the over- or under-absorption of overhead for both departments in year 19.1.
6 How will the amounts calculated in **5** be disposed of at the end of year 19.1?

ANSWERS

1 Overhead rates:

Machining $\dfrac{£150,000}{30,000}$ = £5 per machine hour.

Finishing $\dfrac{£240,000}{120,000}$ = £2 per labour hour.

2 Job cost – order 87:

	Machining £		Finishing £	Total £
Material	269		43	312
Direct labour	111		150	261
Overhead (60 × 5)	300	(60 × 2)	120	420
	680		313	993

3 Accounts affected:

Transferred from:	£	Transferred to:	£
Material stock control	312		993
Wages control	261	Work in progress	
Overhead absorbed	420		
Other final entries:			
Work in progress	993	Finished goods	993
Finished goods	993	Cost of goods sold	993

4 Overhead absorbed:

Machining: 32,000 × 5 = £160,000
Finishing: 110,000 × 2 = £220,000

5

	Machining £	Finishing £
Actual overhead	170,000	200,000
Overhead absorbed	160,000	220,000
Under-absorbed	10,000	
Over-absorbed		20,000

6 The under/over-absorbed overhead will be transferred from overhead absorbed account to the cost of goods sold account at the end of year 19.1.

12 | Ascertaining processed unit cost

Introduction

In Chapter 6 you were introduced to the two basic systems of product costing – job order costing and process costing (see figures 8 and 9). The former was covered in the last chapter and relates to batches or units of work that are unique in terms of processing required, that can easily be identified as they proceed through their manufacturing stages and in respect of which there is a need to identify their separate costs.

By comparison, process costing does not require the separate identification and costing of each unit of output. In its simplest form, usually referred to as *output costing*, there is one uniform product, for example milk or cement, with no unfinished work at the end of a period, or where stocks vary little from year to year. In these instances the cost per unit is simply the total costs incurred during a particular period divided by the total units produced. The costs are thus averaged over an homogeneous mass of output.

The same approach is used in service industries, such as gas, water, electricity, hospitals, bus companies and airlines, where one type of service is rendered and all costs are expressed in terms of a common unit. This is known as *service* or *operating* costing. For example, bus companies will divide their total costs by mileage operated to give cost per mile, each type of expense making up the total cost being expressed in the same way, applying the same total mileage, as shown in the abbreviated statement overleaf (figure 23):

The Westville Omnibus Co. Ltd
Operating statement for the month of . . . .

Expense item	£	pence per mile
Drivers' and conductors' wages	250,000	5.0
Tyres	40,000	.80
Fuel	80,000	1.60
Vehicle maintenance	50,000	1.00
Vehicle depreciation	35,000	.70
Traffic expenses	30,000	.60
General expenses	15,000	.30
	500,000	10.00
Miles operated	5,000,000	

Figure 23. A simple operating statement

There are certain industries, however, such as oil, textiles, beer, food, paint, glass, steel, plastics and paper, where the products have to go through a continuous sequence of processes, each of which needs to be separately controlled.

The costs of each process are accumulated in separate work-in-process accounts, including overhead assigned on an appropriate labour or machine hour basis (see figure 24), and the average cost per unit of output is determined over a period of say four weeks, by dividing the total costs of each process by its output. This presumes that all units are finished, and that there are no opening or closing stocks. Control is exercised at each stage by comparing actual with expected costs in the form of a process operating statement.

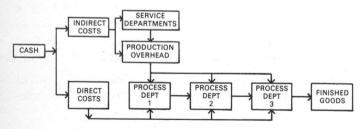

Figure 24. Costs accumulated in separate process department accounts

In some of these industries, however, complications arise because:

- there are part-finished products in each process at the end of the control period;
- losses in processing arise, and these need to be controlled;
- the output from one process may be in the form of two or more joint products, each of which then proceeds through a different series of further processes (see figure 25);
- a small amount of output at any of the processes, not being the main product, and called a byproduct, might have to be accounted for (see figure 25).

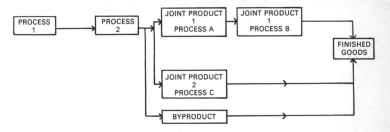

Figure 25. Joint products and byproducts

Each of these problems is dealt with in the succeeding sections of this chapter.

Self-check

1 A continuous process of paper-making would be costed by using a job costing system. (a) True or (b) false?

2 Which of the following refers to service or operating costing:

  (a) cost control of a service department within a firm;
  (b) the costing method used in a service industry?

3 'Process costing is simply a matter of dividing the costs of each process by the output of that process.' Is this statement strictly correct?

ANSWERS

1 (b) False – because paper-making is a continuous process of

producing one product, it is impossible to trace the costs of any particular measure of paper, as is required in job costing. Process costing is applicable to this industry.

2 **(b)** Service costing refers to industries such as public transport, electricity and gas.

3 In its simplest form – yes. But complications of opening and closing stocks, processing losses and byproducts can make the calculation of unit cost a little more difficult.

Complications of unfinished work

In job costing the costs of *each job* are accumulated as production proceeds. At any time, therefore, work-in-progress is exactly calculable. In process costing, however, we have the total costs of an homogeneous mass, and it is impossible to recognize the separate costs of finished and part-finished units. At the end of an accounting period, therefore, we have to adopt some method of averaging to apportion costs between finished units and work-in-progress. A homely example will illustrate how this is done.

Spring and early summer had been very kind to the strawberry crop and there was a prolific harvest. So much so that the Women's Institute decided to invest some of their funds in 150 kilos of surplus fruit, and sufficient sugar to convert it into some of their special-recipe strawberry jam. This they would sell, and typically donate the net proceeds to charity. The price of each half-kilo jar of jam was set so that it covered the cost of fruit, sugar and preserving additives – about 15 pence, and a nominal 5 pence for the ladies' labour, cost of cooking gas and other overheads.

By Wednesday lunchtime 120 kilos of fruit had been processed and put into jars. The remaining fruit, together with the other ingredients, was half-cooked at that time. Unfortunately, a burst gas pipe prevented the Institute ladies completing their work, but one of their members agreed to purchase the half-cooked jam at cost, including an appropriate proportion of labour and overhead. The secretary was asked to apportion total costs to date between the finished and part-finished jam, and the following were the figures produced by her:

		Total £	Finished £	Part-finished £
Cost of ingredients 300 × 15p		45.00	36.00	9.00
Labour and overhead:				
240 complete	240			
60 ½-complete	30			
	270 @ 5p	13.50	12.00	1.50
		58.50	48.00	10.50

The cost of ingredients had been split on a 120:30 basis, all of the fruit, etc. being used up. In calculating the labour and overheads, however, the view had been taken that whilst the costs of completing 240 jars (120 kilos fruit) was all allocable to the finished produce at 5 pence per jar, the half-processed fruit could be charged on an *equivalent units* basis. That is to say, 60 jars, upon which the ladies had only spent half the normal time, and used only half of the normal amount of gas, are the equivalent of 30 completed jars. On this basis, the part-finished jam was costed at £10.50.

This equivalent units concept is applied in process costing to ensure the equitable division of total process cost between finished and part-finished work.

Activity

The costs incurred by process department B in February were as follows:

	£
Material	3,800
Labour	2,400
Overhead	1,200
	7,400

During that period 2,000 units of production were started, of which 1,800 were finished and 200 one-quarter finished by the end of the month. There was no stock at the beginning of February. Material is added continuously throughout the process.

Calculate the division of costs between finished and part-finished units.

The first thing to note in this example is that all costs are incurred in parallel.

(a) Calculation of equivalent units gives:

	Equivalent units
Input 2,000 – finished 1,800	1,800
– unfinished, ¼-complete 200	50
	1,850

(b) Cost per unit:

$$\frac{£7,400}{1,850} = £4.$$

(c) Costs apportioned:

			£
Finished	1,800 × 4	=	7,200
Unfinished	50 × 4	=	200
Total cost			7,400

The Department B process account would appear as follows:

	£		£
Material	3,800	Transfer to finished	
Labour	2,400	goods	7,200
Overhead	1,200	Work-in-process	200
	7,400		7,400

To complicate things further, material may not be added to a process at the same time as labour and overhead, which will result in the different elements of cost being at different stages of completion at the period end. If this is so, the calculation of equivalent units must be related to the separate elements of cost. Furthermore, part-processed material from a previous process may be part of the input, together with its associated cost.

Using the data from the previous activity, but adding:

- that the 2,000 units of input, cost £2,000, came from a *previous* process; and
- that the 200 units still in process at the end of February were

¼-complete as regards labour and overhead, but ½-complete as regards material added in department B

– we get the following result:

(a) Calculation of equivalent units:

	Total	Material from previous process	Added material	Labour and overheads
Finished	1,800	1,800	1,800	1,800
In process	200	200	100	50
		(100%)	(50%)	(25%)
Equivalent units	2,000	2,000	1,900	1,850

(b) Costs per unit:

Costs	£9,400	£2,000	£3,800	£3,600
Per unit		£1	£2	£1.946

(c) Costs apportioned:*

Finished	8,903	1,800	3,600	3,503
In process	497	200	200	97
	£9,400	£2,000	£3,800	£3,600

* Equivalent units multiplied by cost per unit. Note that the work-in-process units are shown at their respective stages of completion in the calculation of equivalent units.

The department B process account now appears as follows:

	£		£
Transfer from		Transfer to finished	
department A	2,000	goods	8,903
Material added	3,800	Work-in-process	497
Labour	2,400		
Overhead	1,200		
	9,400		9,400

Further complications! The closing stock of one period becomes the opening stock of the next. The equivalent production in the following period will therefore comprise:

(a) work done to complete the opening stock of units;

(b) the *complete* processing of most of the units added in that period;

(c) work completed on the units in the ending stock.

Figure 26 summarizes this picture.

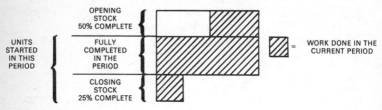

Figure 26. Processed work completed during a period

In order to show how the addition of opening stock affects the calculation of equivalent units, we need to know the number of unfinished units in that stock, and the stage of completion of each of its elements of cost.

Let us assume that there were 300 incomplete units at the end of the last period, with the following costs and stages of completion:

	£	% complete
Material from previous process	240	100
Added materials	270	50
Labour and overhead	290	50
	800	

The units completed in the period comprise opening stock, add units added, less closing stock, that is $300 + 2,000 - 200 = 2,100$, and the statements of equivalent units and costs changes as follows:

(a) Calculation of equivalent units:

	Total	Materials from previous process	Added material	Labour and overhead
Finished units	2,100	2,100	2,100	2,100
less Opening stock	300	300	150	150
		(100%)	(50%)	(50%)

Work on units finished in this period	1,800		1,800	1,950	1,950
add Closing stock	200		200	100	50
			(100%)	(50%)	(25%)
Equivalent units	2,000		2,000	2,050	2,000

(b) Costs per unit:

		Opening stock			
Costs	£10,200	£800	£2,000	£3,800	£3,600
Per unit			£1	£1.854	£1.80

(c) Costs apportioned:

Finished	£8,925		£1,800	£3,615	£3,510
add Cost of opening stock	£800				
	£9,725				
In process at end	£475		200	185	90
	£10,200	£800	£2,000	£3,800	£3,600

Note in particular that the value of opening stock is not averaged with the current period's costs, but is carried through to the end of the statement, to be added to the cost of work done on finished units in the period. This method of apportioning process costs is the FIFO (first in first out) method.

The result of introducing opening stock into the process account is shown below:

	£		£
Opening stock	800	Transfer to finished	
Transfer from		goods	9,725
department A	2,000	Work-in-process	475
Material added	3,800		
Labour	2,400		
Overhead	1,200		
	10,200		10,200

Self-check

1 100,000 metres of material were input into a printing process, and at the end of the accounting period 70,000 metres of material were transferred to the finished goods account; the remaining material being only one-third complete at that time. Total costs for the period amounted to £180,000.

Calculate the cost per equivalent unit, and apportion the total cost between finished output and work still in process.

2 Poacher's Pies and Pâte Co. have 40 kilos of half-processed liver pâté at the commencement of a period. During that period a further 300 kilos of ingredients are added to the pâté production process, and at the end 20 kilos of $\frac{1}{4}$-processed ingredients remain. If the cost applicable to the opening stock was £60, and the costs incurred during this period were £762.50, how much cost would you assign to finished and part-processed pâté, and how would these costs be shown in the pâté-processing account?

ANSWERS

1 (a) Calculation of equivalent units:

	Equivalent units
Input 100,000 metres – finished 70,000	70,000
– part-finished 30,000 ($\frac{1}{3}$)	10,000
	80,000

(b) Cost per unit: £180,000 ÷ 80,000 = £2.25 metre.
(c) Costs assigned:

Finished   70,000 @ £2.25 = £157,500
Unfinished 10,000 @ £2.25 = £ 22,500

£180,000

2 (a) Calculation of equivalent units:

	Kilos
Finished pâté	320
less Opening pâté in process	20 (40 ½-completed)
Pâté finished during the period*	300
add Closing pâté in process	5 (20 ¼-completed)
Equivalent kilos pâté completed	305

(b) Cost per kilo: £762.50 ÷ 305 = £2.50 per kilo.

(c) Costs assigned:

Pâté finished*	300 @ £2.50 = £750	
Add opening stock	60	810
Pâté part-finished	5 @ £2.50	12.50
		£822.50

Pâté processing account

Opening stock	60	Transfer to finished	
Added	762.50	goods	810.00
	———	Work-in-progress	12.50
	822.50		———
			822.50

Accounting for processing losses and gains

'What goes up must come down' is, generally speaking, still profoundly true. But 'what goes in' is not necessarily equal to 'what comes out', particularly if we are considering manufacturing processing operations. Our charitable ladies of the Women's Institute would have discovered this when they bottled their strawberry jam, and found that 150 kilos of mixed fruit and sugar did not produce 300 half-kilo jars of jam. No mystery, of course, for some would be lost through evaporation, some by sticking to the cooking vessels and some by frequent test-tasting. These are referred to as *normal* losses in processing. Any difference between normal loss and actual loss is treated as *abnormal* loss or gain.

Now the management accountant's brief is to report all exceptional happenings. He will therefore have to bring all substantial *abnormal* losses or gains into his calculations when valuing the output of each process.

Normal loss is expected. It is therefore part of the cost of good units produced. Supposing 2,000 units are introduced into a process; 1,800 *good* units are finished, and 200 are lost. If the number of lost units should normally be $\frac{1}{9}$ of good output, which is the same as $\frac{1}{10}$ of normal input, then there will be no abnormal loss or gain in this instance. Assuming that total costs entering the process were £3,600, then this whole amount would be transferred to the next process or to finished goods, including the cost of the 200 normally lost units.

However, if the number of finished good units was 1,710, then the normal loss is $\frac{1}{9} \times 1,710 = 190$ units, and because the normal input for the 1,710 output should have been 1,710 + 190 (or $\frac{10}{9} \times 1,710) = 1,900$, there is an abnormal loss of $2,000 - 1,900 = 100$ units.

Because abnormal losses are not anticipated, they have to be reported to management, and have accordingly to be valued.

Using the figures in the example given immediately above:

Cost of each unit of input: £3,600 ÷ 2,000 = £1.80.
Cost assigned:

	units		£
Normal loss	190 @ £1.80	=	342
Good output	1,710 @ £1.80	=	3,078
Transfer to finished goods			3,420
Abnormal loss	100 @ £1.80	=	180
			3,600

And the process account would appear as follows:

	£		£
Total costs	3,600	Transfer to finished goods	3,420
		Transfer to abnormal loss account	180
	3,600		3,600

Conversely, an abnormal *gain* can arise in processing. In the above example, if good output had been 1,890 units, then normal *input* should have been $\frac{10}{9} \times 1,890 = 2,100$ units. That is to say, the normal outcome of introducing 2,100 units into the process should be 1,890 units of good output.

Costs in this case are assigned as follows:

Cost of each unit of input is the same at £1.80

Cost assigned:	Units	£
Normal loss	210 @ £1.80 =	378
Good output	1,890 @ £1.80 =	3,402
Transfer to finished goods	2,100	3,780
Abnormal gain	100 @ £1.80 =	180
	2,000	3,600

The process account appearing as follows:

	£		£
Total costs	3,600	Transfer to finished goods	3,780
Transfer to abnormal gain account	180		
	3,780		3,780

It is important to show the abnormal loss or gain account separately in the profit and loss account, to highlight the exceptional nature of the item.

The introduction of production losses or gains does, of course, add a further twist to the assignment of costs where equivalent units have to be calculated, but this does not cause too much trouble.

If you refer to the example at the end of the last section you will see that we had to account for 2,100 units. This was made up of:

Opening stock	300
Added units	2,000
	2,300
Closing stock	200
	2,100

If the normal loss expected is 5% of finished good output, and we assume that only 1,900 units were finished, then normal production should have been 1,900 + (5% × 1,900) = 1,995 units. Because we have 2,100 units to account for, there is an abnormal loss of 2,100 − 1,995 = 105 units.

We have now to apportion costs, shown on page 157, to abnormal loss as well as to good output and work-in-process, as follows:

	Unit cost £	Abnormal loss Units	Abnormal loss Cost	Equivalent finished units + normal loss Units	Equivalent finished units + normal loss Cost	Ending work-in-process Units	Ending work-in-process Cost
Opening stock	—	—	—	—	800	—	—
Material from last process	1.000	105	105	1,695	1,695	200	200
Material added	1.854	105	194	1,845	3,421	100	185
Labour and overhead	1.800	105	189	1,845	3,321	50	90
			488		9,237		475

As a consequence of introducing losses into the calculations, the department B process account now appears as follows:

	£		£
Opening stock	800	Transfer to finished goods	9,237
Transferred from department A	2,000	Transfer to abnormal loss account	488
Material added	3,800	Work-in-process	475
Labour	2,400		
Overhead	1,200		
	10,200		10,200

Finally, a word about possible sales of scrap arising from any of the processes. Examples of this include scrap metal in the case of an engineering works and exhausted compost at the end of the mushroom-growing processes. The amount received for such sales is usually treated in one of two ways:

- Show it as separate revenue on the profit and loss account.
- Set it off against the costs of production of the relevant process, and in this case, if the amount received is substantial, credit an appropriate amount to abnormal loss account.

Self-check

1 Is the expected loss resulting from processing called **(a)** scrap, **(b)** residue or **(c)** normal loss?
2 If 12,500 units were introduced into a process, and 12,000 good units were produced, given that there is a normally expected loss of 2% of good units, calculate **(a)** normal loss and **(b)** abnormal loss.
3 Using your answer to **2**, assign total costs of £18,750 to **(a)** good finished output and **(b)** abnormal loss.
4 'Abnormal loss is merged with cost of goods sold.' Is this statement **(a)** true or **(b)** false?
5 'There can be no abnormal gains in processing.' Is this statement **(a)** true or **(b)** false?

ANSWERS

1 **(c)** Normal loss.
2 Normal loss is 2% of 12,000 = 240 units. Abnormal loss is 12,500 − (12,000 + 240) = 260 units.
3 Cost per unit = 18,750 ÷ 12,500 = £1.50.

Costs assigned:

	Units		£
Normal loss	240	@ £1.50 =	360
Finished units	12,000	@ £1.50 =	18,000
Abnormal loss	260	@ £1.50 =	390
			18,750

4 **(b)** False – abnormal loss is charged to a separate account and shown in the profit and loss account to highlight the exceptional nature of this cost.
5 **(b)** False – there would be a gain if the good output plus normal loss exceeds the units put into a process. Such gain would also be shown separately in the profit and loss account.

Joint products and byproducts

This section initially deals with the problem of apportioning common processing costs to joint products, these being two or more dissimilar *end* products derived from the same basic process or material. To be considered a joint product implies that something has a substantial sales value. Examples of joint products include the various derivatives of crude oil, timber processing, meat processing, gas production, and food canning.

Rockview Pottery was recently formed by the Lawson Brothers, and produces two main lines of pottery – plain earthenware and decorated – in the proportion of 2 : 1 respectively.

The basic clay mix is the same for both lines, but thereafter the decorated pots go through far more extensive painting and glazing processes than the earthenware, and this is reflected in their prices. The product cost make-up is, therefore, fairly straightforward. The initial clay preparation and mixing process costs are separately recorded and divided between the two lines of products according to the weight of clay issued to each. Thereafter costs appropriate to each batch of pots processed along the two joint-product lines are recognizable and added accordingly. The finally assembled costs of each batch of product are therefore as accurate as they possibly can be, and can be reasonably used for stock valuation, determining selling prices or profit measurement.

Plainly, the assumption that the costs of processing the material common to all products, that is clay, can be appropriated on the basis of weight is reasonable; but there are other joint products that are physically quite dissimilar when they emanate from the common process – referred to as the 'split-off point'. One may be a liquid, for example, the other a solid, and completely different by nature. A good example of this is in the processing of coal to produce coke, gas, ammoniacal liquor, etc. Weight or volume in these circumstances are not appropriate bases for cost apportionment.

One approach used is relative sales value at the split-off point, this being justified, it is considered, because the product with the highest sales value is able to bear the greatest burden of cost. Though there is no apparent logic in this, it does at least provide a basis for stock valuation purposes. It will no doubt be obvious to you that, however one splits common costs between joint products, the ultimate profitability of the whole operation will remain the same.

Where there is no sales value at the split-off point, and further processing has to be carried out to make a joint product saleable, then the ultimate sales value less the further processing and distribution costs provides an alternative basis.

For example, Agrimek Ltd produce two joint products from a common process. 'Grokwik' is a fertilizer, and is sold without further processing, but 'Zippo' is treated further, before being being sold as a substitute tractor fuel. The following costs and sales information relate to a recent period:

Initial joint processing costs	£50,000
Grokwik tonnage produced	10,000
Further processing costs of Zippo	£4,000
Zippo – gallons produced	22,000
Sales value per ton of Grokwik	£10
Sales value per gallon of Zippo	£2

The following summary shows how the joint processing costs are dealt with:

	Sales value	*less Further processing*	*Net sales value*	%	*Allocated joint costs*
Grokwik	£100,000	—	£100,000	71	£35,500
Zippo	£44,000	£4,000	£40,000	29	£14,500
			£140,000		£50,000

In processing industries there is very often an additional output from processing quite apart from the main product or the joint products. This output is very often sold, but the sales value is relatively insignificant compared to the main product. Such an output is called a byproduct (see figure 25).

Byproducts are best treated in the accounts as separate sales revenue, so that they can be monitored and thus controlled. On the other hand, if the sales value is very small, it is best dealt with by credit to the relevant process account, thus reducing the costs of that process.

Self-check

1 Which of the two following bases would you apply to the apportionment of joint processing costs in a meat-processing plant: (a) weight or (b) relative net sales value?

2 The apportionment of joint processing costs has to be

carried out with care because it affects the overall profit-ability of a firm: **(a)** true or **(b)** false?

3 A byproduct yields income that is best written off against the relevant processing account: **(a)** true or **(b)** false?

4 The common processing costs of two joint products, A and B, were apportioned as £54,000 and £36,000 respectively. If total net sales value was £180,000, and the further processing costs were £5,000 and £3,000 respectively, what was the ultimate sales value of each product?

ANSWERS

1 **(b)** Relative net sales value – though the initial processing of a meat carcass could be said to be related to weight, this bears no relationship to relative sales values of different parts of beef cattle. Sales value can be logically supported, because the price paid for each animal at market would be a composite of the realizable values of its parts.

2 **(b)** False – the method used to apportion joint costs does not affect profitability in total. Total costs and total revenue remain the same, regardless of how costs are divided.

3 **(b)** False – it is *sometimes* dealt with in this way, especially when of insignificant value; but in general terms it is far more informative to management to reveal the income separately in the profit and loss account.

4 *Allocated joint costs*	%	*Net sales value*	*Further processing costs*	*Total sales value*
A £54,000	60	£108,000	£5,000	£113,000
B £36,000	40	£ 72,000	£3,000	£ 75,000
£90,000		£180,000	£8,000	£188,000

The ultimate sales value of each product is shown in the last column.

Review

The Phew Cosmetic Co. includes in its range of products perfumed creams that have two applications. The creams pass through an initial common mixing and blending process, then the mixture splits off into two further distinctive processes to produce face cream and hand cream.

All material is added at the commencement of the common process, and the normal loss in that process is 2% of good mixture produced.

Data relevant to the month of January are given below:

	Material £	Labour/ overhead £
Common process:		
Opening stock 200 kilos (half complete) costs	50	40
Material added 2,500 kilos	650	
Labour and overhead added		550
Closing stock 200 kilos ($\frac{1}{4}$-complete)		

Mixture passed to further processes – hand cream 1,600 kilos
                         – face cream   800 kilos

                               2,400 kilos

Further processes:
No opening or closing stocks
No losses in processing expected or suffered
Hand cream processing costs   £200
Face cream processing costs   £180
Ultimate sales value – hand cream £2 per kilo
                       – face cream £3 per kilo

Required
1 Produce a statement to show the apportionment of the common processing costs between finished and part-finished mixture.
2 Construct the common process account, showing all the final cost entries.
3 Produce a statement showing the sales value, costs and profit applicable to hand cream and face cream.

ANSWERS

1 Working 1. Kilos of finished mixture to account for:

Opening stock	200
Added	2,500
	2,700
less Closing stock	200
	2,500 kilos

Working 2. Calculation of losses:

Actual output	2,400 kilos
Normal loss 2% of 2,400	48
Normal production	2,448
Production to account for	2,500
Abnormal loss	52

(a) Calculation of equivalent units:

	Material added Kilos	Labour and overhead Kilos
Abnormal loss	52	52
Normal loss	48	48
Good finished mixture	2,400	2,400
	2,500	2,500
less Opening stock	200 (100%)	100 (50%)
Kilos of finished mixture this period	2,300	2,400
add Closing stock	200 (100%)	50 (25%)
Equivalent kilos produced	2,500	2,450

(b)

Costs	£650	£550
Equivalent kilos	2,500	2,450
Cost per kilo	£0.2600	£0.2245

(c) Costs apportioned:

	Unit cost	Abnormal loss Units	Abnormal loss Cost	Finished kilos + normal loss Units	Finished kilos + normal loss Cost	Ending stock Units	Ending stock Cost
			£				
Opening stock	—	—		—	90	—	—
Material added	£.2600	52	14	2,248	584	200	52
Labour and overhead	£.2245	52	12	2,348	527	50	11
			26		1,201		63

2 Common process account:

	£		£
Opening stock	90	Transfer to hand cream	801
Material added	650	Transfer to face cream	400
Labour and overhead	550	Transfer to abnormal loss	26
		Closing stock	63
	1,290		1,290

3 Profit and loss statement:

		Hand cream		Face cream
Sales value		£3,200		£2,400
Costs – common	£801		£400	
– further	£200	£1,001	£180	£580
Profit		£2,199		£1,820

13 | Marginal cost per unit

Introducing marginal costing

Mr Charles Simon, the managing director of the Cubic Rude Co., looked up from the draft account he had been closely perusing for the last five minutes. He wore a puzzled frown.

'How can we possibly have made a profit during the last six months when our sales were only about half of our production, and we still had to meet the same heavy burden of fixed costs?' he asked the accountant, adding with a wry smile, 'One of your accounting tricks, John, I'll be bound.'

John Foster, the management accountant, glanced through the summarized profit and loss account, which looked like this:

Cubic Rude Co. Ltd
Profit and loss Account for the six months ended 30 June 19 . .

	£	£
Sales 80,000 units at £5 each		400,000
less		
Variable production costs 150,000 @ £3 each	450,000	
Fixed production costs	150,000	
	600,000	
Stock carried forward 70,000 @ £4	280,000	
Production cost of sales	320,000	320,000
		80,000
Administration and selling expenses (assumed all fixed)		40,000
Net profit		40,000

Referring to this statement, John explained to Mr Simon that profit would obviously have been much higher if sales of 150,000 units had been achieved.

'What would the profit have been in those circumstances?' asked Mr Simon.

║ *Activity*

║ Show what profit would have been if 150,000 units had been sold.

Your statement should read:

	£	£
Sales 150,000 @ £5		750,000
less		
Variable production costs – 150,000 @ £3	450,000	
Fixed costs	150,000	600,000
		150,000
Administration and selling expenses		40,000
Expected net profit		110,000

John was quick to point out that with a unit net profit of £1, that is selling price £5, less variable cost £3 and fixed £1 per unit, total profit was rightly £70,000 less in the first six months of the year because sales were 70,000 units short of the maximum of 150,000.

'I can understand that,' acknowledged the managing director, 'but isn't the profit and loss account to 30 June a bit misleading? After all, fixed costs will still have to be paid whatever the level of sales, and that statement, whilst initially showing them in total, proceeds to reduce them by £70,000 by including that figure in stock carried forward.'

'You are right to be puzzled,' said John. 'There is a certain amount of controversy about the treatment of fixed costs in accounts. Proponents of what is called "marginal costing" would have drawn up our profit statement as follows:

Marginal profit and loss account for the six months to 30 June

	£	£
Sales 80,000 @ £5 each		400,000
less		
Variable production costs 150,000 @	450,000	
£3 each		
less Stock carried forward 70,000 @	210,000	
£3 each		

	£	£
Variable cost of sales	240,000	240,000
		——————
Marginal contribution:		160,000
Fixed costs – production	150,000	
– admin. & selling	40,000	190,000
		——————
Net loss		30,000

which probably reflects your present feeling about the company's performance during that period.'

He paused a little to enable Mr Simon to take in the marginal information, then he continued:

'You will note that the whole of the fixed costs for each period are charged against the sales for that period in the marginal state-ment, because, it is suggested, fixed costs are in the main related to time – not production – and they will be incurred whether we produce or not. These costs are therefore written off in the period for which they are incurred; production cost of each unit is its variable cost; and closing stock is valued at variable cost only. Incidentally, accountants tend to use the words "marginal" and "variable" interchangeably in this context.'

'But which is the correct method?' queried Mr Simon.

'There is really no "correct" method,' replied John, 'but in our case, the full cost approach seems to be more meaningful. We are producing evenly throughout the year to our full annual capacity of 300,000 units, and we plan to continue to do so, because our marketing forecast indicates that we will be able to sell all that we make. As you know, the first six months sales are always worse than those in the second half of the year. Indeed, I understand from the sales manager that he fully expects to sell all the stock held in June, plus the 150,000 units to be manu-factured during the next six months.'

Activity

Produce a full cost profit and loss account for the second six months, based upon the expected sales of 220,000 units.

ANSWER

Profit and loss account for the six months to 31 December 19..

		£
Sales 220,000 units @ £5 each		1,100,000
less	£	
Stock brought forward (70,000 units)	280,000	
Variable production costs	450,000	
Fixed costs	150,000	
	880,000	
Stock carried forward	nil	
Production cost of sales		880,000
		220,000
Administration and selling expenses		40,000
Net profit		180,000

After examining the above figures, Mr Simon agreed that, given Cubic Rude's production and selling plans, the full cost statement was preferable, as it related profit to sales period by period, more clearly than the marginal statement. However, he did observe that, taking the year as a whole, the net profit would be the same whether marginal or full costing was used, that is, £220,000.

Self-check

1 Draw up a *marginal* profit and loss account for the Cubic Rude Co. for the second six months.
2 Do the resultant figures in your answer to question **1** support the observation made by Mr Simon that the profit for the whole year is the same?
3 What is the essential difference between a full and a marginal profit statement?

ANSWERS

1   *Marginal profit and loss account for the six months to*
                                31 December 19..

		£
Sales 220,000 @ £5		1,100,000
less	£	
Stock brought forward		
70,000 units @ £3 each	210,000	
Variable cost of production		
150,000 units @ £3 each	450,000	660,000
Marginal contribution:		440,000
Fixed costs – production	150,000	
– admin. & sales	40,000	190,000
Net profit		250,000

2

First six months – loss	(£30,000)
Second six months – profit	£250,000
Net profit using the marginal method	
– agreed with the full costing method	£220,000

3 In the marginal approach, fixed costs are treated as costs of
the period to which they relate, whereas the full cost method
apportions production fixed overhead to *unit* cost, and therefore carries a certain proportion of fixed costs forward with
stock. Marginal costing values stock at variable cost only.

A closer look at both alternatives

In the last section you were introduced to marginal costing as an
alternative method of valuing unit cost, and thus of valuing stock
and measuring profit. We continue the same theme in this section,
but with more expanded examples, to illustrate that marginal
costing may be the better alternative in certain circumstances.

Consider the XYZ Co. with total fixed costs over a six-month
period of £240,000, variable production costs of £1 a unit, a level
production rate of 40,000 units each month and sales at £3 a
unit over the six-month period as follows:

£
Month 1 – 60,000
Month 2 – 180,000
Month 3 – 120,000
Month 4 – 90,000
Month 5 – 120,000
Month 6 – 30,000

From the above information, profit and loss accounts in both marginal and full cost form are produced below:

Full costing: all figures in £000s

Month	1	2	3	4	5	6	Total
Sales @ £3	60	180	120	90	120	30	600
Opening stock @ £2	—	40	—	—	20	20	—
Variable cost @ £1	40	40	40	40	40	40	240
Fixed costs	40	40	40	40	40	40	240
	80	120	80	80	100	100	480
Closing stock @ £2	40	—	—	20	20	80	80
Cost of sales	40	120	80	60	80	20	400
Net profit/(loss)	20	60	40	30	40	10	200
Marginal costing:							
Sales @ £3	60	180	120	90	120	30	600
Opening stock @ £1	—	20	—	—	10	10	—
Variable cost @ £1	40	40	40	40	40	40	240
	40	60	40	40	50	50	240
Closing stock @ £1	20	—	—	10	10	40	40
Marginal cost	20	60	40	30	40	10	200
Contribution	40	120	80	60	80	20	400
Fixed costs	40	40	40	40	40	40	240
Net profit/(loss)	—	80	40	20	40	(20)	160

Note: in the marginal statement 'contribution' is arrived at by deducting marginal cost of sales from sales.

Activity

With regard to the alternative statements given above, see if you can explain the following:

1 Why is there a difference between total profit under each method?
2 Why is profit the same in months 3 and 5?
3 Why do profits differ in the other months?
4 Under which method is profit more closely related to sales?

ANSWERS

1 The difference in total profit is £40,000. The previous section will have enabled you to spot that this relates to £40,000 of fixed overhead carried forward in stock under the full costing method, but charged against current profit in the marginal statement. Hence the additional profit.
2 When sales and production are equal, stocks do not change. If this is the case, then cost of sales is the same under either method, and so therefore is the profit.
3 When sales and production differ in any month, so does profit. This is because stock levels change. If sales are higher than production then, under full costing, cost of sales includes fixed costs from the previous period as well as the fixed costs of the current period. Hence marginal costing profit is higher. Conversely when sales are less than production.
4 *When production is constant* profit moves in direct relationship to sales under full costing, because both fixed and variable costs charged into the profit statement are proportionate to sales. Under marginal costing, fixed costs are disproportionate to sales when the latter fluctuates.

Self-check

1 Construct full and marginal costing profit and loss accounts using the same cost information as in the last XYZ Co. example, and fluctuating production as follows:

Month 1 – 50,000 units
Month 2 – 30,000
Month 3 – 20,000

Month 4 – 60,000
Month 5 – 30,000
Month 6 – 40,000

Sales for each month were 30,000 units.

2 How do you account for the difference in total profit under the two methods?

3 Where profit is the same in any month, why does this imply that sales and production are equal?

4 Why is profit lower in marginal costing when sales are less than production?

5 Which method relates profit more closely to sales?

ANSWERS

1 *Full costing: all figures in £000s*

Month	1	2	3	4	5	6	Total
Sales @ £3	90	90	90	90	90	90	540
Opening stock @ £2	—	40	40	20	80	80	—
Variable cost @ £1	50	30	20	60	30	40	230
Fixed costs	40	40	40	40	40	40	240
	90	110	100	120	150	160	470
Closing stock @ £2	40	40	20	80	80	100	100
Cost of sales	50	70	80	40	70	60	370
Net profit/(loss)	40	20	10	50	20	30	170
Marginal costing:							
Sales @ £3	90	90	90	90	90	90	540
Opening stock @ £1	—	20	20	10	40	40	—
Variable cost @ £1	50	30	20	60	30	40	230
	50	50	40	70	70	80	230
Closing stock @ £1	20	20	10	40	40	50	50
Marginal cost	30	30	30	30	30	30	180
Contribution	60	60	60	60	60	60	360
Fixed costs	40	40	40	40	40	40	240
Net profit/(loss)	20	20	20	20	20	20	120

2 Over the whole of the six-monthly period production has exceeded sales by 50,000 units. Because the full cost method includes fixed overhead in the cost per unit, £50,000 of fixed overhead has been carried forward in stock value to the next period, resulting in a higher profit of £50,000 under that method.

3 When profit is the same in any month, this can only be because sales and cost of sales are the same under both methods. Cost of sales can only be the same when the same overhead is charged against sales. This can only happen when stock levels do not change, which in turn can only arise when sales equals production.

4 Because under full costing, if production is more than sales, fixed overhead is carried forward with the increased stock, and the lower cost of fixed overhead charged results in a higher profit than the marginal method.

5 The marginal costing method shows a consistent relationship between sales and profit, because when sales are even, fixed and variable costs are proportionate to sales.

Full costing or marginal costing?

Activity

Jot down the conclusions that you have drawn from the discussions in each of the two previous sections. Do not read on until you have thought deeply about the different outcomes arising from using each method.

Your conclusions should include the following:

- For *total* profit reporting over a long period, say a year, it probably makes little difference, especially if stock levels remain at the same volume at the beginning and end of the period. Obviously, consistency in the use of one method is implied.
- With regard to *period* reporting, say monthly or four-weekly, differences in profit may arise because of sales/production variations, and this could mislead management.
- When production fluctuates, but sales are reasonably steady, then marginal costing gives a more acceptable result than full costing because *period* costs are more stable under the former.
- On the other hand, when production is level and sales fluctuate,

full costing gives a better result, because costs are proportionate to sales.

The answer, therefore, with regard to *period reporting* is the well-worn phrase: 'It depends upon the circumstances.'

Proponents of marginal costing would tend not to accept this, however. They point out that the marginal approach with its imposed discipline of having to examine the behaviour of costs, and to differentiate between those costs that are, and those that are not, influenced by changes in volume of production, is far more useful as an indicator of the *contribution* each product or department makes towards the recovery of fixed overhead, and the realization of a profit.

For example under full costing, with its arbitrary apportionment of fixed costs, the trading results of three departments might be shown as follows:

	A £		B £		C £	Total £
Sales		1,000		2,000		3,000	6,000
Variable cost	250		500		750		
Fixed cost	800	1,050	800	1,300	800	1,550	3,900
Profit/(loss)		(50)		700		1,450	2,100

This reveals that A is apparently making a loss, and perhaps ought to be discontinued. But under marginal costing a different picture emerges:

	A £	B £	C £	Total £
Sales	1,000	2,000	3,000	6,000
Variable costs	250	500	750	1,500
Contribution	750	1,500	2,250	4,500
less Fixed costs				2,400
Net profit				2,100

The marginal statement clearly indicates that A is making a contribution to fixed costs and profits. Whether it should be closed down will depend upon (a) the effect that would have upon the sales of the other products, (b) its effect upon the volume of fixed costs – would they be reduced if A were to close down? – and (c) what alternatives are available to replace it.

The marginal concept is obviously of great value in departmental or product decision-making, and ought always to be recognized and used by management whenever applicable. We will have more to say about the concept later in this book under the heading of decision-making.

Most business organizations, however, apply full costing in the costing of production, and thus in the valuation of stock, and profit, for four very good reasons:

- Differentiating accurately between fixed and variable costs is a lot more difficult in practice than theorists would have us believe. Direct product costs present little problem, for they are generally variable, but it is in the division of indirect costs between fixed and variable that problems arise. This will be discussed again at greater length in a later chapter.
- When stock has to be valued at total manufacturing cost, then full costing makes this easier. The professional accountancy bodies recommend that stock should be valued in the annual published accounts, to include a fair proportion of fixed as well as variable manufacturing cost.
- Most manufacturing companies aim to maintain a reasonably stable level of output, and deploy their labour and other resources accordingly. This means that stocks tend to build up or to reduce if sales are not equally stable, but it is, generally speaking, economically more attractive to organize in this way than to switch production facilities on and off simply to accord with the seasonal nature of sales.
- Not apportioning fixed overhead to product costs may lead to selling price decisions that fail to take all costs into account.

Review

The Rosewood Furniture Co. Ltd had taken on a new, recently qualified management accountant, Evelyn Fishant. With recently propounded theories of marginal and full costing still vividly in her mind, she applied her knowledge to the production of marginal profit and loss accounts for the two quarters to 31 December 19...

Proudly presenting her statement to the finance director, she pointed out that the original full-cost statements were misleading, and did not disclose vital information on the contribution being realized. She suggested that the company switch over to marginal costing.

The full costing profit and loss account is given below:

	First quarter			*Second quarter*		
		£	£		£	£
Sales 5,000 @ £5			25,000	Sales 2,000 @ £5		10,000
Opening stock				Opening stock	—	
1,000 @ £3		3,000				
Variable cost				Variable cost		
4,000 @ £2		8,000		4,000 @ £2	8,000	
Fixed cost		4,000		Fixed cost	4,000	
		———			———	
		15,000			12,000	
less Closing stock		—		less Closing stock		
				2,000 @ £3	6,000	
Cost of sales			15,000	Cost of sales		6,000
			———			———
Net profit			10,000			4,000

Required

1 Construct the marginal statements produced by Evelyn.
2 What did Evelyn mean when she indicated that the full cost statement did not disclose 'contribution'?
3 Explain why the profits differ in the two periods.
4 Explain why the total profits differ over the six-month period.
5 The finance director decided to maintain the present system; how do you think he justified his decision?

ANSWERS

1 Marginal costing profit and loss accounts:

	First quarter			*Second quarter*		
		£	£		£	£
Sales 5,000 @ £5			25,000	Sales 2,000 @ £5		10,000
Opening stock	£			Opening stock	—	
1,000 @ £2	2,000					
Variable cost				Variable cost		
4,000 @ £2	8,000			4,000 @ £2	8,000	
	———				———	
	10,000				8,000	
less Closing				less Closing stock		
stock	—		10,000	2,000 @ £2	4,000	4,000

	First quarter		Second quarter
	£		£
Contribution	15,000	Contribution	6,000
Fixed costs	4,000	Fixed costs	4,000
Net profit	11,000		2,000

2 Under the marginal statement the difference between the selling price of a unit and costs that were marginally incurred to produce that unit, is disclosed. This is referred to as 'contribution', and knowledge that a product is contributing is useful in decisions concerning continuance or otherwise of a particular product or department.

3 In the first three months profit is £1,000 less under full costing because £1,000 of fixed costs has been brought forward from the previous period.

In the second three months profit is £2,000 more under full costing because £2,000 of the fixed costs included in the marginal statement are carried forward in the stock value in the full cost statement.

4 Over the whole six months profit is less under marginal costing because more fixed cost is charged to the profit and loss account under that method. Stock has increased from 1,000 to 2,000 units, therefore £1,000 more fixed cost is carried forward in the full cost statement.

5 The finance director probably gave four reasons for not changing to marginal costing:
   (a) the difficulty in classifying costs into fixed and variable;
   (b) as stock has to be valued at full cost in the financial accounts, full costing conveniently provides this information;
   (c) as production is stable at 4,000 units per quarter, profit is more reasonably related to sales under full costing;
   (d) management wishes to know 'full cost' to help in setting prices, or to compare with prices external to the business.

Part 5
Control of resources through standards

14 | How much of each resource should we be using?

Introducing standard costing

Management accounting is concerned with the provision of quantitative information to managers of organizations to assist them in planning and controlling operations, and the bulk of the information provided is related to costs. However, simply reporting *actual* cost to management does little to help them to *control* costs. This has already been acknowledged in earlier chapters. For example, we have seen that actual job costs can be compared with cost estimates; overhead absorption rates help to highlight differences between planned and actual activity; and in process costing we differentiated between normal and abnormal losses. Whilst these approaches undoubtedly improve the usefulness of accounting information, and are probably quite adequate for the small- to medium-sized business, they can be improved upon by the introduction of a formal system of *standard costing*.

The *standard cost* of a product is *what it should cost* to produce under normal conditions, this implying a very careful assessment of the *quantities* and *prices* of all the resources combining to create each product. When this has been accomplished, it is then a relatively easy matter to modify the recording of transactions in the accounting system to reveal differences that arise between actual and standard costs of material, labour and overhead. This method of accounting is known as 'standard costing'. Thus the actual costs of production are still recorded, but are divided so as to value all stock accounts at standard cost, and to direct any differences between standard and actual cost into appropriately labelled *variance* accounts.

Activity

You are the accountant of a manufacturing company which is to introduce standard cost accounting. Bearing in mind that standard cost is what cost should be under normal conditions, what benefits do you think will accrue from this system in the wider context of management planning and control?

Your answer should include some of the following:

1 The study of 'standard' conditions will itself bring some immediate benefits in improved productivity.
2 Performance can be evaluated against standard, and better control of costs attained.
3 Standards are attainable targets, and as such should act as incentives to employees to perform efficiently.
4 Standard costs can be used by management to establish its overall plans (budgets).
5 Standards can assist in the decision-making process; for example, in the determination of prices.
6 Standard costs can form the basis of an incentive payment scheme.
7 Standard costs can lead to a reduction in clerical work; for example, stores records need not be valued as each stock item has a single standard cost.

Standard costing is most effective in industries where products and processes are standardized, for example when there is only one product and where production processes are continuous. Thus it naturally applies to the food-processing industry, to cosmetics and to cement. Where work is non-repetitive, for example in jobbing industries such as motor maintenance, standard costing has limited application.

Self-check

1 'Actual costs are perfectly adequate for control purposes.' Do you agree with this statement?
2 Which of the following is true? The standard cost of a product is:

(a) what it might have cost;
(b) what it did cost;
(c) what it should have cost;
(d) what it will cost.

3 Which of the following terms expresses the difference between actual and standard cost? **(a)** valuation, **(b)** variable, **(c)** variant, **(d)** variance, **(e)** discrepancy.

ANSWERS

1 One of the dictionary meanings of the word 'control' is 'checking or verifying the results'. Verification implies the comparison of what is, against what should have been, therefore we must have an adequate standard with which to compare actual costs if we are to control.
2 **(c)** What it should have cost.
3 **(d)** Variance.

Setting standards for direct materials

Mr Charles Simon, managing director of the Cubic Rude Co. Ltd, was discussing the introduction of a standard costing system with his management accountant John Foster.

'We will not go far wrong in setting standards for direct materials if we analyse our past costing records to find out how much material was used to produce each batch of our educational toys, and how much we have paid for each type of material and part purchased.'

John smiled a little.

'I was expecting that you would make that suggestion, and in anticipation I have made one or two notes of the principles which I think should guide us in the matter of setting material standards.'

He then handed Mr Simon a copy of his notes, and proceeded to read from his own copy.

'1. Cost is a function of quantity and price, therefore it will be necessary for us to *forecast* standard quantities and prices for all direct materials used in the manufacture of each of our products.

'2. The actual amount of material used in the past may not be that laid down in the material specifications for each product; specifications which may be changed at any time for design or cost reasons.

'3. If we use our existing specifications as the bases for standards, we are presuming that their design, and the quality of each of the parts and materials, meets the requirements of our customers.

'4. The standard quantity of each material issued to production should include an allowance for normal production losses.

'5. In settling on standard prices, we concern ourselves with those expected during the period to which standards are to apply. Past prices are not relevant, unless they remain unchanged.

'6. Standard prices are the responsibility of the purchasing department, but standard policy should be to obtain at least two quotations for each material. The cheapest price might not always be the best; delivery, quality and continuity of supply should also be considered.

'7. Standard prices will be net of any quantity discounts allowed by suppliers, but will include delivery charges. In some cases, long-term contract prices will pre-empt the need to forecast future prices.

'8. Investigations should be carried out to see whether it would be more economic for the company to make certain parts internally rather than to purchase them.

'9 The prices used as standard should be those prevailing at the commencement of each accounting period unless an early price rise is expected, when that should be used. If prices are expected to be relatively stable, an average of expected prices could be used.

'10. Rapid inflation can soon render standard prices out of date. If this is the case, they may have to be reviewed at shorter intervals than one year to ensure that reports on variances and stock valuations are realistic.

'These are the principles which apply to most manufacturing operations,' concluded John.

There followed some further discussion, and after Mr Simon had received satisfactory answers to his queries, he instructed the accountant to apply all the principles outlined above to Cubic Rude's standard costing system.

Self-check

1 Indicate and explain whether each of the following statements is (a) true or (b) false.

(i) Standard prices of materials are set by the management accountant.

(ii) Standard quantities of materials can be assessed from past usage.

(iii) Standard material quantities should include an allowance for abnormal losses in production.

(iv) Standard price reflects the highest price to be paid for material during the coming year.

(v) Standards should never be changed during an accounting period.

2 Last year the cost of 2,500 metres of material was £27,500. 2,400 metres was used in finished production of 200 units. Next year the price of material is expected to rise by 10%, but the standard quantity of material should be firm at $1/12$ less than last year's usage. What will the total standard cost of material be next year?

ANSWERS

1 (i) False – the purchasing manager should be responsible for standard prices.

(ii) False – although past usage may be a true indicator of standard quantity, the latter should relate to what *should be* the usage, not what has been.

(iii) False – normal losses are included but not abnormal loss, for it is the latter that our standard costing system is trying to highlight.

(iv) False – standard prices should represent average price for the coming year.

(v) False – if substantial change has taken place during an accounting year, for example, if there has been considerable inflation in prices, then standards ought to be adjusted, otherwise the reporting of variances will not be very meaningful.

2 Standard price will be $£\dfrac{27,500}{2,500} \times 1.10 = £12.10$.

Standard quantity will be $\frac{11}{12} \times 2,400 = 2,200$ metres.
Standard cost $= 2,200 \times £12.10 = £26,620$.

Setting standards for direct labour

Having completed their discussions on material standards, John and his managing director next turned their attention to direct labour.

'As with material, I suppose the basic approach is to determine the quantity of labour required and the price that will have to be paid for it,' said Mr Simon.

'That is so,' replied John, 'but with regard to labour we have a head start because of the work already carried out by our work study engineer. He began by recommending a number of changes in work practices, he then rearranged the layout of machines in the factory, to improve productivity, and specified the grade of employee's skill required for each type of operation. Then, using scientific techniques of observation, he analysed the work content of each operation, making due allowance for the personal and ergonomic needs of employees, and established standard times for all the operations carried out on most of our products.

'For example, the standard direct labour cost of a 10,000 batch of our Magic Shapes metal puzzle is shown in this schedule.'

John handed the director the summary shown below:

Standard direct labour cost – Metal Shapes

Dept	Operation no.	Operation	Standard hours for this batch 10,000	Standard rate per hour £	Standard labour cost £
Cutting	C379	Cut & shape metal	40	1.50	60
Drill	D253	Drill metal	50	1.60	80
Fitting	F293	Fit rod	20	1.70	34
Packing	P127	Pack	20	1.40	28
			130		202

'This kind of detailed cost breakdown enables us to control the manufacture of our products, department by department, and as long as there is no change in the standard operations, we can continue to rely on the summary for standard information.

'Unfortunately, not all jobs have been work-studied to date, which means that we will have to use past experience as a guide until the engineer completes his task.'

'I agree,' acknowledged Mr Simon, 'but I notice that you have specified a standard rate per hour for each operation. Now I know that none of our basic hourly rates of pay are quite as you state. How did you arrive at the figures shown?'

John referred to his working papers for a brief moment, then explained. 'These are averages, calculated by the personnel manager. It is true that rates of pay differ, partly because of the company's long-service and merit increments scheme. However, the differences between the highest and lowest rates in each production department are not too wide, and an average rate has been calculated for each, which should be sufficient to highlight any substantial variances when wages are paid.'

He paused awhile, then continued, 'Of course, we have also included the wages increase expected in January in calculating those rates, because we know that the increase has been agreed, and will be paid from that month onward.'

'I agree that we must be realistic, and include all known changes, whether in rates of pay or hours allowed,' said Mr Simon, 'otherwise the resultant variance analysis will be meaningless.

'Now let us have a look at overhead standards,' he suggested.

Self-check

1 Why would a direct labour standard based only on *total* expected product labour cost be inadequate?
2 Which specialists within a manufacturing concern would most likely be responsible for determining (a) standard times for each job and (b) standard labour rates?
3 Why do you think it is important to differentiate between different grades of labour when setting labour standards?

ANSWERS

1 The standard cost of labour for a product includes (a) standard hours to be worked and (b) the standard rates payable for each hour worked. Both have to be separately specified because cost variances need to be identified for each aspect.
2 The work study engineer who measures the work content of each job determines their standard times. The personnel manager might be responsible for standard rates.

3 If a team of workers is engaged on a production line, some with different skills rewarded at different rates, then a change in the standard composition of the team will lead to variances in cost. It is important to recognize these mix variances.

Setting standards for production overheads

'I suspect that overheads will present more problems than the direct costs,' the managing director observed, 'but are we still to consider setting standards in terms of quantity and price, John?'

'Basically speaking, yes,' replied John, 'but the calculations are a little more obscure than with direct material and labour – mainly because of the "fixed" nature of some of the indirect costs. Not that this problem is unknown to us, because we have been using overhead absorption rates for a while now, and therefore there should be little difficulty in converting to standard costing.'

John then went on to remind Mr Simon how the company currently charged overhead to production by using predetermined overhead rates (see Chapter 11, the section on choosing activity level in calculating overhead rates). Each rate was calculated by dividing an appropriate production activity level for a cost centre into the forecast cost at that level of output.

'Standard overhead rates are calculated in much the same way,' he explained.

'Of course,' continued the accountant, 'there is a fundamental difference between the variable and fixed cost elements of the standard overhead rate. Variable costs such as electrical power are incurred only when production occurs, and therefore, no matter what level of output is chosen as standard, the variable cost *per unit of output*, whether output is expressed in units, standard hours or machine hours, remains the same.

'Not so with fixed overhead, which represents a committed level of expenditure on basic productive resources such as buildings, machinery, plant, services, management and supervisory labour, to provide the capacity necessary to meet the demand for the company's products forecast in our five-year corporate plan.

'Thus the *total quantity* of fixed overhead is determined, but the amount *averaged* to each unit of output will depend upon the chosen standard level of output.'

John then drew the diagram illustrated in figure 27 to show

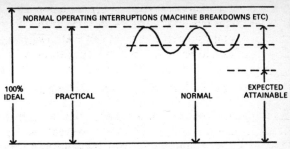

Figure 27. Alternative standard activity levels

Mr Simon the options open to manufacturing companies when choosing a 'standard' level of output.

You will no doubt recognize the terms used in this diagram, for Mr Simon and John are really considering the same problem as that posed in the penultimate section of Chapter 11. What level of output to relate to fixed overhead? Or in the present context, what level to choose as 'standard'?

'*Ideal* at 100% activity is unrealistic in the majority of firms, and certainly is in ours. There are almost certain to be interruptions in production caused by machine breakdowns, inefficiency, waiting for materials and other delays. Which brings us to the *practical* level,' John paused as Mr Simon interrupted him.

'That is the level that we expect to attain, and ought therefore to apply as standard, because our order books are full and are expected to remain so for the foreseeable future,' suggested the managing director, then adding, 'But isn't that level the same as "expected attainable"?'

'In our case, yes,' replied John, 'for we expect to be working at the same "practical" level for some time to come. However, some firms, whose output fluctuates considerably, have to choose between normal and expected attainable.'

Activity

If fixed overhead cost for a firm is £10,000, and practical capacity 10,000 hours, calculate the fixed cost element of the standard overhead rate at expected attainable levels of 10,000, 8,000, 6,000, 4,000, 2,000 and 1,000 standard hours.

At each level you divide £10,000 by standard hours, to give:

Standard hours	10,000	8,000	6,000	4,000	2,000	1,000
Standard rate	£1.00	£1.25	£1.67	£2.50	£5.00	£10.00

'Given that the standard overhead rate is based upon the planned output (expected attainable) in each year, and that this level is achieved, all overhead will be absorbed by production, assuming that prices remain stable. On the other hand, if expected output is not achieved, then managers will be informed of the cost of fixed resources that have been over- or under-utilized. Such information will have some control value when the managers concerned have a considerable influence upon the production in their departments, even though they may have little control over the *total volume* of fixed resources available.' John paused.

'I can understand that adopting the expected attainable output level is probably better for planning and control purposes,' said Mr Simon, 'but won't fluctuating overhead rates mean that stock is differently valued year by year, and that cost estimates for new products will also vary? These are major factors to consider, surely.'

'Very perceptive,' commented John respectfully, 'and these are the very reasons why a large number of firms opt to use the "normal" activity level when demand, and therefore output, fluctuates significantly. As you can see from figure 27, normal is the *average* of the highest and the lowest capacities required to meet the forecast fluctuating sales of the next few years. Its use stabilizes stock valuation and, excepting for inflation adjustment, adds an unchanging amount of cost to selling price "make-up", to cover both good and bad years. However, managers get little help from using normal activity for control purposes, as it is a reflection of the long-term trend of demand, and will only occasionally coincide with actual performance.'

He paused, thought awhile, and added, 'However, some firms solve this problem by using expected attainable for periodic control purposes, and normal activity for year-end stock valuation and for calculating selling prices.'

'A kind of dual rate approach, very clever!' commented Mr Simon. 'But as we are expecting all "good" years, our practical level equates with normal and expected attainable.'

'Precisely,' agreed John.

There was a brief pause in the discussion while Mr Simon consulted some guide notes on his desk. Then he said, 'Well, that deals with quantity of overhead, but what about price?'

'The same considerations apply to indirect costs as to direct costs,' replied John. 'Prices are governed to a large extent by market forces and we have to allow for expected price increases. But our purchasing manager in respect of materials, our personnel manager in relation to labour, and service managers for other expenses, keep a constant vigil to ensure that we pay only the keenest price for each resource acquired.'

Self-check

The fixed costs for next year in the canning department of the Green-Eye Pea Co. Ltd are estimated to be £150,000. Variable costs are estimated at £120 for each hour that the production line operates, and peas are canned at the rate of 20 tins a minute. The company works an eight-hour day, five days a week, for 50 weeks a year, but normal production interruptions amount to 10% of full (ideal) capacity operations.

Required
Prepare a cost schedule to show what the standard overhead cost rate per 1,000 cans would be at practical level, and 75%, 50% and 25% of ideal capacity.

ANSWER

Working 1: output at full capacity:

$20 \times 60 \times 8 \times 5 \times 50 = 2{,}400{,}000$ cans a year.

Working 2: hours at full capacity:

$8 \times 5 \times 50 = 2{,}000$ hours per year.

Schedule of overhead rates at different capacity levels:

	90% (practical)	75%	50%	25%
Output levels				
000s cans	2,160	1,800	1,200	600
Working hours	1,800	1,500	1,000	500
	£	£	£	£
Fixed costs	150,000	150,000	150,000	150,000
Variable cost @ £120 per hour	216,000	180,000	120,000	60,000
Total overhead cost at various output levels	366,000	330,000	270,000	210,000
Standard overhead rate per 1,000 cans	169.44	183.33	225.00	350.00

Review

Norfolk Agrimek Ltd are planning to introduce standard costing into their accounting system, and the management accountant has been given the responsibility of coordinating the compilation of cost standards for all their products.

One of the company's recently introduced, but very popular, products is the mechanical spade, assembled under a licence granted by a Swedish firm. Most of the parts are bought in as a package per spade from Sweden, assembled, spray-painted and packed by the Norfolk firm.

Last year, the direct material and labour cost of producing 2,500 of these spades was as follows:

Materials
2,550 parts packages	£38,250
300 sq. metres sheet steel for blades	£2,700
250 litres of paint	£1,000

Labour
Cutting and shaping blades 230 hrs	£460
Assembling and finishing 5,400 hrs	£13,500

Overhead
Cutting and shaping – total overhead	£18,700
Assembling and finishing – total overhead	£24,000

Direct labour hours available
Cutting and shaping	10,000
Assembling and finishing	17,500

Further investigation showed that:

- The wastage rate on parts packages should be 1% of finished spades.
- Because of a drop in the value of the £, the expected imported cost for each parts package will be £1 more next year than last.
- Blade production time should be extended by 20 hours in total, this would cut last year's usage of sheet steel by 25 sq. metres.
- The price of sheet steel will not change next year, nor will that of paint.
- Labour hourly rates of pay are expected to increase by 10% next year.
- Assembling and finishing time should be 2 hours for each spade produced.
- Variable overhead is incurred on hours worked and is expected to increase by 20% next year.
- Practical capacity for each department achieved last year, and expected to be repeated this year, was as follows:

Cutting and shaping   – 90% of direct labour hours available.
Assembling and finishing – 85% of direct labour hours available.

- Fixed overhead is estimated as follows:

	Last year £	Next year £
Cutting and shaping	11,950	12,600
Assembling and finishing	9,125	9,520

Required

Compile a detailed standard manufacturing cost summary for one mechanical spade for next year. Show both quantity and price details.

ANSWER

Workings

1 *Parts package*

Last year each cost £38,250 ÷ 2,550 = £15.
Next year will cost £15 + 1 = £16.
Plus 1% wastage £16 × 1.01 = £16.16.

2 *Sheet steel*

Will be reduced to $300 - 25 = 275$ sq. metres.
Standard price will be £2,700 ÷ 300 = £9/sq. metre.
Standard usage 275 ÷ 2,500 = .11 sq. metres.

3 *Paint*

Standard quantity 250 ÷ 2,500 = .10 litres.
Standard price £1,000 ÷ 250 = £4/litre.

4 *Cutting and shaping*

Standard labour rate (£460 ÷ 230) × 1.10 = £2.20 per hr.
Standard labour required 250 ÷ 2,500 per product = .10 hrs.

5 *Assembling and finishing*

Standard labour rate (13,500 ÷ 5,400) × 1.10 = £2.75 per hr.
Standard labour required – stated = 2 hrs.

6 *Overhead*

C&S Dept: fixed rate 12,600 ÷ 9,000 * = £1.40 per hr.

—: variable rate $\left(\dfrac{18,700 - 11,950}{9,000*}\right) \times 1.20 = .90$ per hr.

A&F Dept: fixed rate £9,520 ÷ 14,875 * = .64 per hr.

—: variable rate $\left(\dfrac{24,000 - 9,125}{14,875*}\right) \times 1.20 = £1.20$ per hr.

* Practical capacity – C&S 10,000 × .90 = 9,000 hrs.
                  – A&F 17,500 × .85 = 14,875 hrs.

Norfolk Agrimek Limited
Standard cost of one mechanical spade

	Standard quantity	Standard price £ p	Standard cost £ p	Total standard cost £ p
Direct materials				
Parts package	1.01	16.00	16.16	
Sheet steel (sq. metres)	.11	9.00	0.99	
Paint (litres)	.10	4.00	0.40	17.55

	Standard quantity	Standard price £ p	Standard cost £ p	Total standard cost £ p
Direct labour				
Cutting and shaping (hrs)	.10	2.20	0.22	
Assembling and finishing (hrs)	2.00	2.75	5.50	5.72
Overhead				
Cutting and shaping:	*Hours*			
Fixed	.10	1.40	0.14	
Variable	.10	0.90	0.09	0.23
Assembling and finishing:				
Fixed	2.00	0.64	1.28	
Variable	2.00	1.20	2.40	3.68
				27.18

15 | How far are we off target?

Introduction

There is a well-known saying in the world of computers – 'garbage in – garbage out!' – meaning that the output from any process or system can be only as good as the input allows it to be. If a computer is given a set of instructions (a programme), and they are quite meaningless, then the output will be just as lacking in meaning. Likewise, if your tailor makes a suit for you based upon carelessly taken measurements, you would not have a hope of winning the 'best dressed man of the year' competition. Similarly, a system of standard costing will only be as effective as the measured standard costs allow it to be. Great care has to be taken, therefore, in setting the standards discussed in the previous chapter.

If standards are truly what costs should be, then an analysis of differences between actual and standard costs can yield information vital to helping a business achieve its objectives.

But what variances do arise, and how do we calculate and account for them? Before answering these questions in detail, it will be helpful to set out three basic concepts which provide a framework for variance analysis.

Firstly, there is a need to report separately on each of the elements of cost and sales for which standards have been determined.

Secondly, because standards are all based upon quantity and price, we can expect variances to be expressed in similar terms. All variances are basically reporting *quantity* and *price* differences.

Thirdly, all variances are calculated by comparing *what did happen* with *what should have happened*. For example, how much time was taken to complete a job is compared with the time it *should have taken*.

Armed with this common framework of rules, and the following standard and actual cost data relevant to one product, this chapter is devoted to revealing how variances are calculated for each cost element and accounted for.

Cubic Rude Co. Ltd
Standard cost card – Crazy Puzzle standard batch, 200

	Price/rate	Cost	
Direct material:	£ p	£	£
200 units of AB	1.00	200	
200 units of CD	0.50	100	300
Direct labour:			
Assembly 5 hrs	2.00		10
Production overhead:			
Assembly 5 hrs			
Variable	1.00	5	
Fixed	2.00	10	15
Total standard cost			325

Notes

1 For the purpose of calculating the fixed overhead for this batch the fixed overhead rate is based upon a four-weekly budgeted fixed cost of £2,000.

2 Variable overhead cost is incurred on hours worked. During the four-weekly period no. 10, 180 batches of Crazy Puzzle were completed. The following actual cost data apply:

Direct materials used:	£
39,000 units of AB @ £1.10 each =	42,900
35,000 units of CD @ £0.52 each =	18,200
	61,100

Direct labour paid at hourly rate £2.10 = 1,995

Production overhead	
Variable =	970
Fixed =	2,100

Calculating and accounting for direct material variances

Reminders

- Two variances are to be calculated – price and quantity, the latter usually referred to as usage.
- Calculate each by reference to actual less standard cost,
- Variances will either be adverse (A) or favourable (F), according to whether actual is more or less than standard cost respectively.

Price variance:
(actual price − standard price) × quantity used = variance
AB (1.10 − 1.00) 39,000 = £3,900 (A)
CD (0.52 − 0.50) 35,000 = £   700 (A)   £4,600 (A)

This variance is adverse because higher prices than expected were paid.

It has to be remembered of course, that direct materials are usually purchased for stock in the first instance, possibly in large quantities to be used over a period of time. If this is the case, then price variances are normally calculated when material is *purchased*, not when it is *used*. This means that in any accounting period *price* variances will relate to *purchases* during the period, but usage variances will be calculated on material *used* during the same period. As purchases and usage will rarely coincide, it follows that a *total* check on material variances cannot always be carried out, as it can be in this example.

Usage variance:
(actual quantity used − standard quantity for 180 batches) × standard price
AB (39,000 − 36,000) 1   = £3,000 (A)
CD (35,000 − 36,000) .50   =   500 (F)   £2,500 (A)

Usage of AB was excessive, but CD kept within standard.

Total materials variance check:
(actual cost of material used − standard cost for 180 batches)
    = £61,100 − (180 × £300)
    = £61,100 − 54,000
    = £ 7,100 (A) (price £4,600; usage £2,500)

Self-check

Tom had just returned home from a very enjoyable continental holiday. He had planned to travel 3,000 miles, and amazingly had exactly achieved his goal. He had also calculated that his car should run a standard 30 miles to a gallon of petrol, and that he would pay an average £1.80 a gallon. Tom discovered that he had purchased 110 gallons of petrol, at a total cost of £192.50 during his holiday.

Required
Calculate Tom's petrol price and usage variances.

ANSWERS

Price variance:

(actual price − standard price) × quantity used
[(192.50 ÷ 110) − 1.80] × 110
(1.75 − 1.80) × 110 = £5.50 (F)

Usage variance:

(actual usage − standard usage) × standard price
[110 − (3,000 ÷ 30)] × £1.80
(110 − 100) × £1.80 = £18.00 (A)

Total variance check:

actual cost − standard cost
[£192.50 − (£1.80 × 100)]
£192.50 − 180 = £12.50 (A)

Accounting for material variances

As stated at the commencement of Chapter 14, standard cost accounting requires relatively minor modifications to the system described in Chapter 5. (It might be useful to refer back to that chapter before proceeding with the following.) The main change is the creation of variance accounts to record differences between standard and actual costs of resources. All stock accounts are maintained at standard cost.

Accounting entries				Explanations

Suppliers

		Purchases	61,100	1 Amount to be paid to suppliers for material purchased.

Material stock

Purchases	56,500			2 Material added to the stock account at standard price.

Material price variance

Purchases	4,600			3 Difference between amount payable to suppliers and the standard cost.

Accounting for usage variances

Material stock

Purchases	56,500	Work-in-progress	56,500	1 Material issued to production at standard cost.

Work-in-progress

Direct materials	56,500	Finished goods	54,000	2 Output transferred to finished goods at standard cost. Variance represents excess material usage.
		Material usage variance	2,500	
	56,500		56,500	

Material usage variance

Work-in-progress	2,500			3 Excess material used.

Finished goods

Work-in-progress	54,000			4 Standard material cost of finished goods.

Calculating direct labour variances

There is a great similarity between the calculation of direct labour and direct material variances.

Rate of pay variance:
(actual rate paid − standard rate) × hours worked
$(2.10 − 2.00) × (1,995 ÷ 2.10)$
$.10 × 950 = £95 \text{ (A)}$

Labour efficiency variance:
(hours actually worked − standard hours) × standard rate of pay

Note: standard hours represents the time that should have been taken to complete the work.
$[950 − (180 × 5)] × £2$
$(950 − 900) × £2 = £100 \text{ (A)}$

Total labour variance check:
(actual cost of direct labour − standard cost of direct labour)

Note: standard cost of direct labour is the number of batches produced × the standard cost of a batch.

£1,995 − (180 × 10)

£1,995 − £1,800 = £195 (A)

> ### Self-check
>
> State and explain whether the following statements are **(a)** true or **(b)** false.
>
> 1 An adverse rate variance arises when direct wages paid are less than hours paid multiplied by the standard rate.
> 2 Labour inefficiency arises when total wages paid are greater than expected.
> 3 The amount transferred from the wages account to work-in-progress represents the standard cost of hours worked.

ANSWERS

1 **(b)** False – wages paid are less than expected, therefore this is a favourable variance.
2 **(b)** False – total wages could be greater because of an adverse rate variance.
3 **(a)** True – the rate variance is taken out of the wages account, what is left and transferred to work-in-progress must be the standard cost of hours worked.

Accounting for direct labour variances

Accounting entries Wages				*Explanations*
Cash-wages paid	1,995	Work-in-progress Labour rate variance	1,900 95	1 Total wages paid £1,995. Hours worked at standard rate £1,900. Difference £95 transferred to rate variance.
	£1,995		£1,995	
		Labour rate variance		
Wages	95			2 Rate variance transferred from wages account.
		Work-in-progress		
Wages	1,900	Finished goods Labour efficiency variance	1,800 100	3 Output transferred to finished goods at standard cost. Variance represents excess hours worked.
	£1,900		£1,900	

Accounting entries Wages	Explanations
Labour efficiency variance	

Work-in-progress 100 Finished goods		4 Excess hours worked.
Work-in-progress 1,800		5 Standard labour cost of finished goods.

Calculating overhead variances

In the last chapter your prior knowledge of overhead absorption rates provided a very helpful background to the problems of setting standard overhead rates. Similarly, you will find that the reasons given for the over or under absorption of overhead in Chapter 11 are worth recalling:

* activity being different to plan, and
* overhead cost being higher or lower than anticipated, or
* something of both

– for these also provide the basis for the computation of overhead cost variances.

Calculating variable overhead variances

In our Cubic Rude standard cost specification at the commencement of this chapter, variable overhead is stated as being directly related to hours worked. For each hour worked, £1 of variable overhead should be incurred. Further, five hours worked should produce one Crazy Puzzle. It follows that if each hour worked cost more or less than £1, there will be a price variance, usually referred to as *expenditure* variance. In addition, if each hour worked produces more or less than one hour's worth of product, there will be an *efficiency* variance.

Expenditure variance:

(actual variable overhead cost – standard variable overhead cost)
£970 – 950 hours @ £1 hr
£970 – £950 = £20 (A)

Efficiency variance:

(actual hours worked – standard hours produced) × standard variable overhead rate

$(950 - 180$ batches $\times 5$ hrs per batch$) \times £1$
$(950 - 900) \times £1 = £50$ (A)

Calculating fixed overhead variances

The Cubic Rude fixed overhead rate is found by dividing hours expected to be worked (standard capacity), into the budgeted fixed cost, that is, £2,000 ÷ 1,000 = £2.

If the actual fixed overhead cost is more or less than £2,000, there will be an *expenditure* variance. If actual hours *worked* are more or less than 1,000, we have a *capacity* variance, and if those hours worked do not result in an equivalent number of product hours, there is an *efficiency* variance (see figure 28).

Overhead expenditure variance:

(actual fixed overhead cost − standard fixed overhead cost)
$(2,100 - 2,000) = £100$ (A)

Adverse because there was more cost than expected.

Overhead capacity variance:

(actual hours worked − standard capacity hours) × standard fixed overhead rate
$(950 - 1,000) \times £2 = £100$ (A)

Adverse because 50 hours of production capacity have been lost.

Overhead efficiency variance:

(actual hours worked − standard hours produced) × standard fixed overhead rate
$[950 - (180 \times 5)] \times £2 = £100$ (A)

Adverse because 950 hours worked have not produced an equivalent number of hours of product.

All the overhead variances can be checked in total as follows:

Total overhead variance:

(actual total overhead cost − standard overhead absorbed)
Note: standard overhead absorbed = standard hours produced (5×180) multiplied by the standard overhead rate (£3)
$[(2,100 + 970) - (900 \times 3)]$
$3,070 - 2,700 = £370$ (A)

You will see that the total variance of £370 is the equivalent of all the separate variances added together.

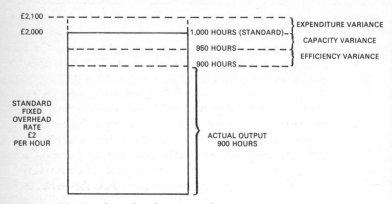

Figure 28. Fixed overhead variances

Accounting for overhead variances

Accounting entries			*Explanations*
Overhead control			
Cash paid:		Work-in-progress:	1 Overhead incurred £3,070.
variable	970	Variable	Overhead transferred to work-in-progress £2,950. Expenditure variance – the balance of £120.
fixed	2,100	950 × £1	950
		Fixed	2,000
		Expenditure variance	120
	£3,070		£3,070
Work-in-progress			
Variable overhead	950	Finished goods	2,700	2 Standard overhead cost of output transferred to finished goods £2,700. Overhead variances transferred to variance accounts.
Fixed overhead	2,000	Efficiency variance	150
		Capacity variance	100
	£2,950		£2,950
Finished goods			
Work-in-progress	2,700			3 Standard overhead cost of finished goods produced.
Expenditure variance			
Variable	20			4 Expenditure variance transferred from overhead control account.
Fixed	100		
Efficiency variance			
Work-in-progress	150			5 Variable (£50) and fixed (£100). Efficiency variances transferred from work-in-progress account.

Capacity variance		
Work-in-progress 100		6 Fixed overhead capacity variance transferred from work-in-progress account.

Self-check

1 If the standard fixed overhead rate of the Compo Co. is £3 per hour, and the standard capacity 21,000 standard hours, what is the standard fixed overhead cost?
2 The actural hours worked at the Compo Co. were 20,000, the standard hours produced 21,000 and the actual fixed overhead cost £65,000. Calculate the expenditure, capacity and efficiency variances and check them in total.
3 If the standard variable overhead rate of the Compo Co. is £1, (a) calculate the variable overhead efficiency variance, (b) give the accounting entries to show this variance.

ANSWERS

1 21,000 × £3 = £63,000.
2 Expenditure variance:

actual overhead − standard overhead
£65,000 − £63,000 = £2,000 (A)

Capacity variance:

(actual hours worked − standard capacity hours) × standard overhead rate
(20,000 − 21,000) × £3 = £3,000 (A)

Efficiency variance:

(actual hours worked − standard hours produced) × standard overhead rate
(20,000 − 21,000) × £3,000 (F)

Total overhead variance:

(actual overhead cost − standard overhead absorbed)
£65,000 − 21,000 × £3 = £2,000 (A)

3 (a) Variable overhead efficiency variance:

(actual hours worked − standard hours produced) × standard variable overhead rate
(20,000 − 21,000) × £1 = £1,000 (F).

(b)

Work-in-progress		Explanation
Variable overhead efficiency 1,000		Efficiency variance transferred
Variable overhead efficiency variance		
	Work-in-progress 1,000	Variance transferred from work-in-progress account

Review

Olympic Sails Ltd, manufacturers of an offshore spinnaker sail, reported the following manufacturing variances for the whole of 1981:

	£
Material price	2,800 (A)
Material usage	1,000 (A)
Labour rate	550 (A)
Labour efficiency	150 (F)
Overhead variable expenditure	250 (A)
Overhead fixed expenditure	350 (A)
Overhead capacity	500 (A)
Overhead efficiency – var.	50 (F)
Overhead efficiency – fixed	100 (F)

The actual production and cost figures for that year were as follows:

Number of sails produced in the year	700
Material used	7,200 metres
Material purchased at £5.40 a metre	7,000 metres
Number of hours worked	5,500
Direct wages paid at £1.60 an hour	£8,800
Variable overhead incurred	£3,000
Fixed overhead incurred	£6,350

Required
Produce workings to show the detailed standard cost of each sail, and show how material is accounted for in detail.

ANSWER

Material standards:

Price
£2,800 more than standard cost was paid for 7,000 metres of material.
Therefore:
£5.40 (purchase price) less 2,800/7,000 = standard price
£5.40 − £0.40 = £5 per metre

Quantity
£1,000 more material than standard cost has been used. Therefore:

$$\frac{\text{material used} - \text{excess material used}}{\text{number of sails completed}} = \text{standard quantity per sail}$$

$$\frac{7,200 - (£1,000 \div £5)}{700} = \frac{7,000}{700} = 10 \text{ metres per sail}$$

Labour standards:

Rate
£550 more than standard was paid for 5,500 hours worked. Therefore:
standard rate = £1.60 − (£550 ÷ 5,500)
$= £1.60 − 0.10$
$= £1.50$

Labour hours
£150 less than standard labour cost has been paid. Therefore:

$$\text{standard hours} = \frac{5,500 + (£150 \div £1.50)}{700}$$

$$= \frac{5,500 + 100}{700}$$

$$= 8 \text{ hours}$$

Overhead standards:

Variable
£250 more than standard cost was incurred. Therefore:

$$\text{standard cost per hour worked} = \frac{3,000 - 250}{5,500} = £0.50$$

Fixed
£350 more than standard cost was incurred. Therefore:
standard cost of fixed overhead = £6,350 − 350
$= £6,000$
and the standard fixed overhead rate per hour

$$= \frac{\text{standard cost} - (\text{efficiency} + \text{capacity variances})}{\text{standard hours produced}}$$

$$= \frac{\pounds 6,000 - \pounds 400}{700 \times 8}$$

$$= \frac{\pounds 5,600}{5,600}$$

$$= \pounds 1.00$$

Olympic Sails Ltd
Standard cost of each sail	£
Material 10 metres @ £5 per metre	50
Labour 8 hours @ £1.50 an hour	12
Overhead – variable 8 hrs @ £0.50 per hr	4
– fixed 8 hrs @ £1.00 per hr	8
	——
	74

Budgeted fixed overhead £6,000
Standard capacity 6,000 hrs

Accounting for material

Accounting entries				*Explanations*
	Suppliers			
		Purchases	37,800	1 Amount payable to suppliers.
	Material stock			
Suppliers	35,000	Work-in-progress	36,000	2 Material added to stock at standard price. Issued to production £36,000.
	Material price variance			
Suppliers	2,800			3 Difference between amount payable to suppliers and standard cost.
	Work-in-progress			
Direct materials	36,000	Finished goods	35,000	4 Completed sails transferred to finished stock at standard cost. Variance represents excess material usage.
		Material usage variance	1,000	
	£36,000		£36,000	
	Material usage variance			
Work-in-progress	1,000			5 Excess material used.
	Finished sails			
W-I-P	35,000			6 Standard cost finished sails.

16 | Informing management through standard costing

What caused the differences from plan?

When you feel ill enough to have to consult your doctor, one of his first tests will be to take your temperature, and if it is above normal, he will note it as a symptom of the condition causing your distress. Your temperature does not tell him *what* is wrong with you, it merely indicates that *something* is wrong. Other tests will no doubt enable him to diagnose the precise *cause* of your feeling unwell, and it is only when he knows this, that he can prescribe treatment to put you on the road to recovery.

Likewise, a football manager unable to attend one of his team's matches will know that all did not go well when he finds out that they lost the game ten goals to nil. The score tells him that his team 'probably' played badly, but it does not reveal the underlying causes for their poor performance. Conversely, had they won by a wide margin of goals, the favourable score does nothing to indicate the features of their play that were the main contributory factors to their winning. When the manager knows the causes, he can rectify bad play by training his players; on the other hand good play can be applauded and players encouraged to incorporate its best features in future games.

And so with standard costing; quantifying and reporting variances is a vital part of the procedure, but analysing the reasons for those variances is the essential feature of the system. Only by tracing differences between actual and standard back to root causes can appropriate corrective action be taken by management.

Given that standards are realistically set, and not changed during an accounting period, reasons for variances can be seen to relate to the two basic approaches to their calculation. These are that:

- *prices paid for resources are more or less than planned;*
- *quantities of resources used are more or less than planned*

– and they form the common thread woven through the variance analysis considered below.

There are frequently interrelationships between variances, however, for example if a material bought at less than standard price leads to a higher than normal production scrap rate. Such interrelationships should be highlighted wherever appropriate.

Analysing material variances

Activity

The accountant of the Cubic Rude Co. was asked to provide the managing director with a summary of the causes of the adverse material price and usage variances reported in the Crazy Puzzle illustration in the last chapter.

Investigation revealed that the AB material had not been purchased from the regular supplier, that part of it was defective and that discount had not been allowed by the supplier. A higher grade of CD material had to be bought because of a shortage of the standard grade. It was also found that machine breakdowns had occurred when processing material AB, and that during an unsupervised period operator efficiency had deteriorated causing excess wastage.

List the reasons for the AB and CD material price and usage variances that you can draw from the above information, indicating against each reason whether this leads to an adverse (A) or favourable (F) variance. Also describe any interrelationships which you consider exist between any of the reported variances.

ANSWER

Your analysis should include:

Price	AB	CD	
Irregular supplier	(A)	Higher grade material than	
Discount not allowed	(A)	standard purchased	(A)
Usage			
Defective material	(A)	Higher grade material than	
Machine breakdowns	(A)	standard used	(F)
Lack of supervision	(A)		
Operator inefficiency	(A)		

Note: 1 A higher grade of material purchased has lead to higher efficiency in usage.

2 Using a non-standard supplier has led to a higher price than standard being paid for defective material which has caused a usage variance.

Analysing labour variances

|| *Activity*

|| Now see if you can suggest reasons for the labour rate and efficiency variance. Are there any connected variances?

ANSWER

Check your answers with the following:

Rate
Unforeseen increase in wage rates	(A)
Higher grade labour than standard used, at a higher rate of pay	(A)

Efficiency
Use of non-standard employee, machine methods or conditions	(A)
Low productivity	(A)
Poor supervision	(A)

Note: The poor supervision probably led to the use of a higher than standard grade of labour being used, and certainly to the low efficiency.

Analysing overhead variances

Variable overhead: expenditure variance will be due to paying more or less than standard prices.

Fixed overhead: expenditure can probably be attributed to changing prices, but may also have occurred because of a higher quantity of service, for example an unplanned additional supervisor might be employed.

|| *Activity*

|| Suggest reasons for the *capacity* and *efficiency* variances in the Cubic Rude illustration in the last chapter.

ANSWER

You will no doubt have included the following:

Capacity: less productive hours than standard have been worked because:

- there is less plant than planned;
- of machine breakdowns;
- of industrial relations problems;
- there were insufficient orders;
- of bad management.

Efficiency: reasons will be the same as those for labour efficiency:

- use of non-standard employee, machine methods or conditions;
- low productivity;
- poor supervision.

Scorekeeping is not enough

Part of an accountant's role in an organization is similar to that of the cricket scorer. Players can derive a great deal of satisfaction from playing the game of cricket, but without knowledge of the score, they would lack motivation and the game would be pointless. Accountants 'keep the score' in business operations, but this task is only the tip of the iceberg relative to their total responsibilities. The business 'game' would be lacking in guidance and direction if no more than 'total score' information was forthcoming from the accounting system, and this applies to all levels of operational management.

At the top management level, the board of directors will not be satisfied with a bare note of the profit or loss for each accounting period. They will wish to know how it compares with expected profit, and how any differences between expected and actual profit have arisen. At the middle level, the production manager wishes to know whether he has attained his production targets and kept within overall cost limits; but he must also have a more detailed breakdown of this information related to the cost centres under his supervision, with explanations of any variances from plan. Further down the management hierarchy, cost centre supervisors will be given very detailed information regarding their outputs and costs compared with planned activity levels and costs; but in addition to receiving total variance figures extracted from the accounting records, they should also be advised of the detailed reasons for these variances arising, as discussed in the previous section. Obtaining such detailed information involves considerable additional analysis and summarizing of sources of variances data, either manually or by machine, and the cost of this extra effort must be more than covered by the benefits yielded by the additional information.

Activity

Assume that you are the management accountant of the Cubic Rude Co. Ltd, manufacturers of educational toys. At the commencement of each week you send a summary to the purchasing manager, of the price variances that have arisen on suppliers' invoices processed during the previous week. You only include variances that are more than + or − 5% of standard prices, and there is a space on the form for a short explanation of each variance. A copy of this form is returned to you after the puchasing manager has completed it.

What explanations for the variances do you think the purchasing manager will include on the form when he returns it to you?

ANSWER

The form used will be similar to that shown in figure 29, and reasons for variances will include:

- Unforeseen increases in prices caused by inflation.
- Higher or lower than standard quantities purchased. Price reductions are usually allowed on bulk purchases.
- Higher or lower than standard quality of material bought.
- Changes in suppliers.
- Renegotiated contract prices.
- Substitute materials – acceptable to specifications.
- Cash discounts for prompt payment received, or not taken.
- Unforeseen changes in prices for reasons other than inflation.

The purchasing manager may already be well aware of some of the differences from standard before he receives this report,

		MATERIAL PRICE VARIANCE REPORT						
TO: PURCHASING MANAGER FROM: MANAGEMENT ACCOUNTANT				WEEK ENDED				
INVOICE DATE	SUPPLIER	MATERIAL	ACTUAL QUANTITY	VALUE AT STANDARD COST	VALUE AT ACTUAL COST	VARIANCE		EXPLANATION
						ADVERSE	FAV.	

Figure 29. Material price variance report

		MATERAL USAGE VARIANCE REPORT							
DEPT							PERIOD............		
COST CENTRE	TYPE OF MATERIAL	QUANTITY		COST		VARIANCE		% ACTUAL TO STANDARD	EXPLANATION
		STANDARD	ACTUAL	STANDARD	ACTUAL	ADVERSE	FAV.		

Figure 30. Material usage variance report

		WAGE RATE VARIANCE REPORT PERIOD				
DEPT						
COST CENTRE AND GRADE OF WORKER	HOURS WORKED	COST		VARIANCE		EXPLANATION
		STANDARD	ACTUAL	ADVERSE	FAV.	

Figure 31. Wage rate variance report

and he may already have taken appropriate action to reverse any adverse trends, but it will still be a useful summary to him and to other interested managers, for example the sales manager and the accountant.

Other reports, directed to departmental and cost centre supervisors, and giving reasons for variances, could be in a form similar to those shown in figures 30, 31 and 32. In each case the total net cost variance will substantially explain the figure shown in the relevant variance account in the accounting records.

The summation of all this detailed information can generally be found in a periodic departmental operating report (figure 33) which is submitted to each of the relevant managers. The format of this and all the other reports will, of course, vary in accordance with the type of business activity carried on.

COST CENTRE AND JOB	HOURS			STANDARD RATE	VARIANCE		% ACTUAL TO STANDARD TIME	EXPLANATION
	STANDARD	ACTUAL	DIFF		ADVERSE	FAV.		

LABOUR EFFICIENCY REPORT
DEPT. .... PERIOD ....

Figure 32. Labour efficiency report

Thus the apparently sterile processes of calculating and recording variances in the accounting records, when supported by the kinds of reports discussed in this section, are seen to be part of a dynamic management information system.

Self-check

1 Labour efficiency variances result when the actual times taken to complete jobs are greater or less than standard

DEPARTMENTAL OPERATING REPORT

PERIOD .... ACTIVITY % ....

EFFICIENCY % ....

DEPARTMENT..................... CAPACITY % ....

YEAR TO DATE	DIRECT MATERIALS	PRODUCTION COST		USAGE VARIANCE	% VARIANCE TO STANDARD
		ACTUAL	STANDARD		
	COST CENTRE: CUTTING WELDING ASSEMBLING	£	£	£	

YEAR TO DATE	DIRECT LABOUR	ACTUAL WAGES PAID	ACTUAL HOURS @ STANDARD RATES	PRODUCED HOURS @ STANDARD RATES	VARIANCES		% EFFICIENCY TO STANDARD
					RATE	EFFICIENCY	
		A	B	C	A-B	B-C	
	COST CENTRE: CUTTING WELDING ASSEMBLING	£	£	£	£	£	

YEAR TO DATE	CONTROLL-ABLE OVERHEAD	ACTUAL COST	ALLOWED COST		EXPENDITURE VARIANCE	% VARIANCE TO ALLOWED COST
			FIXED	VARIABLE		
	INDIRECT MATERIAL INDIRECT LABOUR INDIRECT EXPENSE	£	£	£	£	

		ALLOWED COST	OVERHEAD RECOVERED		CAPACITY VARIANCE	EFFICIENCY VARIANCE
			ACTUAL HOURS WORKED	STANDARD HOURS PRODUCED		
		A	B	C	A-B	B-C
		£	£	£	£	£

Figure 33. Departmental operating report

times. However, in certain exceptional circumstances metal workers at the Norfolk Agrimek Co. are given extra time allowances over standard times to complete jobs. These allowances are recorded, analysed and summarized on a special extra time report, and they form part of the explanation for labour efficiency variances.

Suggest some reasons why extra time allowances might be granted to the metal workers.

2 Why might material price variances not appear on departmental operating reports prepared for production departments?

3 In each of the two following cases specify which variances may be affected:

   (a) a job is completed by a lower grade worker than standard;

   (b) a higher than standard price is paid for a higher than standard grade material.

ANSWERS

1 Possible reasons for extra time allowances:
   (a) Using a non-standard worker (perhaps unskilled);
   (b) Using non-planned tools;
   (c) Using non-planned machines;
   (d) Substituted material;
   (e) Using non-standard material;
   (f) Receiving wrong instructions.

2 Material price variances are normally analysed and recorded separately when suppliers' invoices are processed for payment. Thus stocks of material are recorded and issued to production cost centres at standard cost. Cost centre supervisors are therefore not usually held responsible for price variances because they are unable to control them. Hence price variances do not usually appear on departmental operating reports.

3 **(a)** labour rate – because his pay will be lower;
   labour efficiency – his lack of skill might result in a longer time than standard;
   material usage – lack of skill may result in a higher rate of scrap than normal;
   overhead efficiency – because this naturally follows labour efficiency.

(b) standard price – because it is higher than planned;
material usage – less because of higher quality – less scrap;
labour efficiency – better material – less time taken.

Variance profit reporting

An effective standard costing system informs all levels of management, and the types of detailed variance information provided to assist cost centre and departmental managers was discussed and illustrated in the previous section.

Whilst more senior managers have access to, and may request, the same detailed information, the reports directed to them will normally contain more summarized information of output, sales, profit, orders outstanding, capital expenditure commitments, etc., usually associated with the level of decision that they have to take.

In this section we examine the compilation of a variance profit and loss account, the purpose of which is to show how the budgeted profit or loss for a period can be reconciled with the actual profit or loss by using variance analysis.

Activity

Singular Electronics Ltd produce and sell one type of home mini-computer – the Magic Eye, and the standard price to be charged to customers next year is £200. The standard costs of each machine are as follows:

	£
Direct materials and components	50
Direct labour	30
Variable manufacturing overhead	20
Fixed manufacturing overhead	30
Standard cost per computer	130

Budgeted normal output for next year is 5,000 mini-computers; fixed manufacturing overhead £150,000; and other overheads are budgeted as follows:

	£
Administration overheads	50,000
Selling overheads	150,000

The company plans to sell all its output next year, with no work-in-progress at the end of that year.

Calculate the company's net profit for next year.

ANSWER

	per computer
Standard selling price	£200
Standard manufacturing cost	£130
Standard manufacturing profit	£70

		£
Total budgeted manufacturing profit 5,000 × £70	=	350,000
less Budgeted administration overhead £50,000		
Budgeted selling overhead	£150,000	200,000
		———
Budgeted net profit		£150,000

Observe that the above activity introduces further aspects of standard control: selling prices, quantity of sales, administration and selling overheads.

Selling price variances follow the same pattern as for other price variances, except that they affect revenue rather than costs. For example, if a standard selling price of £10 increases to £12 during the control year, each product sold during that year will contribute a £2 favourable variance.

The number of products planned to be sold, less those actually sold, results in a further difference to planned profit – a sales volume variance. Profit will be increased or decreased according to whether the quantity of a product sold is more or less than planned respectively, by the standard manufacturing profit of one unit. Notice that it is *unit profit* that is adjusted against budgeted profit, for if a product is not sold it will still be in stock to sell later, and therefore its cost value is not lost. What has been lost in the budget period is that part of the planned profit related to the unsold unit.

As regards administration and selling overheads, these will be discussed more fully in the later chapters on budgetary control, but it will be realized that the costs involved under these two heads can be very high indeed, and will therefore require the same measure of care in forecasting their separate costs as is devoted to manufacturing costs. Administration costs will be relatively fixed, but selling costs will invariably contain an element of variable cost incurred as each product is sold. For example, commission paid to salesmen, and delivery costs, will be relatively variable to the *number of products sold*.

Variance profit and loss account – full costing

Let us now assume the following cost and performance data related to the Singular Electronics Ltd during the year from which you have already prepared the budgets earlier in this section.

		£
Sales 4,900 computers at £205 each		1,004,500

Production   5,000 computers.
Manufacturing costs:

	£	
Direct materials	255,000	
Direct labour	160,000	
Variable overhead	95,000	
Fixed overhead	160,000	
	670,000	
less Stock 100 @ £130	13,000	
Manufacturing cost of sales		657,000
Administration overheads	48,000	347,500
Selling overheads	157,000	205,000
Actual net profit		142,500

From the above and the budgeted data we can now produce the following variance profit and loss account:

Singular Electronics Ltd
Variance profit and loss account for the year to . . . .

		£
Budgeted manufacturing profit		350,000
	£	
less Budgeted administration overhead	50,000	
Budgeted selling overhead	150,000	200,000

	£	
Budgeted net profit		150,000
Sales variances: Price	24,500 (F)	
Volume	7,000 (A)	17,500 (F)
		167,500
Manufacturing variances:		
Material	5,000 (A)	
Labour	10,000 (A)	
Variable overhead	5,000 (F)	
Fixed overhead	10,000 (A)	20,000 (A)
		147,500
Administration overhead	2,000 (F)	
Selling overhead	7,000 (A)	5,000 (A)
Actual net profit		142,500

Notes
1 The actual net profit agrees with that shown in the conventional profit and loss statement.
2 The 100 unsold computers are valued at standard cost and carried forward as stock into the following period. They do not feature in the variance profit and loss account.
3 Excess costs are treated as costs of inefficiency and written off against profit in the current period.
4 Variance computations:
   Sales price – 4,900 × £5 (excess price over standard)
      volume – 100 × £70 (manufacturing profit per unit)
   Material – 5,000 × £50 (standard cost) less £255,000 (actual cost)
   Labour – 5,000 × £30 (standard cost) less £160,000 (actual cost)
   Variable overhead – 5,000 × £20 (standard cost) less £95,000 (actual cost)
   Fixed overhead – £150,000 (budgeted cost) less £160,000 (actual cost)
   Administration overhead – £50,000 less 48,000
   Selling overhead – £150,000 less £157,000
5 There is insufficient information to separate price and usage variances for materials and labour.

Variance profit and loss account – marginal costing

Another way of presenting this variance summary is by using marginal costing, discussed at length in Chapter 13. You will recall that fixed costs are not allocated to product cost under this method, are not therefore carried forward in stock valuation, but are treated as costs of the period in which they arise.

Activity

Using the cost data given in the Singular Electronics example, calculate the marginal contribution realized on the sale of one computer.

Your computation should read as follows:

	£	£
Selling price		200
less Variable costs:		
Direct material	50	
Direct labour	30	
Variable overhead	20	100
Marginal Contribution		100

We can now summarize budgeted profit as before, but using *contribution* rather than *net profit* as the starting point:

	£	£
Budgeted contribution 5,000 × £100		500,000
less Fixed costs:		
Manufacturing overhead	150,000	
Administration overhead	50,000	
Selling overhead	150,000	350,000
Budgeted net profit		150,000

Activity

Now have a go at compiling a variance profit and loss account in contribution form, using the Singular Electronics data given earlier in this chapter.

ANSWER

It is not expected that your answer will be perfect, but it should be similar to the following:

	£		£
Budgeted contribution			500,000
Sales variances: Price	24,500 (F)		
Volume	10,000 (A)		14,500 (F)
			514,500
Manufacturing variances:			
Material	5,000 (A)		
Labour	10,000 (A)		
Variable overhead	5,000 (F)		10,000 (A)
Actual contribution			504,500

Fixed costs:	Budgeted	Variance	
Manufacturing	150,000	10,000 (A)	
Administration	50,000	2,000 (F)	
Selling	150,000	7,000 (A)	
	350,000	15,000 (A)	365,000
Actual net profit			139,500

Notes

1 The layout and ordering of data in the above statement is aimed at emphasizing contribution. Both budgeted and actual contribution are shown.

2 The sales volume variance has been calculated by reference to marginal contribution and not to product net profit. Fixed costs, it is argued, will be incurred whatever the quantity of goods sold, therefore each product sale lost diminishes net profit by product contribution.

3 Apart from sales volume variance, all the other variances are calculated as in the full standard costing statement.

Activity

See if you can discover why the profit shown in the marginal statement is less than the full costing statement by £3,000. Do not read on until you have given this problem some thought.

ANSWER

This is the kind of difference that we discussed in Chapter 13. Quite simply, the £3,000 represents £30 fixed overhead per product multiplied by 100 – the number of computers still in stock at the end of the period and carried forward into the following year under full costing. This means that there is £3,000 more fixed manufacturing overhead charged into the contribution statement, resulting in £3,000 less profit than in the full costing statement.

Note that both the full and the marginal standard costing variance statements show only *exceptional* information, and are not cluttered up with too many detailed figures. This enables management to get a clear overall view of past performance related to the firm's profit objective. Much more explanatory information is available should it be required.

Self-check

1 the standard details of a product are as follows:

Selling price		£20
Variable costs	£9	
Fixed costs	£2	£11
	—	——
Net profit		£9

What figure would you use to calculate the sales volume variance in **(a)** a full costing system of reporting variances, **(b)** using marginal costing?

2 'Selling price variance is calculated by multiplying the difference between the actual and standard prices, by the budgeted quantity.' Is this statement **(a)** true or **(b)** false?

3 'There will always be a difference between the net profit reported in a full as against a marginal variance profit and loss account.' **(a)** True or **(b)** false?

ANSWERS

1 **(a)** Full costing: £9 (i.e. net profit).
  (b) Marginal costing: £20 − 9 = £11 (i.e. contribution).
2 **(b)** False – selling price variance is the difference between actual and standard selling price multiplied by the *actual* (not the budgeted) quantity sold.
3 Profit measurement will only be different if there is a change in opening and closing stocks over the period of account. This is because fixed costs are included in the full costing value of stocks. An increase in stocks will therefore result in less fixed

costs being charged in a full cost statement, as there is an increase in the fixed costs carried forward into the next period.

Review

New Day Boats Ltd actual net profit for last year was £49,000. They had planned to make and sell 12 boats, but had made and sold only 8. There was no boats in stock at the beginning of last year. Actual costs of production for the year were:

	£
Direct materials	36,000
Direct labour	42,000
Variable overhead	9,000
Fixed overhead	40,000
	127,000

Standard costs per boat for last year were:

	£
Direct materials	4,000
Direct labour	5,000
Variable overhead	1,000
Fixed overhead	3,000
	13,000

And the total budgeted marginal contribution was £120,000.

Required

1 Using the full costing method, produce a variance profit and loss account for the year.
2 If you were asked to compile a marginal profit and loss account:

  (a) would the actual net profit be any different to that in your answer to question 1? Why?
  (b) what would the sales volume variance be?
  (c) what would the actual contribution be?

Helpful hint: the best way to tackle this problem is to recall the *order* of information required in the variance profit and loss format, then working upon the data given above, pre-

pare workings for each item. Your statement should open
with the budgeted net profit, and close with the actual net
profit.

ANSWERS

1

New Day Boats Limited
Variance profit and loss account for the year . . . .

See
working

		£		£	
				£	
1	Budgeted net profit			84,000	
		£			
2/3	Sales price variance	16,000	(F)		
4	Sales volume variance	28,000	(A)	12,000	(A)
				72,000	
	Manufacturing variances:				
5	Direct materials	4,000	(A)		
6	Direct labour	2,000	(A)		
7	Variable overhead cost	1,000	(A)		
8	Fixed overhead cost	4,000	(A)		
9	Fixed overhead volume	12,000	(A)	23,000	(A)
	Actual net profit			49,000	

Workings

1 *Budgeted net profit*: budgeted contribution less total fixed overhead budgeted:

$120,000 - (12 \times £3,000) = £84,000.$

2 *Standard selling price per boat*: budgeted contribution plus variable cost per boat:

$$\frac{120,000}{12} + 10,000 = £20,000.$$

3 *Actual selling price per boat*: $\dfrac{\text{total costs} + \text{net profit}}{\text{total no. of boats sold}}$

$$\frac{127,000 + 49,000}{8} = £22,000.$$

4 *Standard net profit per boat*: standard price less standard cost:
$20,000 - 13,000 = £7,000.$

5 *Direct materials variance*: actual cost $- 8 \times$ standard cost per boat:
£36,000 $-$ £32,000 = £4,000 (A).

6 *Direct labour variance*: actual cost − 8 × standard cost per boat:
£42,000 − 40,000 = £2,000 (A).

7 *Variable overhead variance*: actual cost − 8 × standard cost per boat:
£9,000 − 8,000 = £1,000 (A).

8 *Fixed overhead cost variance*: actual costs − 12 × standard cost per boat:
£40,000 − 36,000 = £4,000 (A).

9 *Fixed overhead volume variance*:
(budgeted production − actual production) × fixed overhead per boat:
(12 − 8) × £3,000 = £12,000 (A).

2 (a) The net profit would not change, as there were no stocks of boats either at the beginning or the end of the year. Fixed overhead is therefore the same in both statements.

(b) 4 × £10,000 (i.e. contribution per boat) = £40,000.

(c) Actual contribution = budgeted contribution adjusted for sales variances, and variable manufacturing variances:
= £120,000 − £24,000 − £7,000 = £89,000.

Note that net profit £49,000 + actual fixed overhead £40,000 = £89,000 = actual contribution to check with the above.

17 | Some limitations of standard costing

Computing, analysing, explaining and reporting standard costing variances are the essential processes of a standard costing system; but like most accounting techniques it is an art rather than a science. The limitations of such a system begin to show through when we attempt to answer the following questions:

- Who can be made responsible for variances?
- Are the standards attainable?
- When should variances be reported?
- When is a variance significant?
- How does one cope with inflation?

We discuss each of these questions in turn in this chapter.

Responsibility

Effective action is what is required of any control system, and the person most able to act, and therefore to be made responsible, is the one who most *influenced* the variation from standard. It follows that responsibility for prices of direct materials and some services can be ascribed to the purchasing manager, whilst quantity variances are generally the province of cost centre managers.

This does not mean that all we are concerned about is to attach blame to someone for plans not being attained. This kind of philosophy is generally counter-productive, for 'witch-hunting' demoralizes and ~aps the initiative of managers. In any case, though variances may be reported to a particular responsible person, it does not follow that complete control lies in the hands of that person.

For instance, the purchasing manager is unable to forecast with precision what the price of copper will be, as this commodity is extremely sensitive to economic and political influences. Again, in attempting to determine the standard price of grain he cannot forecast whether harvest yields will be good or bad, and therefore whether higher or lower than average prices will be quoted by the supplier.

Further, the inefficiency of one manager may cause excess costs to arise elsewhere. A cost centre manager may be held responsible for excess material usage, but this could well have happened because he was supplied with substandard material. In this instance, the purchasing manager may have reported a favourable price variance because he paid a low price for low-standard material, but this is offset by the adverse variance in production.

These interrelationships need to be recognized, and responsibility reporting adjusted accordingly, to ensure that effective action is taken by the person most able to prevent a recurrence of the same problem.

Self-check

A machine operator completes a job in 16 hours, the standard time for which is 8 hours. Further investigation revealed that he had been transferred to the machining department without completing a full course of training on the machine operated by him. It was also discovered that he had the misfortune to have been issued with substandard material, for which an extra 4 hours allowance was made.

Do you consider that the machining department manager should be held responsible for the labour efficiency variance?

ANSWER

Not the whole variance! The extra time allowance for non-standard material probably lies at the door of the purchasing manager to explain. It could be the result of bad buying, but then it could be that a shortage in supplies led him to purchase below standard quality.

A proportion of the remaining four hours can be charged to the training officer for allocating a partly trained machine operator to the machining department.

Attainable standards

It has been pointed out that managers will become demoralized by 'witch-hunting'. Similarly, they will become completely frustrated if targets of performance set for them are unattainable. Show-jumping horses are not expected to jump fences that are beyond their capabilities, so why should a manager be expected to reach a 'height' in production level that is beyond the capacity of the operatives in his department? Ideally, what the manager and his departmental colleagues *aspire* to achieve should coincide with the expected standard, for then they will be more likely to equal or better the target set for them. Mutually agreed targets are always better than ones that are imposed by authority.

With hindsight, it can sometimes be seen that standards ought originally to have been set at different levels. For example, if a machine operation causes more wastage than was planned, and the additional wastage could have been foreseen by a more astute manager, and incorporated into the standard, then this part of the material usage variance should be referred to as a *planning* variance, and the remainder, the normal *operational* variance.

The drawback to this more dynamic approach to variance reporting, of course, is that it will sometimes be difficult to determine what ought, or ought not to have been known at the time that standards were established. It is always easy to be wise after the event. However, if the effort is made to extract 'planning' variances from the total variances, it could provide far more meaningful information, and enhance the credibility of variance reporting as a vital part of the management information system.

Self-check

This question is an extension of the one at the end of the last section.

After the machine operator had completed the job, it was considered that the standard time ought to have been originally set at 6 hours, not 8, and that the part-training of the operative probably accounted for a further 2 hours of the excess time.

Show a summary of the causes of the variances, together with the hours related to each.

ANSWER

Total variance = total time − new standard: 16 hours − 6 hours = 10 hours.

Comprising:

Planning variance	2 hours (8 − 6)
Non-standard material	4 hours (12 − 8)
Partly-trained operative	2 hours (14 − 12)
Operational i.e. efficiency variance	2 hours (16 − 14)
	10

Getting the timing right

At the present time a lot of people take for granted their comfortable, thermostatically controlled home heating or air-conditioning systems. Indeed, so much so, that not many of us know much about the technicalities of them, nor care too much – until something goes wrong! Our attitude is conditioned by the subtlety with which information regarding room or heater temperature is automatically sensed, *at just the right moment*, by a thermostat, which immediately triggers the sending of an 'on' or 'off' message to the switch controlling the input of the electrical current.

All efficient control systems work in this way, reacting to information fed back to a 'sensing device', at just the right moment. The sensor, in the case of a standard costing system, is the person most able to take action to correct or reinforce variances, as pointed out earlier in this chapter, and variance information must reach him *as frequently as is necessary for him to take effective action*.

It has already been suggested that material price variances are best extracted and reported to the purchasing manager at the time of purchase rather than when material is issued to production – perhaps many weeks later. The 'time of purchase' relates to the stage in accounting procedure when suppliers' invoices are checked and authorized for payment, but of course this is rather like shutting the stable door after the horse has bolted. The most effective way to halt the variance is not to let it happen at all, this implying that the purchasing manager should ensure that he only buys at standard prices, or at least at prices no more than a tolerable level above standard. A further check on this could be imposed by giving the authority for agreeing to purchase at above standard prices, to some other official, when an order of significantly high value is to be placed. In some concerns, price variances are analysed from purchase orders *daily*, and information fed back to the purchasing manager the day after. Obvious errors can then be rectified long before the ordered materials and the related invoices are received.

> ### Self-check
>
> It has been the practice of Norfolk Agrimek Ltd to send to the production manager a voluminous weekly computer printout of labour efficiency variances on all jobs completed during the week by all operatives. Despite this, the cost of labour inefficiency continues to rise in certain cost centres.
>
> What action might you take to make the standard labour cost reporting more effective?

ANSWER

It appears that too much information is being supplied to the wrong person at the wrong time, and that this combination of mishaps has resulted in inaction.

It might improve matters if:

- a *daily* report were to be sent to *each supervisor* of efficiency variances in their cost centre;
- the daily report should only contain details of each operative's labour efficiency when it is significantly off-standard;
- in the longer term, that is when most deviations have been corrected, the report could perhaps revert to being a weekly one.

Highlighting the significant

When Sebastian Coe the great middle-distance runner is speeding round the last lap of a 1,500 metres race, shouts of encouragement and advice are showered upon him. Then suddenly the voice of his coach, his father, pierces the general uproar, proffering just the right measure of tactical advice needed by the runner at that critical moment.

There are many similar situations where a high volume of

irrelevant 'noise' can smother a vital message, and this can certainly happen in connection with a badly designed and administered standard costing system. This was aptly illustrated in the self-check question at the end of the last section, when inaction resulted from information 'overkill'.

Differences between standard and actual performance are only worth highlighting if they are *significant*, but of course significance is a relative term. One can expect and allow for variations that are merely random fluctuations around a standard value, variations which probably cancel one another out over a reasonable period of time. Figure 34 illustrates the kind of record that might be maintained to show the trend of cost variances over a number of periods. It makes allowance for random fluctuations between tolerable limits, and highlights the exceptional occurrence that should trigger off action.

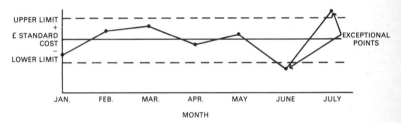

Figure 34. Cost variance trend chart

Again, a small difference may be insignificant in a *single* period, but if a similar difference occurs, and perhaps grows, period after period, then a significant trend is revealed which probably requires remedial action.

A significant variance need not always be adverse. Favourable variances on labour efficiency, for example, might indicate that standard times are too generous and that they need revising, or they could be due to a higher level of operator efficiency, which needs encouraging. Favourable variances require as much attention as adverse ones.

Of course, a judgement upon the significance or otherwise of a variance should always take into account the *cost* of investigating and correcting it. Costs should never exceed the benefits expected from correcting a variance.

Self-check

A cost clerk in the Cubic Rude Co. office kept continuous records of standard costing variances, and the following is a trend chart produced by the clerk showing material usage variances for the last six months:

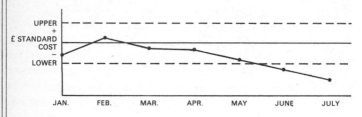

Figure 35. Cubic Rude material usage variance chart

Now answer the following questions:

(a) Are the variances significant?
(b) What do you think is causing them?
(c) What action would you take to correct them, if any?

ANSWERS

(a) The variances show a significantly increasing adverse trend. This trend should be reported so that appropriate action can be taken.
(b) The differences between standard and actual usage could be caused by:
  (i) faulty standards;
  (ii) operator inefficiency;
  (iii) untrained operators;
  (iv) machine breakdowns;
  (v) substandard materials being used.
(c) Depending upon which of the causes listed in **(b)** have resulted in the variances, action would follow:
  (i) the standards could be reviewed by the work study engineer;
  (ii) new or additional training for operatives could be introduced;

(iii) better preventive maintenance would reduce machine breakdowns;

(iv) ascertain from the purchasing manager the reasons for buying substandard material.

Inflation and standard costs

Rising prices are no new phenomenon, but in recent years the pace of increases has quickened, causing consternation everywhere, and no more so than among the business community. The problems of forecasting, planning and controlling are greatly exacerbated by the uncertainty caused by changing price levels, with the result that managers have to be more vigilant in interpreting the effect of the increases upon present and planned operations.

Inflation affects a standard costing system in relation to:

- the setting and updating of price standards for material, labour and overhead;
- the reporting of price variances;
- the valuation of stocks of raw materials, work-in-progress and finished goods;
- the determination of selling prices.

Standard prices of direct materials can be based upon:

(a) the prices current at the beginning of the period to be controlled;

(b) the same prices as in (a), but updating them as thought necessary during the control period;

(c) the anticipated average price during the control period.

Activity

Briefly jot down what you think will be the effect on material price variances during a control period, of using each of the bases for setting standard prices listed above – given that prices continue to rise.

ANSWER

In the case of (a) if prices continue to rise, ever increasing price variances will be reported, and though it may be difficult to do so, variances caused by inflation should be extracted and reported upon separately from those arising from other causes. If standard prices are updated during the period, reported variances will be more closely related to causes other than inflation.

Should the average anticipated prices be adopted, the early months of the period would report *favourable* variances, because standard prices would be more than actual; but in the later periods of the year there would be *adverse* variances, as actual prices overtake and exceed the standards.

When prices are not rising at a very high rate, the use of current or anticipated average prices as standards will be quite adequate for control purposes, but in times of rapidly advancing prices variance reporting will be far more meaningful if standards are changed. This does pose workload problems for the accounting staff, not only in revising standard prices, but also because all stocks held at the revision date have also to be revalued. However, the advent of microcomputers has lightened the burden of clerical work considerably.

Self-check

1 In connection with a standard costing system, which of the following are affected by inflation?

(a) standard capacity   (d) productivity
(b) prices of materials   (e) price variances
    and supplies   (f) labour efficiency
(c) labour wage rates   (g) stock values

2 Norfolk Agrimek set their standard prices in the middle of December each year for the following year. The price of a particular material at 16 December was £100, its expected price on 30 June next was £120, and at 31 March and 30 September next, £110 and £130 respectively. What price(s) would the company use as standard in each case if its policy was to apply:

(a) current prices;
(b) anticipated average prices for the control period;
(c) continuously updated prices through the control period?

ANSWERS

1 **(b)** and **(c)** relate to *prices* of resources which are directly affected in times of inflation.

(e) discloses the difference between standard and actual prices of resources, and is also touched by inflation.

(g) stock values arise by the use of standard costs, and as prices increase, so their values have to be adjusted.

2 **(a)** £100.

(b) £115 – the average price for the year.

(c) £100, £110, £120, £130, progressively through the year.

Review

1 A batch of 1,000 surgical instruments had reached the final stage in their manufacture, but before they could be completed 200 of them had to be scrapped. Inspection revealed that the defective instruments had been badly processed earlier in their manufacture.

How would you deal with the accumulated costs of the defective instruments?

2 At a meeting with his managing director the supervisor of the printing department was asked why he had taken no action to arrest the steady increase in the overhead capacity variance of his department. His reply was that the overhead cost rate was based upon the assumption that all his machines worked continuously. Knowing that this rate of working could never be attained, he had ignored the variance.

Comment upon this situation.

3 The material usage variance reported in the monthly operating statement of the sausage-making department of a meat-processing factory had shown a phenomenal increase in the last three months, but no one could give any satisfactory explanation for the excess usage so long after the sausages were made. What action would you suggest to improve control information?

4 Why do you think that it might be necessary to revise standard prices during an accounting period?

ANSWERS

1 The cause of the scrapping has been traced to a previous pro-

cessing department. The accumulated costs should therefore be charged to that department because it is responsible for the loss. The department in which the instruments were scrapped should not have to bear any of this cost.

2 100% capacity usage is rarely attainable, and to set standards based upon this ideal, with the certainty that capacity variances will occur, will not motivate the printing manager to look more closely at the variance. Part of it might be caused by an abnormal incidence of machine breakdowns and other stoppages which need close investigation.

Standards calculated on practical capacity, which take into account normal stoppages, will be more realistic.

3 A weekly, or even a daily, sausage-meat usage report appears to be called for, until the cause of the excess usage is discovered and rectified. When the variance returns to a level considered not significant in relation to total sausage-meat input, then monthly reporting would be quite adequate for control purposes.

4 If prices are rising rapidly, a revision of standard prices would:

- highlight reasons for price increases other than inflation;
- be more useful for forward planning purposes;
- point up any necessity to revise selling prices of the company's products.

Part 6
Budgeting for control

18 | The budgeting framework

Introduction

Planning and controlling are the essence of effective management, and the management accountant's primary role is to provide quantitative information to aid the planning process, and then to monitor progress after the plans have been implemented. This requires the support of an effective management accounting system, to record the acquisition, allocation and use of resources, and the earlier chapters of this book have discussed the concepts and methods employed in such a system.

Part 5 – 'Control of resources through standards' – introduced the concept of pre-planned targets of performance for revenue and costs. Standards are woven into the fabric of the accounting system to facilitate the production of reports which highlight variances between actual and planned performance. A standard costing system normally operates within the framework of a system of budgetary control, and we saw how standard overhead rates are based upon overhead *budgets*. '*Budgeted* profit for the year' was shown as the starting point in compiling variance profit and loss accounts.

Part 6 focuses exclusively on budgets; how they are compiled, and how they are used. As a budget ultimately becomes a monitoring device, it follows that its compilation draws upon the principles of cost classification and allocation previously discussed. This part of the book, therefore, feeds upon most aspects of management accounting.

This chapter examines why budgets are needed, how they relate to long-term plans and how they are organized and administered.

The benefits of budgeting

John Storey had designed and developed a unique system of double-glazing. He manufactured the units himself and supplied installation contractors. Although his first five years' trading had been very successful in terms of sales, he had given little thought to planning ahead. By the end of the fifth year he found himself extremely short of cash, and it appeared that the business would have to close, just when John's double-glazing system was becoming well known. Then Dame Fortune smiled on John! He came into a large legacy left by his Aunt Agatha, and this was sufficient for him to settle his current financial difficulties and to provide adequate finance for expansion. He moved into a small factory unit on a local authority industrial estate, installed production machinery, hired production and selling staff and a part-time accountant.

Although John did not continue to be personally involved in manufacturing, he insisted upon directing all operations himself, without the aid of supervisors. Orders collected by his sales staff were entered into his order book periodically then passed direct to his production workers. No systematic production plan existed, and consequently customers frequently complained of delays. There was a large demand for standard-sized units, but many non-standard requirements had also to be met.

John redesigned the standard units during the year, passing the revised specifications and prices to his salesmen, but failing to advise his production staff, who were already experiencing difficulties keeping up with orders. Periodically, John placed orders for large quantities of materials, much to the consternation of his accountant, who found it difficult to keep track of all transactions, and who only found it possible to produce a set of accounts at the end of the year to compare with the previous year's results.

By the end of the year there was a large backlog of non-standard unit orders, though stock of standard units was very high. Material stocks were also high, as were the amounts owing by customers. Although he appeared to have made a profit during the year, so much of it was tied up in stock and other assets that his cash position was again serious.

Activity

A budget can be defined as 'a quantitative expression of the operational plans for an organization for a future accounting period'. It is proposed to introduce a formal system of budgeting into John's double-glazing business. Given the difficulties experienced by the business during the past two years, what benefits do you consider will arise from introducing such a system?

ANSWER

If you have covered all of the following points you will have done very well:

- A *formal* system would at least *compel* John to think ahead, to forecast sales and to consider the production and resources required to meet the sales targets.
- Planning for sales, production and other services would highlight the need to *assign responsibility* for carrying out each part of the plan to functional supervisors, thus allowing John to concentrate on design and general management.
- Because supervisors will *participate* fully in the compilation of budgets they will be completely informed, and therefore more *motivated* to achieve their objectives. Imposed budgets would not have the same effect.
- All aspects of the business would be *coordinated*, instead of the present chaotic situation, and supervisors would be aware of each other's difficulties and work more as a team.
- Detailed planning would focus on *present weaknesses* such as unplanned overspending and the lack or waste of resources.
- The budget will be used as a standard with which actual performance can be *compared* for control purposes. Comparison with last year's performance is not as meaningful.
- The need for a more efficient and responsive *accounting system* would be recognized, to produce periodic progress reports.

How far ahead do we need to plan?

We all know how difficult it is to obtain a seat for a popular concert or sports event without booking weeks ahead. Similarly, it is the norm these days to make holiday reservations many months in advance, especially if we insist on taking vacations during peak periods.

These are personal short-term decisions, but it is equally important to scheme for the long term. Our children's education, house purchase, retirement pension, life assurance, these are all commitments on our long-term income. Failure to plan and to take decisions well in advance restricts our future activity and can leave us unprepared for an uncertain future.

The extent and timing of planning is governed by our overall objectives and the need to commit ourselves to certain lines of action, and this applies as much to organizations as it does to individuals. A plan to increase profit by building a branch factory in Brazil requires extensive long-term planning.

Planning – deciding what action to take – is therefore a continuous process, as constantly changing conditions will not allow us to be indecisive for long. Businesses, like individuals, plan on two time scales. They have to decide:

- *long-term* objectives and strategy, including major marketing, production, investment and financing decisions;
- *short-term* operational plans (budgets), of a more detailed nature which activate the next year of the long-term plan, and are used to monitor progress.

A large number of businesses operate a systematic approach to long-term planning, referred to as corporate planning, usually covering a period of at least three to five years ahead on a 'rolling' basis; that is, each year a new long-term plan will be created which incorporates necessary revisions to the previous plan and adds one year.

Self-check

As John Storey's double-glazing business expanded, the need for long-term planning also grew. Which of the following decisions do you consider to be long-term?

1 Temporary repairs to the factory roof.
2 An agreement to merge with a similar business.
3 An increase in wages for all the staff.
4 The employment of temporary staff in peak periods.
5 The introduction of new products.
6 An agreement with the bank to borrow £50,000 over ten years.
7 The setting up of a training school inside the firm.

8 The scrapping of obsolete windows, still in stock.
9 The replacement of worn out machinery.
10 The setting up of a cavity-wall insulation department.
11 Agreement with the trade union regarding tea-breaks.
12 The introduction of a pension scheme for employees.

ANSWERS

2 Part of long-term expansion strategy. Negotiations would be protracted.
5 New products require a long-term programme of research and development.
6 A long-term commitment.
7 Part of long-term manpower planning.
9 Part of a long-term replacement policy.
10 Diversification strategy being implemented.
12 Pension plans take some time to negotiate, and the decision is part of long-term manpower planning.

Short-term operational planning

Earlier in this chapter a budget was described as 'a plan for a future accounting period'. The short-term budget normally covers a period of one year, as in the case of the national budget presented by the Chancellor of the Exchequer, but it could be for a shorter period. Most fashion-clothes and footwear firms, for example, budget in six-monthly periods to coincide with seasonal fashion changes. It must be remembered, however, that although detailed operational plans for next year are being assembled, they must be prepared within the framework of the long-term plan, with the objective of achieving long-term rather than short-term goals.

The budget is, at one and the same time, a plan of action and a control medium. As a *plan* it stipulates agreed targets for sales, production, stocks, cash, etc. which managers responsible for its separate functions translate into action. As a *control medium* it is used to compare with actual performance for the purpose of taking necessary corrective action, and is usually divided into monthly or four-weekly periods.

Budgeting procedure will vary from the simple to the complex depending upon the size and nature of the business. In a one-man business planning may be non-existent or at the very best consist solely of cash forecasts. At the other extreme, in a large enterprise budgetary control will be a formalized procedure specified in a 'budget manual', supervised by a budget officer and overlooked by a budget committee.

The budget manual will make provision for:

- a list of all the budgets to be prepared, specifying who is responsible for each;
- a timetable specifying the latest date for the preparation of each budget, and for its final approval;
- guidance on the procedure and principles to be applied, and the documentation to be used in connection with each budget.

The function of the budget committee is to:

- reconcile differences between the managers responsible for producing the component parts of the budget;
- ensure that the forecasts are within the framework of the long-term plan;
- coordinate and consolidate the budget;
- present the budget to the board of directors for their approval and distribution to responsible managers;
- review the budgets in the light of actual performance, and recommend any necessary revisions.

Outline of a system of budgetary control

Figure 36 charts each of the steps in the preparation of a complete system of budgets. Each of the steps is briefly described below, and in the following three chapters the component budgets are examined and illustrated in detail.

1 *Long-term policy* Profit and other objectives are agreed, and strategic decisions made to achieve those objectives.
2 *Implementation* Of financial, investment and marketing strategic decisions
3 *Short-term forecasts* Of sales, production and associated costs.
4 *Choice of optimum forecast* From the alternatives presented in 3 with long-term objectives and current limiting factors the principal factors influencing this decision.

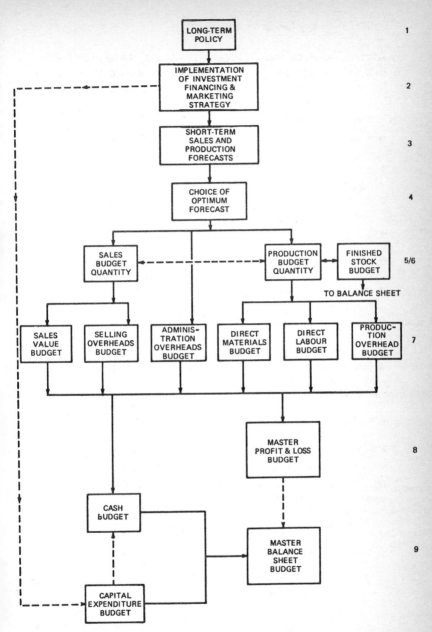

Figure 36. Outline of a system of budgetary control

5/6 *Sales and production quantity budgets* Reconciled after taking account of any factors limiting the firm's ability to produce or sell, and also existing and planned stock levels.

7 *Sales revenue and cost budgets* Naturally derivatives of the sales and production budgets. However, there may be policy decisions made regarding, for example, the level of sales promotion expenditure, which may not be directly linked to the expected volume of sales.

8 *Master profit and loss budget* Consolidates the totals of the sales revenue and cost budgets to arrive at budgeted profit.

9 *Master balance sheet budget* Consolidates all the financial budgets, comprising debtors, creditors, stocks, cash and capital expenditure.

A further three steps that are not shown on the budget flowchart are worth adding here to complete the cycle:

10 *Actual* sales and costs will be recorded in the management accounting system, and periodic results presented in a form similar to the way in which the budgets have already been prepared, to facilitate comparison at the control stage.

11 *Variations* between budgeted and actual performance are reported, explained, and acted upon.

12 *Review* long term plans.

Review

1 It is claimed that the major benefits arising from a system of budgetary control are that it:

  (a) compels an organization to think ahead;
  (b) improves communication within an organization;
  (c) coordinates the decision-making and activity of the separate functions;
  (d) provides a standard with which to compare actual performance. Briefly explain and illustrate these benefits.

2 Indicate whether each of the following statements is true or false, briefly explaining your choice.

  (a) Long-term planning covers operations one year ahead.
  (b) Once a long-term plan is agreed it is not changed.
  (c) Investment decisions arise out of long-term planning.

(d) Long term planning is not as detailed as short-term planning.
(e) There is no connection between short and long-term plans.

ANSWERS

1 (a) Advance planning makes for better decisions. For example, if cash forecasts are compiled for a future period, a business will be able to judge whether it will have sufficient cash to carry out its plans and, if not, to take some action in advance to ensure that it does.
 (b) Effective budgeting involves managers at all levels. They should actively participate in creating the plan, can appreciate what a vital part each of them plays in carrying out the plan, and thus are more highly motivated than if they were 'left in the dark'.
 (c) If managers of different functions are making conflicting decisions, overall company objectives may not be achieved. For example, if the production manager is working to a production plan which does not take account of the current level of sales, this will result in over- or under-production, both of them undesirable conditions. Coordination of sales and production plans will overcome this.
 (d) Certain assumptions are made and criteria adopted when preparing budgets. For example, that high unemployment in an area will reduce sales in that area; or that a chosen selling price will optimize profit. If we then compare what actually did happen with what we thought would happen, we have a better basis for making future decisions than if we merely make comparisons with last year's performance, or even make no comparison at all.
2 (a) False. Long-term plans require decisions on investment etc., which will affect periods well over a year ahead.
 (b) False. Changing economic, competitive, and technological circumstances force a periodic review of long-term plans. Most progressive businesses produce a revised three- to five-year plan each year.
 (c) True. Investment decisions are at the very heart of long-term planning as they initiate financing, marketing, production, manpower and other major decisions.

(d) True. Long-term plans are usually specified in more rounded terms and deal with the major aspects of strategy such as product planning, whereas short-term plans are detailed specifications of the agreed plan of action for the coming budget year or other shorter period.

(e) False. The short-term plan operates within the framework of the long-term plan. Long-term aims should not be sacrificed to apparent short-term advantages.

19 | Planning sales and production

Introduction

One disappointing year after moving into his new factory on the industrial estate, John Storey, of double-glazing fame, decreed that he would not let his dear departed Aunt Agatha down any longer. Her legacy had given him a new lease of life, and he was determined to deploy her money wisely. He decided that a system of long-term and operational planning would help him to do this.

Initially, he sought the professional advice of a firm of management consultants. Their advice was expensive, but after examining various alternative future strategies, and discussing these with his newly appointed selling and production managers, he adopted a relatively ambitious five-year plan. This incorporated new product development, investment in more plant, expansion of premises, and training and expansion of staff.

There would be no major change in operations next year, the first of the five-year plan, although an increase in sales was forecast, and the production of standard units was to be restricted to two types – A and B.

John's balance sheet at the end of the current year was as follows:

Fixed assets:

	Cost £	Depreciation £	Net value £
Plant and machinery	80,000	16,000	64,000
Motor vehicles	20,000	8,000	12,000
	100,000	24,000	76,000

	Cost £	Depreciation £	Net value £
Current assets:			
Cash	5,000		
Stock – Finished goods	14,915		
– Work-in-progress	5,000		
– Materials	19,000		
Debtors	45,000	88,915	
less Current liabilities:			
Creditors – supplies	30,000		
Taxation payable	5,000	35,000	
Working capital:			53,915
			£129,915
Financed by:			
John Storey – capital			£129,915

The following information relates to the year just ended:

Sales:	*Quantity*	*Value*	*Stock – year end*
Standard unit A	1,000	£300,000	50
Standard unit B	800	£160,000	30
Non-standard units	300	£72,000	

The standard costs of material and labour are not expected to change next year, and the current standard costs of each unit are as follows:

	Unit A	*Unit B*	*Non-standard (average)*
Direct material	£80	£50	£70
Direct labour	(24 hrs) £72	(15 hrs) £45	(20 hrs) £60

Sales are forecast to increase by 20% next year, but this increase could be limited to 10% due to lack of machine capacity. Sales prices are to be increased by 5%.

It is planned to reduce finished stock by the end of next year to:

Unit A – 30 units
Unit B – 10 units

but materials stock will increase to £30,000.

Sales budget

Activity

Produce a sales budget for next year showing the quantity, price and total value of each product, based upon the above information and assuming that the sales forecast is accepted without any limitations being imposed.

SOLUTION

John Storey
Sales budget for the year to ....

Type	Quantity	Price £	Value £
Standard A	1,200	315	378,000
Standard B	960	210	201,600
Non-standard	360	252 (avg)	90,720
Total sales budgeted for the year			670,320

Notes:
1 Quantity is 20% more than last year.
2 Prices have been increased by 5%.
3 Non-standard must be treated on an average basis as there is no information to do otherwise.

The sales budget is the responsibility of the sales manager, and in most firms would be the keystone upon which all the other budgets build. This may not always be the case, however, for production or other limitations may prevent the maximum sales forecast from being attained. This is discussed further in the next section.

Note the use of the word 'forecast' at the end of the last section when referring to sales. A forecast is a *possible* plan, perhaps one of many alternatives, the forecast ultimately adopted becoming the budget.

It must be emphasized that budgets are concerned with the future, not the past, although past experience may be a guide to the future. The sales manager must 'crystal-ball gaze' as clearly as possible, therefore, and in so doing he will adopt the best techniques and sources of information. He may adopt one or all of the following approaches:

- *Analysis of past sales trends* – particularly of a seasonal or cyclical nature using statistical techniques and knowledge of industry growth, competition, general trade prospects and planned sales promotion expenditure – to forecast future trends.
- *Estimates by own field staff* – sales representatives have a unique local knowledge and 'feel' for the market that head office staff will not possess, especially when judging the future of new products.
- *Market research* – by own staff or by consultants who would advise on possible product demand, taking into account customer habits, how they are motivated and effect upon them of different promotional techniques.

For control purposes, further analysis of the sales budget may be carried out. For example, sales may be analysed by products, areas, representatives, home and export, or by methods of distribution.

Self-check

What factors do you think John Storey's sales manager may have taken into account in deciding to recommend a 20% increase on last year's sales?

ANSWER

Factors influencing the forecast 20% increase in sales might have included:

- that the limitation in machine capacity could be overcome – perhaps by temporary overtime working;
- the proposed sales price increases would not reduce volume of sales;
- a current full order book with well-founded forecasts that demand will remain high;
- the national energy conservation policy would help to keep his business buoyant;
- planned sales promotion expenditure;
- the correlation between the level of housebuilding in the area and demand for double-glazing.

Production budget (quantity)

Because the production manager will ultimately be held responsible for achieving production targets, he should play the major role in compiling the production budget.

The main purposes of the production budget are:

- to reconcile production with sales and stock requirements;
- to facilitate a smooth production flow;
- to help forecast requirements and costs of materials, labour, machines and services.

Which is the 'chicken' and which the 'egg'? Do sales or production govern activity in the short term? The answer must, of course, be determined either by the limitations set by projected sales demand, or by the availability of production facilities. The need to reconcile and coordinate sales and production plans is fundamental to the planning process, and anything short of effective collaboration will either result in lost sales opportunities, or in overproduction, with consequent effects upon employment and profit targets.

Limiting factors

Before the production of a manufacturing firm can be agreed, a plant utilization forecast must be completed. This indicates the available machine-hour capacity in each department. Alternatively, where operations are labour- rather than machine-intensive, available capacity will be expressed in labour hours. Available capacity is then matched with the sales forecast, and if production facilities fall short of what is needed, an effort is made to overcome the 'limiting' factor or factors. Limitations could include not only machine or labour hours, but also material in short supply, or even the finance required to purchase these resources.

> *Activity*
>
> What alternative actions do you think are available to John Storey's production manager if production is limited by machine capacity?

ANSWER

A decision could be made to:

(a) work overtime;
(b) work machines more intensively by introducing shift working;
(c) subcontract work to outside contractors;
(d) improve productivity by introducing training for machine operators;
(e) redesign the product to reduce the machine time required;
(f) hire additional machinery;
(g) in the long term purchase additional machines.

Activity

Another constraint on production might be a shortage of materials. How might this limitation be overcome?

ANSWER

Various alternatives open to you would include:

(a) substitute another suitable type of material;
(b) obtain materials from another supplier;
(c) redesign the product so as to use less material or a different material;
(d) cut down on wastage and scrap by changing the process, or by improving operating efficiency;
(e) take over the supplier of material so as to ensure availability and to reduce delays in supplies.

Having reconciled productive capacity required with that available, the production manager can go ahead and compile his budget. If it were not for the need to hold stocks of finished products to act as a buffer against production delays, his production quantities would be the same as those in the sales budget. Planned changes in stockholding through the budget period will therefore affect the quantity to be produced.

Activity

Prepare John Storey's production budget for the coming year.
    Hint: production required of each type of unit will need to satisfy the sales budget and the planned changes in stock between the beginning and the end of the budget year.

ANSWER

John Storey
Production budget for the year to . . . .

Product	Sales budget	less Opening stock	add Closing stock	Production required
	Units	Units	Units	Units
Standard A	1,200	50	30	1,180
Standard B	960	30	10	940
Non-standard	360	—	—	360

Production cost budget – direct materials

Completed sales and production budgets are the catalyst for the creation of budgets for all the resources needed to meet the year's master plan. It is the responsibility of the various production and service departmental managers to prepare their budgets for direct materials, direct labour, and indirect expenses for submission to the person responsible for coordinating the budget procedure.

The purchasing manager is responsible for the procurement of direct materials and other supplies, and his direct materials cost budget will take account of production requirements, planned prices, stocks held at present and planned stocks for the end of the budget period. In large multiproduct companies the role of the purchasing manager is complicated and onerous. He has to be knowledgeable about current sources of materials, as well as possible substitutes for them, should be able to buy at the keenest prices consistent with quality, and skilled in negotiating advantageous purchase contracts.

Activity

Using the figures given in the production budget of John Storey, draft a direct materials budget, in quantity and value.

Hint: calculate the quantity and cost of material required for the production budget first, then make an adjustment for the difference between the opening stock of material (see the balance sheet in the first section of this chapter), and the planned closing stock, also given in the first section. The final resultant figure will be the cost of direct material to be purchased.

ANSWER

John Storey
Direct material requirement and purchase budget for the year to ....

	Budgeted production units	Price per unit £	Total cost of material required £
Standard A	1,180	80	94,400
Standard B	940	50	47,000
Non-standard	360	70	25,200
Material usage budget			166,600
less Opening stock	19,000		
add Closing stock	30,000		11,000
Material purchase budget			177,600

Note: the material usage and material purchase budgets are produced separately by the production and purchasing managers respectively, but are shown together here to illustrate how they are interconnected.

Production cost budget – direct labour

Assuming that standard production times have been established for each product by work study techniques, the direct labour hours required to satisfy the production plan will be the product of production quantities × standard hours per product. Assuming that direct labour employees are all of one grade, the number of them needed can be arrived at by dividing budgeted labour hours by the hours in a normal working week. Of course, where products are built up through a series of operations in successive production departments, the calculations have to be broken down into departmental requirements, but the principle is still the same. The task is further complicated because operatives may be paid at varying rates of pay, and standard rates will have to be established for the grade of labour employed on each operation. The setting of standard costs has already been discussed in Chapter 14.

The calculation of hours required may show that more employees have to be engaged, but conversely it may reveal that the firm has more direct employees than it needs to cover budgeted production. In these circumstances, a policy decision has to be made regarding the employment of these 'surplus' employees. If they are skilled, a decision to retain them is likely, because, once released, they may never return if required in the future. If they are retained, their wages will be treated as an indirect cost.

Further, in these days of automation, or at least a high degree of mechanization, the number of direct operatives required for production is considerably fewer than when using more labour intensive methods. Direct employees have become 'machine-minders' more and more, and even if production is halted the cost of direct labour might not change. In these circumstances, direct labour is virtually a fixed cost, not varying with volume of production as is usually supposed.

Self-check

Given the production budget and applying the standard times and rates stated in the first section of this chapter, construct a direct labour budget for John Storey.

ANSWER

John Storey
Direct labour budget for the year to . . . .

	Budgeted production units	Hours per unit	Total hours required	Rate per hour £	Total cost £
Standard A	1,180	24	28,320	3	84,960
Standard B	940	15	14,100	3	42,300
Non-standard	360	20	7,200	3	21,600
			49,620		148,860

In conclusion, it must be emphasized that the budget example used in this and the following two chapters has been kept purposely simple in order to illustrate *principles* involved in budget preparation rather than detailed calculations.

Review

1 The sales director presented three alternative sales 'budgets' to the budget committee for their consideration. Was the sales director correct in calling them budgets?

2 The Accord Company produces three products – A, B and C. The following information is available regarding each product:

	A	B	C
Last year's sales (units)	2,000	3,000	1,500
Budgeted prices – next year	£5	£6	£7
Material required for each product (units) X	2	—	—
Y	—	1	—
Z	—	—	2
Direct hours required for each product	1	2	3
Finished stock:			
End of last year (units)	400	300	300
End of next year (units)	600	600	400
Direct hours available	2,400	10,000	5,300
Direct material available (units) i.e., in stock and from suppliers	3,500	6,500	3,500

Note: it is anticipated that sales of products A and C will increase by 10% next year, and that a planned £1 reduction in the price of B from its previous level of £7 will double the sales of that product.

Required

(a) What will be the budgeted production for next year, assuming that any constraints on production cannot be lifted?

(b) Explain the term 'limiting factor' and illustrate its application in your answer to **(a)**.

(c) What action could the Accord Company take to achieve its forecast level of production?

ANSWERS

1 A *budget* is the agreed plan for a period of time. It will be adopted when all the alternatives have been examined and rejected. Each of the alternatives is referred to as a *forecast*.

2 (a)

	A	B	C
Last year's sales	2,000	3,000	1,500
add 10% increase	200		150
100% increase		3,000	
Sales forecast (units)	2,200	6,000	1,650
add Planned increases in stock	200	300	100
Production forecast (units)	2,400	6,300	1,750
Hours per unit	1	2	3
Production forecast (hours)	2,400	12,600	5,250
Total hours available	2,400	10,000	5,300
Material per unit	2	1	2
Total material required (units)	4,800	6,300	3,500
Total material available (units)	3,500	6,500	3,500
Limiting factor	Material	Hours	None
Production budget (units)	1,750	5,000	1,750

(b) A 'limiting factor' (also known as a 'governing' or 'key' factor) is a resource shortage or other constraint, restricting the level of production or sales activity. In the above example, the production of:
- A is restricted to 1,750 units because *material* is in short supply, even though there are sufficient hours;
- B is limited to 5,000 units by the shortage of *hours*; material is sufficiently available;
- C is not limited by lack of resources, and can therefore fully satisfy the production requirement.

(c) To break the material restriction on the production of A the following action could be taken:
(i) use a substitute material;
(ii) change suppliers;
(iii) redesign the product (long-term action);
(iv) be more efficient in the use of materials.
To overcome the hours restriction on B Accord might:
(i) work overtime;

(ii) work additional shifts;
(iii) improve efficiency;
(iv) subcontract production;
(v) hire machinery;
(vi) redesign the product.

20 | Planning overhead costs

Introduction

In Chapter 19 we found that the budgeted level of direct costs of material and labour are geared to the production budget. It is generally assumed that these costs vary in direct proportion to volume of output.

We now consider the budgets for indirect costs of selling, production and administration, but we do so with the help of a great deal of background knowledge developed in previous chapters.

Chapter 10 is of particular significance in relation to the classification of indirect costs, cost behaviour and allocation and apportionment of overheads, and you are strongly recommended to re-read that chapter together with the section in Chapter 14 dealing with the setting of standard overhead rates, before proceeding with this chapter.

The influences governing the behaviour of indirect costs are not as clear as those affecting direct costs. We look first of all therefore, at basic cost behaviour, then at methods of analysing that behaviour. We then go on to consider how that knowledge is applied to the construction of indirect cost budgets, both at the planning and at the control stages of a system of budgetary control.

Basic cost behaviour

Activity

Water authorities are considering charging for water on the basis of actual consumption, rather than on the rateable values of the properties supplied.

Assume that water is charged at the rate of 1.25 pence per

gallon and that the average consumption for a household is 10,000 gallons a year. Construct a graph to show the cost to households of consuming between nil and 15,000 gallons.

Read off your graph the cost at consumptions of 13,000, 10,000, 9,000 and 7,000 gallons, and check by calculation.

ANSWER

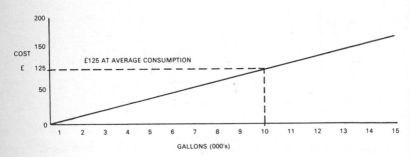

Figure 37. Graph of water charges at a fixed price per gallon

NOTES ON THE ABOVE CHART

1 Costs at 13,000, 10,000, 9,000 and 7,000 gallons respectively are £162.50, £125, £112.50 and £87.50.
2 Because the costs vary directly with consumption, this is known as a 'variable' cost.

Activity

Now draw two further graphs:

1 For a household with a rateable value of £400 and assuming that water is charged at 20 pence per £ of rateable value.
2 Assuming that the water authority compromise, and charge on a two-part tariff basis. That is, at 8 pence in the £ on rateable value, and 0.5 pence per gallon for water consumed.

ANSWER

FIRST GRAPH

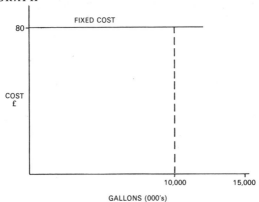

Figure 38. Graph of water charges at a fixed total cost at all levels of consumption

NOTES

1 Cost is a constant £80 at all levels of consumption and is therefore referred to as a 'fixed' cost.
2 Because the fixed charge only covers a period of one year, it is also known as a 'period' cost, i.e. it is relevant to time rather than volume.

SECOND GRAPH

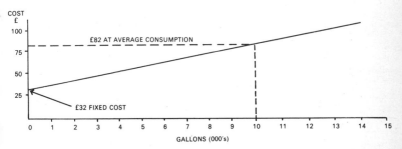

Figure 39. Graph of water charges based upon a two-part fixed/variable tariff

NOTES

1 Minimum cost is £32 plus a variable element based on consumption.
2 This 'hybrid' is known as a 'semi-variable' cost because it is part fixed and part variable.

These three basic cost patterns portray some indirect costs exactly, and are acceptable approximations of the way other costs behave. However, the fixed or variable nature of costs only applies within certain ranges of output because:

- *fixed costs* tend to increase by 'steps' at progressively higher levels of activity. For example, doubling output would probably double fixed costs (see figure 40(a));
- *variable cost* of each unit of activity, e.g. products, may increase or decrease after a certain level of activity has been reached (see figure 40(b)).

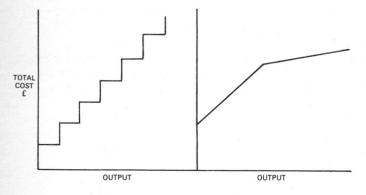

Figure 40(a) (left): 'Stepped' fixed cost, e.g. supervisors

Figure 40(b) (right): Semi-variable with a change in cost per unit after a certain level, e.g. electricity

Self-check

Costs can be categorized as: **(a)** fixed, **(b)** variable, **(c)** semi-variable, **(d)** stepped fixed costs, **(e)** variable, with a change in cost per unit after a certain level has been reached, **(f)** a combination of any of the above.

Indicate into which category each of the following domestic expenses belong:

1 Annual total food cost as the family grows in number.
2 The quarterly telephone bill.
3 Property insurance.
4 Fuel oil for heating.
5 Regular purchase of soft drinks from the milkman, with a reduction in price per bottle after 200 have been bought.
6 Weekly wage paid to the odd-job man/gardener.
7 Total costs of running the family car.
8 Property rates paid to the local authority.

ANSWER

1 **(d)** 'Stepped' fixed – going to a higher step, say per annum, for each addition to the family.
2 **(c)** Semi-variable – comprising a fixed rental, and variable charges for calls.
3 **(a)** Fixed – does not change unless the value of the property increases. This ignores inflation of course.
4 **(b)** Variable – directly proportional to oil used.
5 **(e)** Variable + change – same variable cost per bottle, until the 200 point, after which the variable cost per bottle reduces.
6 **(a)** Fixed – same wage each week, not correlated to level of activity.
7 **(c)** Semi-variable – fixed insurance and tax; variable running costs.
8 **(a)** Fixed – for each year, the charge remains the same.

Why are some costs fixed and others variable?

You now know *what* fixed and variable costs are, but what makes them behave the way they do?

Basically, when we *commit* ourselves to a certain level of expenditure on a resource, over a *specific period of time*, regardless of activity, then we have a *fixed* cost. For example, if we wish to put our car on the road, the annual road fund tax has to be paid, whether or not we actually cover any mileage.

Other costs are *variable* because they are only expended when activity occurs. For example, we only spend money on petrol for our cars if we drive the car on the road. The more mileage, the more petrol consumed.

To illustrate the difference a little further, let us introduce Mr and Mrs Bill Stevens, a retired but extremely active and adventurous couple who are planning a world tour. They have not set any particular time limit on their adventure, and plan to commence their journey in New York, USA. They will travel overland by motor-caravan which they will purchase in America but trade in for a specific sum when they return. The following is a list of some of the items which they will need:

Sea passages	Clothes
Air fare to New York	Tent
Vehicle cost	Bedding
Vehicle running cost	Cash for luxuries and entertaining
Personal insurance	Food – essential
Camping site fees	Toiletry needs
Cooking and heating fuel	First-aid equipment

> *Activity*
>
> Arrange the above items under three cost headings:
>
> > *Fixed*   *Variable*   *Semi-variable*
>
> Do not refer to the list below until you have completed your own.

ANSWER

Fixed	*Variable*	*Semi-variable*
Sea passages	Food – essential	Vehicle running costs
Airfare to New York	Toiletry needs	
Personal insurance	Camp site fees	
Clothes	Cooking and heating	
Tent	fuel	
Bedding		
First-aid equipment		
Vehicle cost		
Cash for entertaining		
Cash for luxuries		

Note that all but the last two *fixed* items cannot be avoided. We are committed to paying for transport whether the tour lasts six months or a year, and this applies also to insurance, clothes, tent, etc. In the sense that a certain level of funds will be set aside for entertaining and luxuries, the last two can also be classed as fixed, but with the difference that Mr and Mrs Stevens can change their planned spending on these two items during the tour, if they feel it prudent to do so. These are therefore '*discretionary*' fixed costs, because they can be avoided or abandoned at a later date.

In business organizations, fixed costs are also referred to as 'policy' and as 'period' costs. 'Policy' in the sense that the planned level of production, selling or other activity determines the need for such expenditure; and 'period' because such costs are incurred to cover a specific period of time rather than a volume of activity. Insurance on buildings is a typical example of the latter.

Items in the 'variable' column will cost roughly the same each day, and are therefore strictly dependent upon how long the tour lasts.

Variability of business costs mainly refers to direct costs, but there are many indirect costs that are influenced by volume of activity. The latter is referred to as the independent variable, and can include labour hours, machine hours, number of employees, sales value and sales quantity. Some indirect costs may be influenced by more than one independent variable.

Finally, vehicle running costs include some fixed costs – taxes and insurance for example – and some variable costs such as petrol, tyres, oil and maintenance. The fixed element is *committed* expenditure because it will not change no matter what mileage the Stevens cover. On the other hand, the variable costs will be avoided if no mileage is run.

This combination of a necessary minimum level of cost plus a variable element is to be found widely in business; examples being telephone charges, and maintenance. Separating the fixed from the variable element is not always easy, however, and the next section shows how this problem might be tackled.

Self-check

Head four columns as follows:

Fixed discretionary	Fixed committed	Variable	Semi-variable

Now list under the appropriate heading, each of the following indirect expenses:

1 Painting of buildings	8 Storekeeper's wages
2 Electric power for machines	9 Factory office stationery
3 Industrial clothing	10 Telephones
4 Depreciation	11 Research and development
5 Rent	12 Property rates
6 Salesmen's commision – a % of sales value	13 Maintenance of machines
	14 Market research
7 Vehicle running costs	15 Lubricant oil for machines

ANSWER

1 FD – the amount is fixed, but can be avoided or delayed.

2 V – dependent upon the number of machine hours worked.

3 V – with the number of employees.

4 FC – this is fixed by the prepaid cost of the asset, and cannot be avoided.

5 FC – usually a fixed, contracted, period payment.

6 V – directly proportionate to value of sales.

7 SV – some costs fixed, e.g. insurance; others variable, e.g. petrol.

8 FC – the storekeeper is a necessary member of staff, so this is committed fixed expenditure.

9 V – documentation will tend to vary with output.

10 SV – fixed rental per instrument, plus variable charge for calls.

11 FD – policy will decree the fixed amount, but this could change.

12 FC – owning property commits one to paying rates fixed for a period.

13 SV – fixed amount of expenditure required even when no output.

14 FD – as **11** above.

15 V – dependent upon number of machine hours worked.

Determining the behaviour of indirect costs

In Chapter 14 reference was made to scientific method study and work measurement as techniques used to set standards for direct materials and direct labour. This 'industrial engineering' approach is very appropriate when applied to direct costs as there is a recognizable and measurable output with which to link the necessary inputs. Each table produced in a furniture factory for example, requires a measurable amount of timber. Not so with indirect costs. The factors influencing these may vary, and are not so clearly recognized. What, for example, determines the level of telephone usage in a business?

The use of *scientific work study* is the most efficient approach to setting cost levels as it entails a detailed investigation into all the factors influencing a particular expense, and attempts to answer the question, What level of cost is really necessary to carry out this task? Some success has been achieved in this field, particularly where repetitive, routine tasks are involved such as typing documents and packing parcels.

An associated formalized technique known as '*zero base budgeting*' is of more recent origin, placing emphasis upon the need to make a constant appraisal of the considerable resources expended upon overheads. Starting from a 'zero' cost position, cost centre supervisors are asked to justify their levels of costs by the benefits to be derived from the expenditure. Analysis of alternative ways of carrying out the same functions is encouraged, with the object of choosing the one that is most efficient in its use of resources. More often, most firms start from their current cost levels, without justifying them, and add an appropriate amount for inflation to set next year's costs.

One cannot ignore the present patterns of expenditure completely, however, and a sensible analysis of each indirect cost, its benefit and its behaviour would appear to be a logical first step in the process of estimating future costs.

Three other methods which examine *past* records of costs to analyse cost behaviour are:

- high/low activity analysis;
- scattergraph analysis;
- statistical regression analysis.

Each of these methods progressively seeks for more accuracy.

Activity

John Storey's production manager is examining the last six years' indirect costs to try to discover cost behaviour patterns to use in estimating future costs. The following information is extracted from the accounts.

John Storey

Analysis of production indirect costs for the last six years

		Year 1 £	2 £	3 £	4 £	5 £	6 £
Number of hours worked		17,000	21,000	26,000	30,000	34,000	42,000
Supervision	F	14,000	14,000	14,000	29,000	29,000	29,000
Other indirect labour costs	SV	15,650	17,400	18,750	20,550	21,500	24,500
Consumable stores	V	6,400	8,600	10,300	12,400	13,600	17,000
Scrap	V	550	850	850	1,200	1,100	1,500
Electric power	SV	2,800	3,300	3,550	4,100	4,150	5,000
Depreciation – machines	F	2,000	2,000	2,000	3,000	3,000	3,000
Maintenance	SV	3,900	4,600	4,900	5,700	5,900	7,000
Tools	V	1,700	1,850	2,600	2,600	3,400	4,000
Rent and rates	F	25,000	25,000	25,000	25,000	35,000	35,000

Note: F = fixed; V = variable; SV = semi-variable.

Using the total labour hours of 49,620 calculated and shown in the direct labour budget of John Storey, schedule an estimate of indirect costs for next year.

Hint: choose your estimates by judgement alone. Do not make any precise calculations, but take note of the cost classifications against each item.

SUGGESTED ANSWER
(yours could be different)

	£
Supervision	29,000
Other indirect labour costs	27,350
Consumable stores	20,200
Scrap	1,880
Electric power	5,800
Depreciation – machines	3,000
Maintenance	8,050
Tools	4,570
Rent and rates	35,000
	134,850

Fixed costs have been repeated, and the variable element of each cost has been judged by comparing the last two years' figures. Inflation has not been taken account of, but would obviously have to be built into the estimates, together with any planned changes such as additional depreciation consequent upon the installation of new machines.

This simple scheduling approach leaves a lot to chance, but might be quite adequate for a relatively small business. To obtain a higher degree of accuracy, however, the trends in the historic cost schedule need to be more closely examined.

The *high/low method of cost analysis* takes the costs at the highest and lowest levels of activity during a period, and compares them. It is then assumed that the increase in costs between the two levels is directly due to the increase in activity, and represents the variable cost. Dividing that increase by the increase in volume of activity should therefore give the variable cost per unit of activity.

Taking 'other indirect labour costs' in John Storey's schedule as an example, we have:

	Costs £	Hours	*Variable cost per hour* £
Year 6	24,500	42,000	
Year 1	15,650	17,000	
	8,850 ÷	25,000 =	0.354

We then calculate the variable cost at each of the high and low levels of output, and deduct it from the total cost at that level to give the fixed cost:

	Year 6 £		Year 1 £
Total cost	24,500		15,650
less Variable cost – 42,000 × .354	14,868	17,000 × .354	6,018
Fixed cost	9,632		9,632

The cost function for other indirect labour costs is £9,632 + £0.354 per hour, which, if applied to next year's budgeted hours of 49,620, gives £9,632 + (49,620 × .354) = £27,197, which compares with our scheduled estimate of £27,350.

Activity

Using the high/low method, calculate **(a)** the cost function for maintenance in the original schedule and **(b)** the estimated cost of maintenance for next year.

ANSWER

(a)

	Costs £	Hours	Variable cost per hour £
Year 6	7,000	42,000	
Year 1	3,900	17,000	
	3,100	÷ 25,000 =	0.124

	Year 6 £		Year 1 £
Total cost	7,000		3,900
less Variable cost – 42,000 × .124	5,208	17,000 × .124	2,108
Fixed cost	1,792		1,792

(b) Estimated total cost of maintenance for next year: £1,792 + (49,620 × .124) = £7,945. This compares with the scheduled estimate of £8,050.

We could probably obtain a higher level of accuracy in our

estimating by testing other combinations of high/low activity, but the simplicity of this method has much to commend it. Costs which are strictly variable can also be analysed by use of this method, although more accuracy can probably be obtained by dividing the total of the six years' costs by the total hours worked during the six years. For example, the total costs of consumable stores – £68,300 divided by total hours of 170,000 – gives £0.402 per hour, whereas the high/low method shows £0.424 per hour.

Scattergraph analysis is carried out by plotting the cost/activity relationships drawn from historic records on to a graph, and drawing a visual best fitting line through the points.

Activity

On a sheet of graph paper draw a vertical axis to record cost, and a horizontal axis to show hours worked in the firm of John Storey over the last six years. Now plot the cost/hours worked coordinates for electric power for each year. Then draw a line through these points to cross the vertical axis.

Your graph should appear as follows:

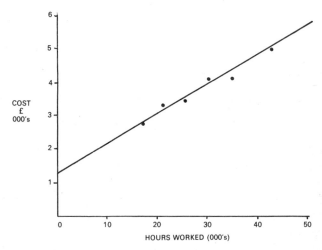

Figure 41. J. Storey – scattergraph analysis of electric power expense for the last six years

The fixed cost is where the line crosses the vertical axis, and the variable cost per hour is represented by the slope of the line drawn through the points. Fixed cost is £1,300. Variable cost is calculated by dividing the difference between fixed cost – £1,300 – and say £5,000, i.e. £3,700, by the hours worked at £5,000 cost. That is £3,700 ÷ 42,000 = £0.088. This is the same figure as that derived from the high/low method (check this for yourself).

Because scattergraphs take account of the 'scatter' of many previous cost/activity relationships, they may be more accurate than the high/low method. Their major drawback is that the 'line of best fit' is the result of visual interpretation, which is largely a matter of judgement.

Statistical regression analysis can place the 'line of best fit' with more precision than the visually produced scattergraph, by producing an equation showing:

total cost = fixed cost + (cost per unit of activity × activity)

It can be seen, however, that more accuracy can only be produced at higher cost, and the latter can only be justified by the benefits resulting.

Self-check

1 'Last year's figure, plus an amount for inflation, is the best measure of next year's cost.' Do you agree with this statement? Why?
2 Plotting historic cost coordinates on a cost/activity chart, and drawing a 'line of best fit' is referred to as:

   (a) break-even analysis
   (b) fixed/variable analysis
   (c) scattergraph analysis
   (d) high/low activity analysis

   Which of the above is correct?
3 During the past four years the highest and lowest mileages run by Simon Poacher's Pies and Pâté delivery vehicles, together with their associated costs, were as follows:

	Highest	*Lowest*
Mileage	160,000	90,000
Cost	£34,000	£19,650

Calculate the cost function for delivery cost using the high/low method.

ANSWERS

1 Although such an approach may be a good guide and approximate the best estimate, it completely ignores the question, What level of cost is necessary to carry out this task? It also fails to examine the level of next year's operations, and ignores planned changes in methods and technology.

Work study and zero base budgeting are two techniques that adopt a 'starting from scratch' approach to cost estimation. However, one should never take a sledgehammer to crack a nut, and the cost of more sophistication in cost estimation must be more than matched by the benefits to be derived.

2 (c) Scattergraph.

3

	Cost £	Mileage	Variable cost per mile £
Highest	34,000	160,000	
Lowest	19,650	90,000	
	14,350	÷ 70,000 =	0.205

	Highest £		Lowest £
Total cost	34,000		19,650
less Variable cost – 160,000 × .205	32,800	90,000 × .205	18,450
	1,200		1,200

Therefore the cost function is £1,200 + £0.205 per mile.

Flexible budgets

Having analysed the behaviour of indirect costs over the past six years we have now obtained sufficient information to compile John Storey's production overhead budget for next year, and this is scheduled below.

John Storey
Production overhead budget for year to . . . .
Budgeted hours worked – 49,620

Expense type		Cost function	Fixed	Variable	Total
Controllable		£	£	£	£
Supervision	F	29,000	29,000	—	29,000
Other indirect labour	SV	9,632 + .354	9,632	17,565	27,197
Consumable stores	V	.402	—	19,947	19,947
Scrap	V	.036	—	1,786	1,786
Electric power	SV	1,304 + .088	1,304	4,367	5,671
Maintenance	SV	1,792 + .124	1,792	6,153	7,945
Tools	V	.095	—	4,714	4,714
Non-controllable					
Depreciation – machines	F	3,000	3,000	—	3,000
Rent and rates	F	35,000	35,000	—	35,000
			79,728	54,532	134,260

Notes:
1 For the sake of simplicity no provision is made for inflation, or for any change in methods.
2 Fixed costs are assumed to be as last year.
3 Semi-variable cost functions are calculated using the high/low method.
4 Variable cost per labour hour is calculated by dividing the total costs of each variable item over the last six years by the total labour hours for the same period, viz. 170,000 hours.
5 The total is little different from that arrived at by scheduling by judgement (see previous section). Where there is little change, this may be perfectly acceptable, but the question as to whether all costs can be justified is left unanswered.
6 It is assumed that direct labour hours worked is the only independent variable influencing production indirect expenses, and that the cost functions listed are applicable to the range of output levels that might be achieved during next year. We can also assume that this is the 'expected attainable' budget, upon which the overhead absorption rate will be based (or standard overhead rate if a system of standard costing is in operation).
7 Controllable costs are grouped separately to indicate those expenses which are the direct responsibility of the production manager.

The main advantages of preparing the budget in the above form are:

- the effect of change upon profit can quickly be assessed when costs are analysed into their fixed and variable classes,
- for periodic *control* purposes actual costs can be compared with costs adjusted (flexed) to the actual level of activity during each period, hence the term 'flexible budgets'.

Activity

Using the cost functions relating to the first three items in John Storey's production overhead budget, prepare a control statement for the year showing, in respect of each item, the original budget, a flexed budget, the actual costs and the variances. Assume that the actual hours worked were 45,000 and that costs were:

	£
Supervision	30,000
Other indirect labour	29,500
Consumable stores	17,900

SOLUTION

Operating report
Production overhead cost

	Fixed budget £	Flexed budget £	Actual costs £	Variances £
Supervision	29,000	29,000	30,000	1,000 A
Other indirect labour	27,197	25,562	29,500	3,938 A
Consumable stores	19,947	18,090	17,900	190 F
	76,144	72,652	77,400	4,748 A

The fixed budget in the above statement is the original plan. Circumstances have conspired against its achievement and explanations for this might help future planning, but it is not the model to use in the control of *actual* costs. The only objective comparison must be with a budget 'flexed' to the activity *actually achieved* during the period. If flexible budgets are not used the purpose of control is lost, for comparison must always be between what *did* happen, with what *should have* happened.

The above statement is only an extract from a full cost centre operating report. In a complete budgetary control system a statement in similar form is prepared for each cost centre. In the case of production centres the costs of direct material and direct labour are also included, for the latter can be flexed to the actual level of output in a similar way to overheads.

Cost centres include those covering the selling and administration functions of course, and budgets and control statements will be compiled using the same 'flexible' approach to costs. However, although some expenses related to these two functions will have a variable element, for example sales delivery costs, a large percentage of their total costs will be fixed – both committed and discretionary.

A budgetary control system can be operated with or without a full standard costing system as described in Part 5. A business using standard costs will prepare variance statements similar to those illustrated in Chapter 16, but with more detailed supplementary information of overhead cost variances relating to each expense head, as shown above. A variance reporting system can be applied to any type of organization, but because of the additional planning and control problems attending a manufacturing concern emphasis has been placed upon this type of operation in this text.

Self-check

An item for 'maintenance – £10,000' was included in the original production overhead budget of Norfolk Agrimek Ltd.

Budgeted activity for the year was 10,000 hours, actual hours worked were 9,000 and the actual cost of maintenance was £10,000. The production manager claimed that he had succeeded in meeting his expense target for maintenance. Do you agree with him? Why?

ANSWER

Maintenance is usually a composite of fixed and variable elements of cost. Machines still have to be maintained even during a period of no production, to keep them in working order. The cost of doing this is the fixed element, and when the machines are in operation they will incur a further variable cost – relating to the number of machine hours operated.

The flexible budget for 9,000 hours will therefore be less than that for 10,000 hours, and a cost of £10,000 results in an adverse variance. The manager has exceeded his budget.

Review

Note: question number **2** draws together some of the work in this chapter together with some in previous chapters. Before you answer that question, therefore, you will no doubt find it helpful to revise Chapter 14, 'Setting standards for production overheads', and Chapter 15, 'Calculating overhead variances'.

1 In order to stimulate sales John Storey is planning a new sales strategy. He plans to:
  (i) introduce a new sales incentive scheme, whereby he pays each of his two salesmen a fixed salary of £5,000 plus a commission of 1% on sales value; and
  (ii) increase sales advertising by £2,000 a year.

  (a) Into which behavioural categories would you put these two costs?
  (b) Draw a simple chart to illustrate the behaviour of the salesmen's earnings from zero to £700,000 sales.
  (c) What would the total salesmen's remuneration be at sales of **(i)** £560,000 and **(ii)** £400,000?

2 Refer to the section in this chapter on flexible budgets, and particularly to John Storey's production overhead budget. Assume that John Storey operates a full budgetary control and standard costing system. During the year to which the budget relates the hours worked were 45,000. The actual production overhead costs recorded for the year were as follows:

	£
Controllable	
Supervision	30,000
Other indirect labour	29,500
Consumable stores	17,900

	£
Scrap	1,670
Electric power	5,800
Maintenance	6,900
Tools	4,600
Non-controllable	
Depreciation – machines	3,000
Rent and rates	36,750
	136,120

(a) Using the information in the production overhead budget, calculate the standard overhead cost rate.

(b) Compile a production overhead operating report showing the original fixed budget, the flexible budget for the year's level of activity, the actual costs and the variance for each item of expense.

(c) Given the standard overhead cost rate calculated by you in answer to question (a) above, calculate the *total* overhead variance, the overhead *expenditure* variance and the overhead *volume* variance. (Note: the overhead expenditure variance ought to agree with the total of the 'variance' column in the report produced by you in answering question (b).)

ANSWERS

1 (a) (i) The salesmen's remuneration is a semi-variable cost being part fixed (salary of £5,000) and part variable with sales value (1% on sales).

(ii) Sales advertising is a discretionary fixed cost. Once the policy has been agreed, the expense is 'fixed', but unless the advertising is contracted, it could be abandoned.

(b)

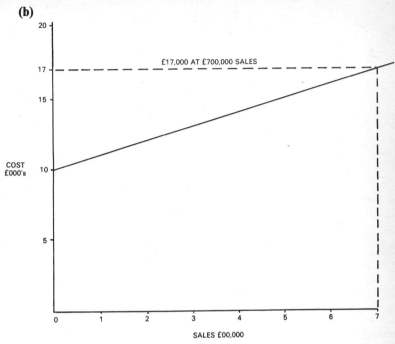

Figure 42. J. Storey – graph of sales commission expense

(c) (i) £15,600 = (£10,000 + 1% of £560,000). (ii) £14,000 = (£10,000 + 1% of £400,000).

2 (a) Standard overhead rate = £134,260 ÷ 49,620 hours = £2.7058 per hour – variable: £1.0990; fixed: £1.6068.

(b)

Production overhead operating report

	Fixed budget £	Flexible budget £	Actual costs £	Variance £
Controllable				
Supervision	29,000	29,000	30,000	1,000 A
Other indirect labour	27,197	25,562	29,500	3,938 A
Consumable stores	19,947	18,090	17,900	190 F
Scrap	1,786	1,620	1,670	50 A
Electric power	5,671	5,264	5,800	536 A
Maintenance	7,945	7,372	6,900	472 F
Tools	4,714	4,275	4,600	325 A

	Fixed budget £	Flexible budget £	Actual costs £	Variance £
Non-controllable				
Depreciation – machines	3,000	3,000	3,000	—
Rent and rates	35,000	35,000	36,750	1,750 A
	134,260	129,183	136,120	6,937 A

(c) Overhead variances:

Overhead expenditure variance
   Budget allowance – actual cost
£79,728 + (45,000 × 1.0990) – 136,120
    129,183 – 136,120   =   6,937 A

Overhead volume variance
   Overhead absorbed – budget allowance
    45,000 × 2.7058 – 129,183
     121,761 – 129,183   =   7,422 A

Total overhead variance
   Overhead absorbed – actual cost
    121,761 – 136,120   = £14,359 A

Notes:
1 The expenditure variance agrees with the total of the individual expense items in the production overhead operating report. The latter is able to pinpoint the most significant variances for investigation.
2 The volume variance relates wholly to the fact that hours worked were 4,620 less than budgeted, which meant that 4,620 × £1.6068 (the fixed overhead rate) = £7,422 was under-absorbed. You will recall that this could be analysed further into capacity and efficiency if details of hours actually produced are given.

21 | The investment, finance and profit plan

Introduction

Before operational budgets are compiled and agreed, there is a prior exploratory stage when the effects of alternative sales and production forecasts on cash flow and profit are examined. This is step 3 of figure 36. The forecasts are completed in rounded terms, perhaps by assessing costs of direct materials and labour as percentages of sales, based upon previous experience, and estimating overhead costs in total. The alternative scenarios which emerge from this preliminary investigation will have, as an end product, profit and cash forecasts, and it is upon these two vital indicators that the choice of optimum forecast will depend. This is not to imply that the forecast resulting in the largest profit and cash balance is the inevitable choice. The short-term plan is not considered in isolation from the long-term plan, and maximization of short-term profit may not be compatible with long-term aims.

When the operational budgets are eventually completed, their effects are summarized in the profit and cash budgets. This chapter examines the preparation of these two statements, the capital expenditure budget, and then finally the master balance sheet budget, which pulls the whole plan together in a statement of the organization's financial position at the end of the budget year.

The capital expenditure budget

If you were to take stock of all your personal possessions at some time in the future, you would probably include your house (mortgaged), car, furniture, hi-fi equipment, food, kitchen and laundry equipment, clothes, camera, pictures, books, savings, sports and recreational equipment. Some of these possessions, for example food and clothing, will be consumed and replaced regularly within a year and paid for in that year.

Most of your other 'assets', however, would have been purchased over many years, and whilst none of us would claim to be inveterate forward financial planners, we probably do have some medium- to long-term plans in mind. We plan to purchase our houses by instalments over a number of years, and our cars and furniture over shorter periods. On the other hand, many of the other items just lie temptingly in the backs of our minds as desirable future acquisitions, when we have saved sufficient cash.

Each year then, we buy some things that are consumed and replaced within the year, but we also purchase items that will be enjoyed by us over a number of years.

In business terminology, the former is referred to as 'revenue' expenditure, and the latter 'capital' expenditure. Businesses spend money on materials, labour and other services which are consumed and periodically replaced within the year, but they also pay for land, buildings and machines which will be in use for many years. You will recall from Chapter 10 that only a part of the cost of an asset is charged against profit each year, in the form of depreciation. The remaining part of the cost is included in the balance sheet as a fixed asset until it is completely written off over its useful life. However, the *cash* for these long-term assets is all paid in the year of acquisition, unless of course they are paid for by instalments.

Efficient business organizations plan long-term as you know, and this embraces plans to finance investment in long-term assets.

Formal approval procedures ensure that commitment to the organization of these resources is accomplished as part of an overall business strategy, summarized in the capital expenditure budget. It is worth noting that research and development expenditure is dealt with in much the same way as capital expenditure, although a high proportion of these costs will be charged to the budgeted profit and loss account.

Our double-glazier, John Storey, plans to purchase and pay for one machine next year, but it will not be installed until the end of the year, and certainly will not be in operation in that year. It will cost £5,000, but no amount for depreciation will be charged in the budget, although the cash payment will be reflected in the cash budget. John's capital expenditure budget for the year will show:

John Storey
Capital expenditure budget for the year to . . . .

Project no.	Dept	Description of expenditure	Est. life	Total cost £	Month of payment
671B	Machining	Forming machine	10 yrs	5,000	July

The long-term capital expenditure budget shown in figure 43 would include the above item, together with other capital projects approved and to be implemented during the coming years.

DEPARTMENT	PROJECT NO.	DESCRIPTION	TOTAL COST TO DATE 1981	ESTIMATED COST PER ANNUM				TOTAL ESTIMATED COST
				1982	1983	1984	1985	
			£	£	£	£	£	£
PRODUCTION	61	CUTTING MACHINE			10,000			10,000
BOILER	64	NEW BOILER	2,000	18,000				20,000
TRANSPORT	66	NEW VAN				15,000		15,000
OFFICE	67	FURNITURE					10,000	10,000

Figure 43. Long-term capital expenditure budget

Cash budget

'Ah yes, cash budgeting,' I hear you remark, 'now, that is something that everyone knows about', and this is true. Of course, some people are better at handling cash than others, but whether as individuals or as families, our finances would be less uncertain if we put some semblance of planning into our cash dealings. Problems of cash shortage would still exist, but we would be better able to predict this position and plan in advance to take appropriate action such as selling the family heirlooms, growing a beard to disguise ourselves, or joining the next Antarctic research team on a ten-year contract!

More constructively, a cash forecast will point up the range of actions open to you. You could increase your income by part-time working, reduce your payments by cutting living expenses, spread certain payments by instalments, delay payment or borrow. Should you anticipate a period of cash surplus you have time to examine the alternative investments. Eventually you will decide a cash plan which takes you confidently into the future.

The cash budget of a business organization is no different in concept – just larger, with different classes of receipts and payments. The same principles of efficient forward planning apply, to ensure that cash, the 'lubricant of the business world', is available when required, and invested efficiently when not required immediately.

It is completed largely by reference to all the operational budgets, but takes into account other receipts and payments not reflected in those budgets. These will include:

• Capital receipts by way of loans or share issues (part of the long-range financing plan).
• Sales of assets such as land or buildings.
• Payment of taxation and dividends to shareholders.
• Purchase of assets such as machines, motor vehicles and buildings (included in the capital expenditure budget).

The most important principle to recognize in constructing a cash budget is that of the timing of cash flows. Cash payments do not necessarily coincide with either the receipt or the use of a resource. Material may be received in January, not paid for until February because the supplier allows time to pay, and not used until March. Goods may be sold in April and recorded as sales in that month, but not paid for by the customer until May because we allow him time to pay. More subtly, a machine purchased and wholly paid for in October will be used over many years; its use being recorded as depreciation over that period of time.

The construction of John Storey's cash budget will help illustrate the above points. Whilst the budget would be analysed into quarterly or even monthly periods in practice, we show it in two six-monthly periods for simplicity.

Information is drawn from the budgets already prepared and illustrated in Chapters 19 and 20, with further information provided as follows:

	1st 6 months £	2nd 6 months £	Total £
Sales	300,000	370,320	670,320
Debtors at end of period	50,000	60,000	
Direct materials purchases	80,000	97,600	177,600

	1st 6 months £	2nd 6 months £	Total £
Creditors at end of period	14,000	16,000	
Direct labour	66,000	82,860	148,860
Production overhead	60,000	74,260	134,260
Selling overhead	30,000	40,000	70,000
Administration overhead	24,000	30,000	54,000
Capital expenditure		5,000	5,000
Taxation		5,000	5,000
Withdrawn for personal use	10,000	10,000	20,000

Notes:

1 It is assumed that there are no debtors or creditors for overheads.

2 Do not forget that depreciation on machines of £3,000 is included in the production overhead budget. As already emphasized this is not a cash payment, and should be omitted from the overheads paid for in the second six months' figure.

3 Assume that there is £2,000 depreciation on motor vehicles in selling overhead, and treat it as though it were all in the second six months' figure above.

4 Assume that debtors and creditors in the opening balance sheet of £45,000 and £30,000 respectively are received and paid in the first six months.

	1st period £	2nd period £
Workings – sales receipts		
Sales – see above	300,000	370,320
add Opening debtors	45,000	50,000
	345,000	420,320
less Closing debtors	50,000	60,000
	295,000	360,320
Workings – material payments		
Purchases – see above	80,000	97,600
add Opening creditors	30,000	14,000
	110,000	111,600
less Closing creditors	14,000	16,000
	96,000	95,600

John's cash budget for the year should now appear as follows:

John Storey
Cash budget for the year ended . . . .

		1st 6 months £	2nd 6 months £	Total £
Sales receipts	A	295,000	360,320	655,320
Payments:				
Direct material		96,000	95,600	191,600
Direct labour		66,000	82,860	148,860
Production overhead		60,000	71,260	131,260
Selling overhead		30,000	38,000	68,000
Administration overhead		24,000	30,000	54,000
Capital expenditure			5,000	5,000
Taxation			5,000	5,000
Drawings		10,000	10,000	20,000
	B	286,000	337,720	623,720
Surplus/(deficiency) A − B		9,000	22,600	31,600
Add Balance b/fwd		5,000	14,000	5,000
Balance at period end		14,000	36,600	36,600

John's cash budget looks healthy enough, although a finer break-down into months might indicate a period of cash inadequacy. As it is, there is a steady build-up of cash, and the financial manager should make forward arrangements to invest at least some of the surplus in short-term investments, so that this valuable resource can continue to make a contribution to profit until it is required for other purposes.

Self-check

The management accountant of the Cubic Rude Co. has been requested to produce a cash budget for the three months April to June as the company appears to be running into cash problems. The following data is produced for this purpose:

	February £	March £	April £	May £	June £	July £
Sales	100,000	120,000	130,000	100,000	150,000	160,000
Wages & salaries	20,000	21,000	21,000	22,000	21,000	22,000
Rent & rates		4,000	3,000		4,000	
Insurance				3,000		
Depreciation	3,500	3,500	3,500	3,500	3,500	3,500
Machine bought				40,000		
Tax paid	20,000					
Dividend paid		5,000				

Other information provided is as follows:

10% of sales were made for cash; 60% of the remainder of each month's sales being paid for in the following month, and the balance the month after that.

Direct materials represents 60% of the value of sales, and are purchased and paid for in the month before they are incorporated into the finished product and sold.

Other expenses are £2,000 fixed per month, plus 2% of sales, all paid for in the month following sale. Sales commission is 3% of sales paid a month in arrears.

The cash balance at the beginning of April is expected to be £12,000.

Required

1 Prepare the cash budget of Cubic Rude for the three months April to June inclusive.

2 What action would you take regarding Cubic Rude's planned cash position?

ANSWER

1 Working – sales receipts:

	April £	May £	June £
Sales – cash	13,000	10,000	15,000
– credit 60% of previous month	64,800	70,200	54,000
– credit 40% of two months ago	36,000	43,200	46,800
	113,800	123,400	115,800

Cubic Rude Co.
Cash budget for the three months April to June 19. .

		April £	May £	June £
Sales receipts	A	113,800	123,400	115,800
Purchases – materials		60,000	90,000	96,000
Wages and salaries		21,000	22,000	21,000
Rent and rates		3,000	—	4,000
Insurance		—	3,000	—
Other expenses – fixed		2,000	2,000	2,000
– variable		2,400	2,600	2,000
Sales commission		3,600	3,900	3,000
Machine		—	40,000	—
	B	92,000	163,500	128,000
Surplus/(deficiency) A–B		21,800	(40,100)	(12,200)
Balance b/fwd		12,000	33,800	(6,300)
Balance c/fwd		33,800	(6,300)	(18,500)

2 The company is running a deficiency in cash from May onward, partly due to the payment for the machine, but also because it prepays its materials in advance of increasing sales, but receives cash from those sales in arrears. However, if sales continue at their July level, and expenses do not materially alter, the position should reverse in the coming months. A chat with the bank manager to arrange an overdraft facility for the months of deficiency should cope with the situation.

Summarizing the plans – profit or loss?

None of the budgets already discussed stand in isolation. They all interlock, and the master profit and loss and balance sheet budgets are part of the total procedure. Many revisions will be made to first forecasts with consequent effects upon the whole plan. Only when the summarized profit and loss, and the final financial position evidenced in the balance sheet receive the approval of the management of the organization, will the budget procedure be complete.

The profit and loss budget for a manufacturing organization would essentially be in the form shown below:

Specimen profit and loss budget

	£	£
Sales		700,000
Cost of goods sold:		
Direct materials used	200,000	
Direct labour	180,000	
Production overhead	150,000	
	530,000	
add Work-in-progress – opening	60,000	
less Work-in-progress – closing	(80,000)	
Cost of production	510,000	
add Finished goods – opening	20,000	
less Finished goods – closing	(30,000)	500,000
Gross profit		200,000
Selling overheads	60,000	
Administration overheads	40,000	100,000
Net profit before tax		100,000
Taxation		50,000
Net profit after tax		50,000

Remember that the profit and loss budget does not measure receipts and payments. The total sales for a period, whether of goods or services, may include sales for which customers have not yet paid. Conversely, the cost of material used features in the profit and loss budget even though it is planned that it may not all have been paid for by the period end. Indeed, some of the material would be in stock at the commencement of the period, but may have been paid for in a previous period.

Activity

Using the information contained in the opening balance sheet of John Storey, and in the budgets prepared in Chapters 19 and 20, and at the commencement of this chapter, construct a budgeted profit and loss statement. Assume that work-in-progress was the same in value at the end of the period as at the commencement, and that profit is taxed at 50%. Use the format suggested in the specimen above.

Helpful hints:

1 The first four items can be extracted from the relevant budgets in Chapters 19 and 20.
2 Opening work-in-progress can be found in the opening balance sheet.
3 Finished stock – both opening and closing – is valued at the standard costs per unit shown in the opening section of Chapter 19, plus overhead at the budgeted rate of £2.7058 per hour (see answer to review **2(a)** on page 287). These standard costs are summarized below:

	Unit A		Unit B	
	£		£	
Direct material	80		50	
Direct labour	72		45	
Production overhead	(24 hours)	64.939	(15 hours)	40.587
	216.939		135.587	

The finished stock (quantities) can also be found in the introduction to Chapter 19.

4 Sales and administration overhead are as stated in the 'cash budget' section of this chapter.

SOLUTION

John Storey
Budgeted profit and loss account for the year to ....

		£
Sales		670,320
Cost of goods sold:	£	
Direct materials used	166,600	
Direct labour	148,860	
Production overhead	134,260	
	449,720	
add Work-in-progress – opening	5,000	
less Work-in-progress – closing	(5,000)	
Cost of production	449,720	
add Finished goods – opening	14,915	
less Finished goods – closing	(7,864)	456,771

Gross profit		213,549
Selling overhead	70,000	
Administration overhead	54,000	124,000
Net profit before tax		89,549
Taxation		44,774
Net profit after tax		44,775

Master balance sheet budget

John Storey's financial position at the commencement of the
budget year is revealed in the balance sheet at the commencement
of Chapter 19. Changes in that position are planned through all
the budgets of John Storey, and will culminate in a revised
financial position shown in the budgeted balance sheet.

Activity

Draw up John Storey's budgeted balance sheet at the end of
the budget year.
  Helpful hints:
1 Draw up your balance sheet in the same format as that
  used in the opening statement at the beginning of Chapter
  19.
2 John Storey's capital will, of course, have to be adjusted
  for the planned profit for the year, less cash withdrawn
  by him for personal use (see cash budget).
3 Start with the first item on your draft balance sheet, and
  ask yourself if any of the figures have been changed by the
  information available to you. For example, machinery has
  been purchased for £5,000, so add this to the pening
  'cost' figure. Add to the cumulative depreciation figures in
  the same way.
4 For cash, see the cash budget. Debtors and creditors can
  also be found in the same section.
5 For ending stocks, see the profit and loss budget and the
  direct materials budget.
6 Taxation in the opening balance sheet is planned to be
  paid during the budget year. The closing amount for
  taxation is to be found in the profit and loss budget.

ANSWER

John Storey
Budgeted balance sheet for the year to . . .

	Cost £	Depreciation £	Net value £
Fixed assets:			
Plant and machinery	85,000	19,000	66,000
Motor vehicles	20,000	10,000	10,000
	105,000	29,000	76,000
Current assets:			
Cash	36,600		
Stock – finished goods	7,864		
– work-in-progress	5,000		
– materials	30,000		
Debtors	60,000	139,464	
less Current liabilities:			
Creditors – supplies	16,000		
Taxation payable	44,774	60,774	
Working capital:			78,690
			154,690
Financed by:			
John Storey - opening capital		129,915	
add Profit for the year		44,775	
		174,690	
less Drawings		20,000	154,690

The plan in action

We have referred to budgeting as both a planning and a control technique. To a large extent Part 6 has dwelt upon the *planning* aspects, although control is an implicit element in the construction of budgets, for we are not only setting targets for future performance, but are also allocating resources in the most efficient way. More explicitly, the discussion on the use of *flexible* budgets in Chapter 20, and the review question at the end of that chapter, brought the two phases closer together.

As plans are implemented and operations proceed, the *control* phase comes into its own. Periodic reports to responsible managers provide them with the guidance needed to attain the original plan. With regard to a plan that is not subject to too much change, the control information will indicate that a 'touch of the accelerator' here, and a 'wee bit of braking' there, will keep the plan steadily on course.

When volatile changes in customer demand, resource cost or availability are the normal conditions faced by an organization, however, then planning and controlling, certainly in the short term, come face to face. Their juxtaposition is always more evident in times of rapid change and uncertainty.

To deal with swiftly changing conditions, a system of *'rolling' budgets* has been introduced by some firms. Figure 44 illustrates its operation. The long-range plan will be revised on a 'rolling' basis each year. That is, the plans for years 2 to 4 will be reviewed at the end of year 1, and a further year added. The annual short-term budget is determined in the usual way, but at each review date, say quarterly, a revised 'forecast' is produced for the remainder of the budget period plus a further quarter. Thus the plans are 'rolled' forward.

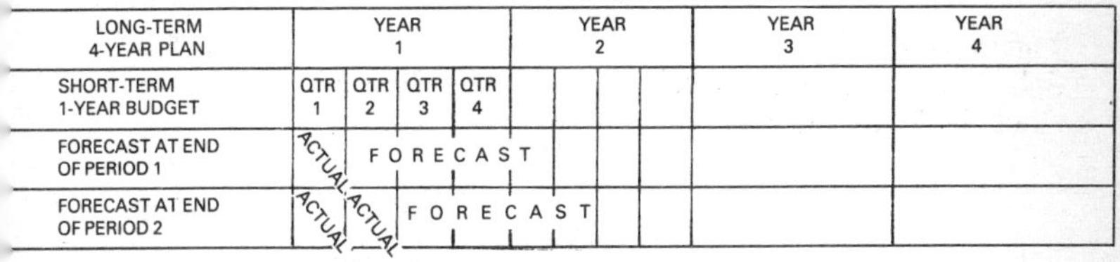

LONG-TERM 4-YEAR PLAN	YEAR 1				YEAR 2			YEAR 3	YEAR 4
SHORT-TERM 1-YEAR BUDGET	QTR 1	QTR 2	QTR 3	QTR 4					
FORECAST AT END OF PERIOD 1	ACTUAL	FORECAST							
FORECAST AT END OF PERIOD 2	ACTUAL	ACTUAL	FORECAST						

Figure 44. The 'rolling' budget

Control reports at each review date will show comparisons of actual, budget and forecast results, with a lot more credence being placed upon the comparison of actual with 'forecast' than actual with budget. The emphasis is upon *controlling the future* rather than the past. Rolling budgets can be justified on the grounds that:

- conditions can change drastically within a year, especially in times of high inflation, therefore pricing and other policies will need to be reviewed more frequently;

- an annual review is too limiting in rapidly changing conditions;
- budgets and standards tend to be set on the high side, when determined for a long period ahead.

Obviously, the periodic reviews cause additional analytical and clerical work, therefore one has to be fairly certain that the benefits from the system are worth its cost. Fortunately, the development of low-cost microcomputing facilities has brought the possibility of this more dynamic mode of control within the range of relatively small organizations.

One area that warrants particular attention in times of uncertainty is that of cash control. Even if a system of rolling budgets is thought not to be justified, a regularly updated cash forecast for say twelve months ahead, and reviewed and moved forward every month, is a 'must' for even the smallest business.

Review

1 The cash balance of the Acme Laundry Co. at 1 June is £23,000, and unpaid debtors amount to £148,000.

	Cash	*Credit*
Actual sales for April were	£20,000	120,000
Actual sales for May were	£30,000	140,000
Expected sales for June are	£25,000	136,000

Credit sales are paid for as follows:
    20% in the month of sale;
    50% in the month following sale;
    25% in the second month following sale;
     5% of debts are estimated to be bad.

Actual purchases for May were	£70,000
Expected purchases for June are	£80,000

Purchases are paid for as follows:
    80% in the month of purchase;
    20% in the month following purchase.

Other estimated cash payments for June are:

Salaries and wages	£50,000
Three months' rent paid in advance	£15,000
Other expenses	£10,000

There is a 10% loan outstanding of £100,000, upon which Acme have to pay a half-year's interest in June.

Required

(a) Prepare a cash budget for the month of June.

(b) Prepare a budgeted profit and loss account for Acme for June, assuming that:

  (i) purchases are all consumed in the month of purchase;

  (ii) interest is apportioned on a monthly basis.

(c) By reference to your answers to questions **(a)** and **(b)**, explain the difference between cash and profit.

(d) If a machine costing £50,000 was delivered and paid for in June, how would it affect the cash balance for that month, the profit and loss account, and the balance sheet?

2 Explain whether each of the following statements is true or false:

(a) A capital expenditure budget shows how production is to be financed next year.

(b) Once prepared, a budget can be compared quite safely with actual operations.

(c) A rolling budget is one revised periodically by adding a further period to the end, and dropping the period just ended.

(d) The cash balance at the end of a period should equal the profit for that period.

ANSWERS

1 (a)

Acme Laundry Co.
Cash budget for the month of June

	£	£
Sales receipts		
– cash	25,000	
– credit – 20% of current month	27,200	
– 50% of previous month	70,000	
– 25% of two months ago	30,000	
	———	152,200
Purchases		
– May – 20% of previous month	14,000	———
– June – 80% of current month	64,000	
	———	78,000

Salaries and wages	50,000
Rent (1 month only)	15,000
Other expenses	10,000
Interest on loan	5,000
Total payments	158,000

Estimated surplus/(deficiency) on the month	(5,800)
add Balance brought forward	23,000
balance carried forward	17,200

(b)   *Budgeted profit and loss account – June*

	£	£
Sales		161,000
less Purchases	80,000	
Salaries and wages	50,000	
Rent (1 month only)	5,000	
Other expenses	10,000	
Interest on loan	833	
		145,833
Profit for the month		15,167

(c) The fundamental difference between a cash flow statement and a profit and loss account is one of timing. Profit and loss accounts include all the sales for a period whether they have been paid for or not. Likewise, they include all *expenses incurred* in connection with that level of sales, whether or not those expenses have been paid. For example, cash paid for a machine is in the cash budget for the period in which it is paid. The value of the machine will, however, be charged to the profit and loss account by instalments over the period of its estimated life.

(d) The *cash balance* would be reduced by £50,000, that is, would turn the present surplus into a deficiency of £32,800. If the machine is brought into operation in June, an appropriate amount for depreciation is included in each month's *profit and loss account*.

In the *balance sheet*, the machine is added to the other fixed assets at cost, less the depreciation deducted for the month.

2 (a) False – this budget details the fixed assets to be purchased during the coming budget period.

(b) False – unless flexible budgets are used, radically changing circumstances will invalidate comparison with original budgets.

(c) True – the rolling budget provides an updated comparative with which to check current performance.

(d) False – the receipts and payment of cash do not necessarily coincide with the items included in the profit and loss account for the same period. This is partly due to the time lag caused by delayed payment by customers of their debts, and to suppliers who grant time to pay the amounts owing to them. As already stated, payment for machines and other fixed assets will almost always precede the appearance of those assets in the profit and loss account as depreciation.

Part 7
Selecting the right information for decision-making

22 | What are relevant costs?

Decisions and relevant costs

Decision-making is the process of deciding what action to take. This involves choosing between alternatives, if only to do, or not to do, a certain thing. In business terms, each alternative will have its own investment, cost and revenue implications, and will therefore require forecasts of the cost of any capital investment needed, together with any other costs to be incurred over the project life, and estimates of sales revenue if the latter is involved.

A decision will then be made and its implications incorporated into the long- or short-term plans of the organization. The plan is implemented, and as it proceeds actual costs and revenues are compared with budgets, and the information drawn from the comparison fed back into a further cycle of forecasts, decisions and plans.

Figure 45 depicts this decision and control cycle.

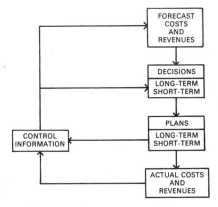

Figure 45. Decision and control cycle

Note that *past* costs in the form of 'actual costs and revenue', are only used for *control* purposes. Forecasts of the outcomes of further decisions will make use of past information, but only to assist in the determination of *future* costs and revenues.

Decision-making, therefore, concerns only *future* changes in cash flows resulting from the decision; *past* cash flows are so much 'water under the bridge'.

Harf Crankschafte, a well-known rally driver, is considering entering one of two alternative car rallies. Everyone agrees that he can win either event with certainty, such is his superiority in skill over his rivals.

He purchased his present car for £20,000 very recently, and has signed a contract for some structural changes to be made to it, which will cost a further £5,000.

He pays a full-time mechanic and assistant £10,000 per annum, and he also pays about £1,000 a year for other expenses including insurance.

Details of each rally are as follows:

	Paris	*Oslo*
	£	£
Cost of transport and hotels	3,000	4,500
Entry fees	200	300
First prize awarded to the winner	20,000	25,000

Before he decides which event to enter, he receives an invitation from French Television to commentate on the Paris rally instead of competing. He is offered a fee by them of £25,000 with all expenses paid. What decision should Harf make?

Before the alternative costs and rewards are considered, it will help if we lay down two guiding principles applicable to all decisions of this kind. These are:

- The costs relevant to any decision are those which cause changes in *future* cash flows. This implies that –
  - (a) costs incurred in the *past* are not relevant, for example machines already paid for;
  - (b) costs that will be incurred whether the decision is taken or not, that is, *committed costs*, are not relevant, for example agreements for services to be supplied.
- Decisions are between alternatives, if only to do, or not to do, a particular thing. Therefore, only the *differences* in costs

between alternatives are relevant. Costs common to both, such as the rent of a building to be used for either of two projects, are thus irrelevant.

Activity

Ignoring the television offer, show by using the relevant figures which rally Harf should enter.

ANSWER

Only *future* costs are relevant, therefore the amount already paid for the car is ignored. Further, the reconstruction of the car cannot be avoided, whichever decision is made, and is also irrelevant.

The cost of the full-time mechanic, £10,000, and the other £1,000 costs are fixed costs common to both, and can also be ignored.

The relevant figures are those that differ between the alternatives, and these are:

| | Paris | | Oslo | |
	£		£	
First prize		20,000		25,000
less Transport and hotel	3,000		4,500	
Entry fees	200	3,200	300	4,800
Surplus		16,800		20,200

The Oslo rally would appear to be the most profitable venture.

But what of the television opportunity? At £25,000 it seems too good an opportunity to miss, being better than the surplus on either of the rallies. The opportunity, if forgone, represents a cost to the other alternatives. The concept of *opportunity cost* is widely used in decision-making as a relevant cost in appropriate circumstances.

Applying the principle of opportunity cost to the choice of either Oslo or television, we have:

		£
First prize		25,000
less Transport, entry fees, etc.	4,800	
TV opportunity fees	25,000	29,800
Net loss		4,800

The loss indicates that Harf ought to choose TV on financial grounds, but a decision to go to Oslo might be taken for other than monetary reasons. Qualitatively, rallying might appeal to Harf more than commentating, and of course the rally could be one of a competition assessment series. Qualitative aspects arising in connection with decisions are those that are difficult to quantify but which exercise a considerable influence on the process of decision-making, as will be seen later in this chapter.

Self-check

1 Tom Smithson, builder and decorator, had repaired a customer's fence and was deciding how much to charge. He would have to cover his costs and then add a reasonable profit. He had used some timber boards of a kind that he stocked and used regularly on other jobs. They had cost him £70, but since he bought them their replacement price had increased to £90. What should he charge his customer for timber? Explain your decision.

2 Tom had painted the fence a bright green at the request of his eccentric customer. The paint had cost £10 some years ago, would never have been used on any other job, although he had recently been offered £3 for it. What should Tom charge for paint and why?

3 Tom was investigating the possibility of leasing one of two alternative micro computers on which to record his accounts and other information. Comparative costs were as follows:

	Model 'Orange' £	Model 'Captain' £
Machine rent per annum	500	400
Programs	500	500
Stationery cost per annum	300	400
Maintenance per annum	250	nil (provided free of cost by supplier)
Rent of room (this is part of the total rental on the building used by Tom in his business)	300	300

	Model 'Orange' £	Model 'Captain' £
Filing cabinets previously used for other purposes	100	100

There were no operating advantages between the two models.

Required

(a) Show by using the relevant costs which machine you think Tom should purchase.

(b) Are there any qualitative factors that might affect your choice?

ANSWERS

1 Tom should charge £90 as this is how much it would cost him to replenish his stock of timber boards at present. If he charged only £70, the original cost, he would not have sufficient cash to bring his stock back to its previous level.

2 The green paint had a disposal value of £3 if sold to another customer. This is therefore the opportunity cost of using it on his customer's fence and the amount to charge him.

3 (a) The relevant costs in each case are:

	Model 'Orange' £	Model 'Captain' £
Machine rental	500	400
Stationery	300	400
Maintenance	250	—
Total costs	1050	800

On a cost basis, model 'Captain' is the choice.

These are the *future* costs, and the ones that *differ between the alternatives*. Programs are the same in each case so are irrelevant to the choice of model. The filing cabinets are a *past* cost and can be ignored. The room rental is an already *committed* cost and need not be taken into account.

(b) Qualitative factors influencing the decision might include:
   (i) knowledge of other users' operating experience of each model;

(ii) the operating capabilities and flexibility of the programs;

(iii) whether the maintenance service offered under each option is prompt and reliable, given that the machine would become a vital part of running the business;

(iv) the comparative opportunities to extend the equipment.

Cost and profit relevant to volume

Charles Simon, managing director of the Cubic Rude Co. Ltd, and John Foster, the management accountant, had completed their discussion on the relative merits of the marginal costing and full costing methods of presenting periodic trading results (see Chapter 13). Mr Simon now understood the reasons for the profits being different when measured in the two alternative ways.

His new-found knowledge of the effect of cost behaviour on profit, and particularly the part played by 'contribution', had merely whetted his appetite however.

'Given that sales less variable costs provides contribution towards company fixed costs and profit, we ought to be able to calculate the expected profit at any level of sales. Total contribution minus fixed costs equals profit. Is that right John?'

'Absolutely,' replied John, delighted that Mr Simon was beginning to realize the value of accounting information. He pressed the matter further.

'One way of showing an instant picture of the relationship between costs and profit at different volumes of sales, is to construct a simple chart.'

He then sketched the graph shown in figure 46.

'Total costs and sales revenue are shown on the vertical axis, and sales volume in units on the horizontal,' he explained.

'Reading from the bottom of the chart, variable cost at £3 per unit increases in direct proportion to sales. Fixed costs of £380,000 then form a layer above and parallel with variable cost to give a line of total cost at any level of sales.

'If the sales function is then added, commencing at zero and increasing by £5 for each additional unit sold, the resultant sales line is seen to cross the total cost line. At this point, total sales equals total costs, there is neither profit nor loss, and it is known

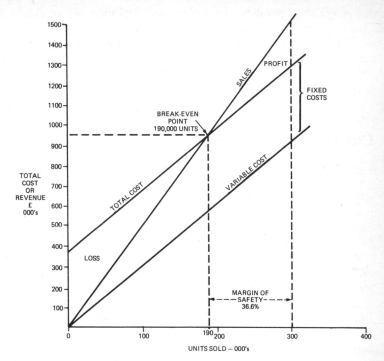

Figure 46. Volume, costs and profit chart

as the "break-even" point. Sales volumes below it result in a loss because costs are not all recovered, and volumes above it, a profit, because costs are more than recovered. The total profit or loss can be measured vertically between the sales and total cost lines at any volume of sales.'

The managing director nodded. 'That is very clear,' he said, and continued, 'in fact this chart shows more clearly than any profit and loss account can how the difference between sales value and variable cost, that is contribution, gradually recovers fixed costs and then beyond the break-even point provides the profit. Patently, knowledge of the "break-even" volume is very helpful, for it indicates the volume of sales that has to be attained before operations become profitable.'

'Exactly,' agreed John, 'and conversely it reveals how much

sales can fall from the current level before a loss is suffered. The "margin of safety", as it is called, measures this as a percentage of total sales – in our case $110 \div 300 = 36.6\%$.

'One must recognize that the chart has its limitations, however, the main one being that the linear assumptions of sales and costs are only applicable between the relevant range of activity. At very low levels, fixed costs would have to be reduced, whilst at higher levels of output, total fixed costs would increase. Variable costs might possibly decrease as suppliers allow quantity discounts for bulk purchases, but this might be countered by higher scrap costs and lower labour efficiency. For most practical purposes, however, the linear assumptions provide a useful representation of cost and revenue behaviour.'

John continued, 'Actually, the picture of contribution gradually "nibbling away" at fixed costs provides an indication of how the break-even point can be calculated without having to go to the trouble of drawing a chart. Fixed costs divided by contribution per unit gives the number of contributions, and thus products, required to recover the whole of the fixed costs.

'In our case this is $£380,000 \div 2 = 190,000$ units, or in terms of sales revenue, $190,000 \times £5 = £950,000$.

'Expressed in another way, the break-even point is where sales are equal to total costs, or $SX = VX + F$, where S = selling price, X is the break-even volume, V is the variable cost and F the fixed costs. Applying our figures gives:

$$
\begin{aligned}
5X &= 3X + 380,000 \\
5X - 3X &= 380,000 \\
2X &= 380,000 \\
X &= 190,000 \text{ units or £950,000 in sales revenue.}
\end{aligned}
$$

'Yet another way to calculate the break-even point expressed directly in sales value is to recognize the fixed relationship between contribution and sales value, known as the "contribution to sales ratio". In our case this is $2:5 = 40\%$. As break-even is attained when contribution recovers fixed costs, the latter must represent 40% of its break-even sales value. Thus:

$$
\text{Break-even point} = \frac{380,000}{.40} = £950,000.
$$

This can be proved as follows:

	£
Sales	950,000
less Variable cost –	
190,000 @ £3 per unit	570,000
Contribution	380,000
Fixed costs	380,000
Net profit	nil

John then managed to persuade Mr Simon to test his understanding of the previous discussion by completing the following activity.

Activity

Using the break-even formula $SX = VX + F$, and applying it to the Cubic Rude costs and price per product, calculate the sales volume required to realize a profit of £30,000.

Hint: sales must now cover profit as well as fixed and variable costs.

ANSWER

Extending the formula to embrace profit (P), we have:

$$SX = VX + F + P$$
$$5X = 3X + 380,000 + 30,000$$
$$5X - 3X = 410,000$$
$$2X = 410,000$$
$$X = 205,000 \text{ units or £5} \times 205,000 = £1,025,000 \text{ sales value.}$$

The more direct approach of dividing fixed costs and profit by contribution per unit gives:

$$\frac{380,000 + 30,000}{2} = 205,000 \text{ units.}$$

Applying the contribution to sales ratio method shows:

$$\frac{380,000 + 30,000}{.40} = \frac{410,000}{.40} = £1,025,000.$$

Flushed with his success in producing the correct answer, the managing director grew more enthusiastic about break-even analysis.

'We ought to be able to adopt this simple model of break-even to show the effects of any proposed change in policy or circumstance affecting costs, volume and profit,' he suggested.

'We can,' replied John. 'For example, our profit last year was £220,000, although we were looking for a target profit of £280,000. Figure 46 reveals that we ought to have sold 330,000 units, but we only sold 300,000. Assuming that we cannot increase the quantity sold, and that it will not change even if we increase our price, what price should we charge for each unit to realize our profit target?'

|| *Activity*
|| Work this problem through with Mr Simon.

SOLUTION

$$SX = VX + F + P$$
$$S \times 300,000 = (3 \times 300,000) + 380,000 + 280,000$$
$$S \times 300,000 = 1,560,000$$
$$S = \frac{1,560,000}{300,000}$$
$$S = £5.20$$

'Of course, we cannot ignore the possible effect on sales of increasing our selling price,' commented John.

'We will have to give that problem some thought,' agreed Mr Simon. 'One problem I do foresee, John, is the effect of introducing two more products next year. Surely this will change the structure of the break-even chart and the calculations?'

'It certainly will,' John replied. 'In fact, break-even calculations will have to be restricted to total sales value, as fixed costs will relate to all products. Given that we adopt a common contribution policy, however, this will cause no problem. If for example fixed costs increase to £500,000, but the contribution to sales ratio of 40% remains the same, the sales value break-even point will be:

$$\frac{500,000}{.40} = £1,250,000.$$

Self-check

1 The social secretary of the Norfolk Agrimek Sports Club was looking at the feasibility of running a dinner-dance. He estimated the costs as follows:

	£
Hire of club reception room (maximum number of people allowed – 500)	100
Hire of two groups	300
Printing 500 tickets	50
Posters	20
Novelties, balloons and prizes	30
Cost of dinner per head (only charged for those attending as long as one week's notice is given of the total number attending)	5
Wine per head (estimate)	1

Required

(a) If 500 people are expected to attend, what price should be charged for each ticket?

(b) If £10 were charged, (i) what number of people would have to attend to break even? (ii) Using the contribution to sales ratio approach, calculate the total value of ticket sales to break even.

2 To which of the following does the 'margin of safety' refer?

(a) The difference between sales value and variable cost;

(b) the difference between fixed costs and the break-even point;

(c) the difference between expected sales and the break-even point;

(d) the quantity required to break even.

ANSWERS

1 (a)
$$S \times 500 = F + (V \times 500)$$
$$S \times 500 = 500 + (6 \times 500)$$
$$S = \frac{3{,}500}{500}$$
$$S = £7$$

(b) (i)
$$10X = VX + F$$
$$10X = 6X + 500$$
$$10X - 6X = 500$$
$$4X = 500$$
$$X = 125$$

(b) (ii) Contribution to sales ratio $= \dfrac{10-6}{10} \times 100 = 40\%.$

Break-even value $= \dfrac{\text{fixed costs}}{\text{contribution/sales ratio}} = \dfrac{500}{.40} = £1,250.$

2 (c) the difference between expected sales and the break-even point.

Review

1 Frank Crane had recently been made redundant from his job as a carpenter and, because there was no other work available, had agreed to make a model yacht for the son of a friend of his. The agreement was that he would charge 'full cost' for the work. The following are the resources used to make the model:

(a) Plywood that had cost him £5 two years ago, but would cost £8 to replace now.
(b) A machine costing £400 a year ago. Depreciation is estimated at £3 for the period during which the yacht is to be made.
(c) Other wood to be purchased will cost £6.
(d) Other supplies needed would have to be withdrawn from another job on which he was working. They had originally cost £2, but would cost £4 to replace.
(e) Various fixtures that he could sell for only £2, but which had cost him £3 six months ago. He had no other use for them.
(f) Time spent in making the boat would be 12 hours. Other jobs upon which he was working currently were 'do-it-yourself' jobs around the house. His previous rate of pay was £2 per hour.
(g) Electricity used £1.
(h) He paid rent for his garage of £6 per week, but used it

as a workshop because he could not afford to run a car.

Required

How much should Frank charge his friend? Explain your treatment of each of the items above.

2 High Fly PLC trading results for last year were as shown in the following profit and loss account:

	£	£
Sales @ £6 per unit		480,000
less Direct material	140,000	
Direct labour	110,000	
Variable overhead	30,000	
Fixed overhead	80,000	360,000
Net profit		120,000

During that year High Fly worked at only 60% capacity. The managing director suggested that a reduction in price to £5.50 would increase the number of units sold by 50% next year. The reduction in price would, however, have to be supported by additional advertising costing £20,000.

Required

(a) Draw a break-even chart to show the effects of the proposal.

(b) Ascertain from your chart the profit at the expected sales level.

(c) Confirm your answer to (b) by drawing up a forecast profit and loss account.

(d) Read off your chart the break-even point of the proposal, and then check it by calculation.

(e) Should the managing director's proposal be implemented?

ANSWERS

1

Relevant costs of building the model yacht

	£	Explanation
Plywood	8	Replacement cost – past cost irrelevant
Other timber	6	To be purchased – future cash flow

	£	*Explanation*
Other supplies	4	Replacement cost for use on other work
Fixtures	2	Opportunity cost – past cost irrelevant
Electricity	1	To be purchased – future cash flow
	21	
Machine	—	Past 'sunk' cost. Does not affect future cash flow
Labour	—	Irrelevant – Frank would not be earning from his jobs around the house
Rent	—	An already committed cost

2 (a) Chart showing the effects of the managing director's proposal:

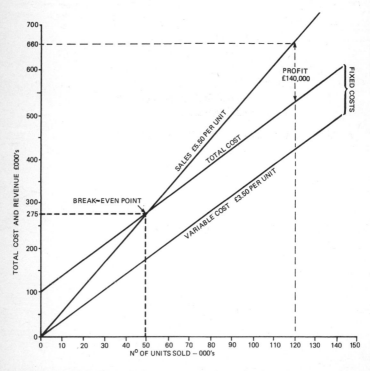

Figure 47. High Fly – volume, costs and profit chart

(b) £140,000.

(c)

Profit and loss account – forecast

		£
Sales 120,000 units @ £5.50 each		660,000
less Direct materials	210,000	
Direct labour	165,000	
Variable overhead	45,000	420,000
Contribution		240,000
Fixed costs (including additional advertising)		100,000
Net profit		140,000

(d) Break-even from chart 50,000 units, or £275,000 sales revenue. Calculation:

$$SX = VX + F$$
$$5.50X = 3.50X + 100,000$$
$$5.50X - 3.50X = 100,000$$
$$2.00X = 100,000$$
$$X = 50,000 \text{ units or } 50,000 \times £5.50$$
$$= £275,000 \text{ sales.}$$

(e) Yes – it increases net profit by £20,000.

23 | Making best use of existing capacity

Introduction

In the long term a business will plan to extend its production and selling facilities to meet an expected growth in demand for its products or services. However, the capital assets required in the form of land and buildings, plant and machinery, ships, aircraft, etc. can take a long time to construct or to deliver, and will be phased in to coincide with planned growth.

In the short term, therefore, the best possible use must be made of existing resources without compromising long-term goals, and in making decisions regarding their deployment particular attention must be paid to the notion of *relevant costs*.

Chapter 22, which dealt with relevant costs, also developed the important theme of *contribution*, by emphasizing the relationship between costs, volume and profit. Because fixed costs cannot be changed to any great extent in the short term, the contribution concept makes a considerable impact upon short-term decisions.

In this chapter we examine how best use can be made of limited capacity and what criteria to apply to the acceptance or rejection of additional work in the short term. Relevant costs and contribution loom large in our discussions.

Limiting factors and product mix

We all try to obtain the most from our limited resources, allocating our spending so as to maximize our satisfaction or 'utility' as economists refer to it.

Businesses experience similar constraints on the extent to which they can expand, at least in the short term, and therefore concentrate their limited resources on the mix of products or services that will recover all their fixed costs, and then add most value to the business in the form of profit. In other words, they plan to maximize contribution.

To illustrate, let us look at John Storey's double-glazing product costs and selling prices used in constructing the various budgets in Chapter 19. They show:

	Unit A	Unit B	Non-standard
	£	£	£
Selling price	315	210	252
Variable cost (approx.)	178	111	152
Contribution	137	99	100
Hours required per product	24	15	20
Sales forecast (units)	1,200	960	360

If we presume that the sales forecast indicated the absolute limit of the number of each product that could be sold, then sales demand is the factor that limits output. In the circumstances, as long as each product makes a contribution towards fixed costs and profit, it should be produced. This presumes, of course, that fixed costs will not change within the range of present output, and that all other costs continue to vary directly with volume of output.

On the other hand, if sales demand for each product is extensive, a higher total contribution can be attained by concentrating production in the first place on the product with the largest contribution per unit. In our example we would produce unit A until the demand for this product is satisfied, then non-standard units, followed by unit B. At least this would be the optimum plan if there were no factors limiting output.

Supposing, however, that skilled labour was in short supply and limited to a total of 42,000 hours. In order to maximize contribution now we have to concentrate production in turn upon the products yielding the highest contribution per hour.

Activity

(a) Calculate the contribution per labour hour for John Storey's products.
(b) Ignoring adjustment for stocks, how many of each product should be produced?
(c) What is the total contribution?

SOLUTION

(a)

	Unit A	Unit B	Non-standard	Total
Contribution	£137	£99	£100	
Hours per product	24	15	20	
Contribution per hour	£5.708	£6.60	£5.00	

(b)

	Unit A	Unit B	Non-standard	Total
Production (units)	1,150	960	nil	
Total hours required	1,150 × 24 = 27,600	960 × 15 = 14,400	nil	42,000 hrs

(c)

	Unit A	Unit B	Non-standard	Total
Contribution	1,150 × 137 = £157,550	960 × 99 = £95,040	nil	£252,590

Note that we choose to produce unit Bs first because they have the highest contribution per limiting factor; then unit As, but only up to the limit of remaining hours. We cannot totally satisfy the demand for unit A, and decide not to produce any non-standard units because they have the lowest contribution per hour.

However, a decision based solely upon limiting factor quantitative analysis may not optimize profit because:

- demand for products might be interdependent. For example, non-standard unit sales may depend mainly upon customers' orders for either unit A or B;
- closing down production on one or more products may encourage competitors to pick up the lost orders, or cause customers to believe that the business is not a reliable one to deal with;
- the shortage of capacity might be overcome by overtime working, subcontracting or shift-work.

Self-check

Details of five products manufactured by a company are as follows:

Product	Cost per unit	Variable cost per per unit	Selling price per unit	Production hours required per unit	Maximum demand in units
	£	£	£		
A	27.00	23.00	30.00	5	90
B	81.00	70.00	84.00	20	200
C	65.50	63.50	66.00	10	300
D	43.40	36.00	48.00	10	50
E	39.00	35.00	44.00	5 ·	150

Present factory capacity is 3,500 hours.
Fixed costs are £2,900.

Required

(a) Recommend a product mix to maximize profit.

(b) Would you recommend increasing capacity to 5,500 hours if fixed costs rise to £3,700?

ANSWER

(a)

Product	Contribution per unit	Hours per unit	Contribution per hour	Make	Total hours required
	£		£	Units	
A	7	5	1.40	90	450
B	14	20	0.70	90	1,800
C	2.50	10	0.25	—	—
D	12	10	1.20	50	500
E	9	5	1.80	150	750
					3,500

Note: demand for B is not completely satisfied, and C is not produced at all; these products have the lowest contribution per limiting factor.

(b)

Available hours will increase by 5,500 − 3,500 = 2,000 hours.

Quantity of additional Bs produced = $\dfrac{2,000}{20}$ = 100.

Additional contribution 100 × 14	= £1,400
less Increase in fixed costs £3,700 − £2,900	= £800
Net increase in contribution	£600

Additional capacity is worth installing.

Deciding whether to keep an activity going or close it down

This kind of decision follows on naturally from the previous section, for in the normal course of events products and services lose their customer appeal. Management of all organizations have therefore to be informed of the contribution being made by each activity to the achievement of overall goals. This applies equally to non-profit and to profit-based organizations.

For example, support for activities offered by sports centres need reviewing regularly in order to 'weed out' those using resources to little effect and replace them with facilities that will command more public support. Health authorities are having constantly to review the wide range of facilities offered by some hospitals in rural areas, and are inclined towards a policy of more centralization of services. In maternity care, for example, the benefits of maintaining a comprehensive local service may not be worth the cost of doing so.

Commercial concerns will normally adopt a sensible long-term policy of introducing new products to replace established ones, when the contribution from the latter begins to wane. However, this usually requires a much wider appraisal of the additional investment involved as well as cost and sales cash flows. We look at the implications of investment appraisal in the next chapter.

In the short term a business should continue to include in its product range only those products which make a contribution towards fixed cost and profit.

Activity

The Ajax Pottery Co. Ltd manufacture and sell a range of six ceramic products. The total sales, costs and profits for the last six months are as follows:

————————————— £000s —————————————

	Sugar bowl	Milk jug	Condiment set	Vase	Thimble	Fruit dish	Total
Sales	10	12	11	19	4	22	78
Variable costs	4	13	3	6	3	4	33
Fixed costs	2	2	2	3	3	3	15
Net profit/(loss)	4	(3)	6	10	(2)	15	30

It is proposed to discontinue the milk jug and thimble because they appear to be unprofitable. As the firm's management accountant, advise the managing director.

Hint: the central question to ask is, Does each product make a contribution?

SOLUTION

In order to make a meaningful decision the profit and loss statement should be redrafted as follows:

	Sugar bowl	Milk jug	Condi-ment set	Vase	Thimble	Fruit dish	Total
				£000s			
Sales	10	12	11	19	4	22	78
Variable costs	4	13	3	6	3	4	33
Contribution/ (loss)	6	(1)	8	13	1	18	45
Less fixed costs							15
Net profit							30

It can now be seen quite clearly that all the products make a contribution to fixed costs and profit, excepting the milk jug. As the selling price of the jug is less than its variable cost it should be discontinued. This would increase total contribution to £46,000, and net profit to £31,000. Note that the allocation of fixed costs does not change their total.

Activity

What factors might deter you from withdrawing the milk jug from the product range?

SOLUTION

The jug may be retained in the product range if:

• The sugar bowl and milk jug are complementary products. Withdrawal of the jug could reduce the sugar bowl sales and lose more contribution than is saved by not making the jug.
• The selling price of the jug could be raised or variable costs lowered.
• The reduction in the product range might lead to increased competition by encouraging a competitor to extend his range of products.

Self-check

Norfolk Agrimek PLC produce a variety of agricultural and horticultural machines. The following are the sales, costs and profits for each of the production centres:

	Motor mowers	Small hand tools	Small motor implements	Spares	Mini-tractors	Total
			£000s			
Sales	600	230	500	300	370	2,000
Variable costs	340	200	290	290	260	1,380
Departmental fixed costs	30	40	10	20	20	120
General fixed cost	10	20	10	20	20	80
Net profit/(loss)	220	(30)	190	(30)	70	420

Required

1 Based purely on the figures summarized above, show whether you would close down the small hand tools and spares departments.
2 If the spares department were to be closed down, the motor mower department would lose 5% of its current sales. Does this affect your decision in 1?
3 What other action might you take and why?

ANSWERS

1 The profit statement should be reconstructed to show the contribution being made by each department.

	Motor mowers	Small hand tools	Small motor implements	Spares	Mini-tractors	Total
			£000s			
Sales	600	230	500	300	370	2,000
Variable costs	340	200	290	290	260	1,380

			£000s			
Departmental fixed costs	30	40	10	20	20	120
Departmental contribution	230	(10)	200	(10)	90	500
General fixed costs						80
Net profit						420

Based upon the figures shown, both the small hand tools and the spares departments should be closed down, as neither is making a contribution.

2 Closing the spares department results in a loss of 5% of motor mower sales, i.e. 5% × (£600 − 340) = £13 in contribution. As this loss is greater than the £10 gain from closing the spares department, the latter should be left open. Another reason for not closing this department is that all other departments will depend upon a reliable spares service. If it ceased to exist within the firm, the turnover of other departments could suffer.

3 Other action that could be taken includes:
   (a) Increasing the selling prices of products, and reducing variable and fixed costs.
   (b) Close the small hand tools department and expand one or all of the remaining profitable products in its place.
   (c) Spend more on marketing to stimulate sales.

Should we ever reject orders?

The answer to this question depends upon the comparative contributions from the alternative use of resources.

Given full capacity working, and if a potential customer's order cannot be delayed or subcontracted, the decision will rest upon whether a contribution is realized after taking into account not only the sales revenue and related variable costs but also the opportunity cost (i.e. contribution foregone) associated with the alternative use of resources.

For example, if a bus company received separate enquiries for the hire of their last available forty-seater coach on the same day, the one yielding the highest contribution would be accepted. The comparison would be as follows:

		£
Hire of coach to Jones Brothers		200
less Variable cost	100	
Opportunity cost of other inquiry	70	170
Excess contribution over alternative		30

If a firm is not using all its capacity, then additional work should be undertaken so long as the price received covers the additional cost incurred in producing that work.

Activity

The manager of the Hotel Continental was concerned about the reduction in the number of guests staying at his hotel during the past year. This had resulted in a decrease in profit. One of his problems was that he had to maintain a full establishment of staff and services even when the number of guests was minimal. This was particularly so at weekends.

As part of his effort to stimulate trade, he was looking into the possibility of offering 'away weekends' at reduced prices. The average costs incurred per guest per day currently were:

	£ p
Food and beverages	4.50
Labour	3.00
Laundry and cleaning	.40
Heat and light (50% variable)	.50
Depreciation	.60
Other fixed costs	2.00
	11.00

What is the minimum that could be charged per guest for a two-day weekend?

SOLUTION

The costs incurred for each guest would be:

	£ p
Food and beverages	4.50
Laundry and cleaning	.40
Heat and light	.25

$$2 \times \qquad\qquad 5.15 = £10.30 \text{ for two days}$$

Any price charged over £10.30 would contribute towards the remaining fixed costs, and would be determined largely by competing prices at other hotels.

From this last example it can be seen that a firm is able to charge different prices for the same product subject to the following conditions:

- that the products are being supplied to different markets. In the above example, only weekend guests received the benefit of favourable terms. Another well-known differential pricing example is the cheap rail ticket at off peak times;
- that it will not have a depressive effect upon other prices, or affect demand for the remaining products;
- that the price at least covers differential costs plus a contribution towards fixed costs;
- that there is no possibility of other work with a higher contribution becoming available during the same period.

Differential pricing is used in times of trade recession to hold skilled labour and keep capacity occupied, and might also be used as a trading tactic to attract larger orders in the future – 'a sprat to catch a mackerel' as it were.

Self-check

1 A business should always charge 'full cost' for its products, otherwise it will lose money. True or false?
2 In deciding whether to accept one of two mutually exclusive orders, the one contributing the highest selling price should be chosen. True or false?

ANSWERS

1 False – when a business is not working to full capacity, it should consider accepting orders at prices that at least cover variable cost and provide some contribution. It will lose more money

by not doing so. This policy is subject, however, to the understanding that a separate market is being served, and that the
prices charged will not have a detrimental effect upon future
sales and prices.

2 False – the order offering the higher contribution, that is, the
difference between selling price and variable cost, should be
chosen. The contribution forgone on the order not taken up
is an opportunity cost of the one accepted. For example, if the
selling prices and variable costs of two competing orders were
as follows:

	A	B
	£	£
Selling price	10	9
Variable cost	8	6
	2	3

B is chosen because it has the higher contribution. Its selling
price and costs can be depicted as follows:

	£	£
Selling price		9
less Variable cost	6	
Opportunity cost A	2	8
Differential contribution		1

Sell now or process further?

This is a problem frequently met with in processing industries,
where the single output from a process or the joint products from
an initial process can be sold at that stage or processed further.
For example, a textile company can sell yarn or weave it into
cloth.

If capacity for the further processing required already exists,
the decision rests upon the difference between incremental revenue
and incremental cost. Past costs are irrelevant to the further
processing decision.

For example, a joint process with total costs of £30,000 produces
two products: one, a varnish, and the other a cleaning fluid, which
can be sold for £25,000 and £20,000 respectively at that stage.

Joint costs allocated to each product are £18,000 and £12,000 respectively. The profit on disposal of the joint products would be £45,000 − £30,000 = £15,000.

Supposing the cleaning fluid could be put through a further process that would convert it into a high-octane fuel. The additional processing and selling costs would be £30,000, and fuel could ultimately be sold for £45,000. Should the cleaning fluid be converted into fuel?

Firstly, the joint costs are past costs, and therefore irrelevant to the 'process further' decision. The relevant revenue and costs to use are:

	£
Sales value as fuel	45,000
less Sales value as cleaning fluid	20,000
Incremental revenue	25,000
less Incremental 'further processing' costs	30,000
Differential loss	5,000

The cleaning fluid should not be converted, because the *additional* sales value received is less than the *additional* costs incurred in processing further.

Should the additional processing require further investment in the form of buildings and plant, the decision is then based upon whether the differential income from further processing yields a satisfactory return on the capital invested. This is dealt with in the following chapter.

Self-check

In a meat-processing factory, the joint costs allocated to a ton of pie meat are £20. As pie meat it can be sold for £30. If processed into finished pies, however, the additional labour, ingredients and preparation costs will amount to £45, and the pies can then be sold for £80. Is it worth making and selling pies, or should the pie meat be sold without further processing?

ANSWER

Ignore the allocated joint costs – these are *past* costs and therefore irrelevant to the *further processing* decision.

	£
Sales value of pies	80
less Sales value of pie meat	30
Incremental revenue	50
less Incremental processing costs	45
Differential revenue	5

Pie-making yields an additional £5 net revenue over selling as pie meat, therefore process further.

Should we make it or buy it?

At first sight this appears to be a very simple decision. If it costs less to make, why buy it? It is that little word 'cost' that 'puts the cat amongst the pigeons' every time!

A dentist may enjoy painting his house, and of course the quality of enjoyment cannot be ignored in making decisions – especially decisions of a domestic nature. When one considers the opportunity cost, however – his professional hourly earnings rate – it would benefit him financially to employ a decorator.

A decision to make or buy is basically a cost decision, but is influenced by the availability of capacity and quite possibly by other qualitative factors.

If a business has capacity but it is under-utilized, the comparison will be between the variable cost of making and the 'buying-in' price.

Activity

Ace Electronics purchase a component that is incorporated into the control instrument that they make and sell. The supplier charges £50 for each component. Ace are currently working at 60% capacity, and this condition looks as though it will last for a year or so. The management accountant submits the following costs of making the component internally.

	£
Direct materials	30
Direct labour	20

	£
Indirect variable manufacturing	10
Indirect fixed manufacturing	5
Selling and administration	5
	—
	70

Skilled workers who have been retained, but who are not fully occupied on productive work, could make these components. 20% of selling and administration cost is variable.

Should Ace make the component or buy it?

SOLUTION

The relevant costs are:

	£
Direct materials	30
Indirect variable manufacturing	10
Selling and administration	1
	—
	41

Direct labour, fixed manufacturing and 80% of selling and administration costs are all incurred whether or not the component is manufactured internally, and are therefore irrelevant.

As the cost of making – £41 – is less than buying – £50 – the decision should be to make.

When capacity is being fully utilized and cannot be increased in the short term, work will probably have to be subcontracted to other firms. In these circumstances, make or buy decisions will draw upon the following principles:

- Make those products that cannot be purchased.
- Ignore selling prices – they will normally be the same in both cases.
- Ignore fixed costs – they will be incurred anyway.
- Include all the *incremental* costs of making.
- The aim of the decision should be to maximize *contribution*.
- Buy those products that show the least excess of purchase price over incremental cost *per unit of limiting factor*.

The following example illustrates how the decision is made:

Product		A	B	C	D
Labour hours per unit	**1**	3	4	5	6
Machine hours per unit	**2**	5	3	4	3
		£	£	£	£
Incremental cost of making per unit		15	20	25	30
Purchase price per unit		30	18	45	42
Excess of buy over make cost (*or the gain from making*)	**3**	15	−2	20	12

Excess cost per unit of limiting factor:

		A	B	C	D
Labour hours (divide line **1** into line **3**)		5	−.5	4	2
Machine hours (divide line **2** into line **3**)		3	−.67	5	4

The decision will then be:

1 Buy B – it costs less to buy than to make.
2 Where labour is the limiting factor: buy D; then C; then A – according to capacity available.
3 Where machine hours are the limiting factor: buy A; then D; then C – according to capacity available.

In each case it will be seen that the largest gain is realized by making those products that show the largest excess of 'buy' over 'make' cost per unit of limiting factor.

If we are already working capacity to the full, but require more, we may be able to extend it by:

- overtime working;
- shift working; or
- by investing in additional production capacity in the form of new machines, buildings, etc.

Whichever option we choose to extend the available production facilities, we compare the costs of doing so with the cost of buying as discussed above. More will be said about this in the following chapter.

Most decisions of the 'make' or 'buy' variety are influenced just as much by qualitative as by quantitative factors. In favour of making these will include:

- a desire to retain a skilled labour force, who might otherwise leave if there were no work for them;
- a desire to control quality;
- a need to ensure continuity of supply;
- a desire to retain the secrecy of a process;
- the possibility that a supplier may change his prices later.

Self-check

State, and briefly explain, whether each of the following statements is true or false:

(a) The make or buy decision is basically one of comparing the incremental costs of the alternatives.

(b) If a decision to make involved the addition of another supervisor, the latter's salary would be included as a relevant cost.

(c) Qualitative factors may be just as influential as quantitative ones in make or buy decisions.

(d) When there is a limiting factor in production it will pay to buy those products that show the greatest excess of 'buy' over 'make' cost.

ANSWERS

(a) *True* – all costs that are already incurred are ignored, and we take account of 'out-of-pocket' costs only.

(b) *True* – this would be an incremental cost. It would not be incurred if the decision was not taken.

(c) *True* – and especially those concerned with management control such as quality.

(d) *False* – those products showing the *smallest excess* of buy over make costs will be bought first. Thus we make those products that are *relatively* cheap.

Review

1 Fashion Shoes PLC manufacture and sell five styles of shoes. Each style is made in a separate department. The selling prices, costs and other information relating to each style are given below:

	Contour	Glide	Softie	Hi-Back	Lilo
	£	£	£	£	£
Selling price	30	18	14	25	22
Variable costs – material	8	4	8	6	6
Variable costs – labour	2	6	4	8	4
Departmental fixed costs	2	4	4	3	2
General fixed costs	4	5	3	4	3
Total costs	16	19	19	21	15
Net profit/(loss)	14	(1)	(5)	4	7
Forecast demand (pairs) for next year	10,000	8,000	6,000	5,000	3,000

Labour can easily be switched from one department to another should demand require it, but there will be only 48,000 labour hours available next year. Labour is paid at £2 per hour.

Required
(a) Produce a statement showing the contribution made by each style of shoe.
(b) Would you continue to produce all five styles based upon the information revealed in (a)?
(c) Given the labour hours constraint, which models would you produce, and in what quantities?
(d) Are there any other factors that might influence your decisions in (b) and (c)?

2 The Unique Hair-Dryer Company is approached by a mail-order business which offers to purchase 30,000 dryers at £1.70 each, to be marketed under its own name and sold solely to mail-order customers.

Unique is at present only working at 60% capacity, and its trading results for the recently completed year were as follows:

	£	£
Sales (60,000 dryers) £2 each		120,000
less Direct materials	45,000	
Direct labour	30,000	
Variable production cost	12,000	
Fixed production cost	36,000	123,000
Gross loss		(3,000)

	£	£
less Variable selling costs	6,000	
Fixed selling costs	12,000	
Variable administration costs	9,000	
Fixed administration costs	3,000	30,000
Net loss		(33,000)

The mail-order firm will collect and pack the dryers, so there will be no variable selling costs. Variable administration will increase by £1,000, whilst other variable costs will be in the same proportions to sales quantity as in the above trading statement.

Required
(a) Should the order be accepted? Show your supporting workings.
(b) What other factors would you consider?
(c) One of the components on the dryer can be bought for 50 pence, but it is made internally at present at the following cost:

	pence
Direct materials	20
Direct labour	25
Fixed production costs	10
	55

Would you continue making or would you switch to buying?
(d) Would your answer to (c) be different if you were working at full capacity?

ANSWERS

1 (a)

	Contour	*Glide*	*Softie*	*Hi-Back*	*Lilo*
	£	£	£	£	£
Selling price	30	18	14	25	22
Variable costs	10	10	12	14	10
Departmental fixed cost	2	4	4	3	2
Contribution	18	4	(2)	8	10

(b) The Softie shoe is losing contribution, and on this count alone should be discontinued.

(c) To answer this question we have to calculate the contribution per limiting factor on all but the Softie shoe:

	Contour £	Glide £	Hi-Back £	Lilo £
Contribution	18	4	8	10
Number of hours per product (variable labour ÷ £2)	1	3	4	2
Contribution per hour	18	1.30	2	5
Demand (pairs)	10,000	8,000	5,000	3,000

Decide to make Contour first, then Lilo, then Hi-Back, then Glide, until all the available hours are exhausted:

	Hours per pair	Total hours
Make 10,000 Contour	1	10,000
„ 3,000 Lilo	2	6,000
„ 5,000 Hi-Back	4	20,000
„ 4,000 Glide	3	12,000
		48,000

(d) Other factors to consider in this decision are:

(i) Will the dropping of Softie from the product range be taken as a sign of failure by retailers and other customers?

(ii) Can the selling price or costs of Softie be improved, to turn the loss into a contribution?

(iii) Can labour hours be extended by working overtime?

(iv) If labour efficiency was improved this would lower the cost of labour and improve the contribution per limiting factor.

(v) Are there any other shoe styles being developed that will offer a higher contribution?

2 (a)

	£	£
Net loss before acceptance of proposed order		33,000
less Additional sales revenue 30,000 × £1.70	51,000	

	£	£
less Additional costs		
Production variable costs –		
30/60 × £87,000	43,500	
Variable administration	1,000	44,500
Incremental income		6,500
Net loss after acceptance of proposed order		26,500

The order should be accepted because it reduces the current loss.

(b) Other factors to take into account:

(i) Will this order have an adverse effect upon the existing price and sales to present customers? It ought not, because the dryers are being sold in a distinct and separate market.

(ii) Is there any other work available which might provide a higher contribution?

(iii) Is the existing operation worth continuing? The current position shows:

	£
Sales (at 60% capacity)	120,000
less Variable costs	102,000
Contribution	18,000
If the company worked at full capacity the additional contribution would be	
40/60 × £18,000	12,000
	30,000
less Fixed costs	51,000
Net loss	21,000

The business is obviously fundamentally unsound, and the additional mail-order business will not change that.

(c) As the variable cost of making – 45 pence – is less than the buying-in price of 50 pence, the decision should be to continue making.

(d) If the company was working at full capacity, the alternative use to which the hours being utilized by the component could be put must be considered as an opportunity cost. For example, if those hours could yield a contribution of 10 pence, the total cost of making would be $45 + 10 = 55$ pence, against 50 pence if bought in. The decision in **(c)** would now be reversed and the component would be purchased from outside.

24 | Relevant costs and long-term decisions

Introduction

In the previous chapter we looked at various short-term problems concerned with utilizing *existing* resources to best advantage. In each case the solution depended crucially upon selecting the relevant costs and revenues.

Relevance continues to be a central theme of this chapter, in which we consider the longer-term decisions which stem from the strategic planning of an organization.

Having decided upon its products and the markets in which it plans to sell them, a business must make major decisions about how to produce them, how to distribute them and at what prices to sell them. Consideration of pricing is left until the last section of this chapter.

If facilities already exist, we may consider using them more intensively by shift-working or overtime. We look at the costs relevant to extending existing resources later in the chapter.

When new or extensive additions to existing productive resources are required, however, large initial capital spending will be incurred. Hopefully, this will be followed by an inflow of cash that will more than replace the initial capital outlay.

How the capital expenditure is to be financed is not the concern of this book, although we do need to know how much the finance will cost, in the same way as a person buying a house on mortgage needs to know the interest rate he will have to pay on his outstanding loan.

Salient features of investment appraisal

Apart from the initial requirement to sink large volumes of cash into long-term investments, the most obvious difference between short- and long-term problems is that of time.

You saw in the last chapter that the aim of short-term decisions is to maximize contribution, either during a temporary period of under-capacity working or until additional capacity can be provided. There was no capital outlay to recover, so we only had to examine the other relevant costs and revenues.

Investment projects are normally for much longer periods, however, requiring forecasts of the cash expected to flow from the investments during their anticipated lives. For example, if a haulage contractor is evaluating the purchase of an additional lorry, he will prepare forecasts of the estimated useful life of the vehicle, of the cash expected to be received each year from additional customers, less the cash to be paid for additional running costs. The cash flow projections could cover a five- to ten-year period.

The essence of every investment decision is that funds otherwise available for consumption are committed to a project in the expectation that they will be recovered intact over the life of the project, together with a reasonable additional amount of value to compensate for the waiting period and the risk involved. For example, if you invest £1,000 in a 10% one-year bond, you do so in the expectation of receiving your £1,000 back in a year's time together with £100 interest. If the same £1,000 is put into a 12% five-year bond, you will look forward to the return of your £1,000 in five years' time, but because you are locking your money away for a longer period at perhaps greater risk, you expect to receive a higher rate of interest each year.

Investments in productive assets, for example machinery and vehicles, as against financial assets such as bonds and shares, are different only in that the initial sum invested is recovered *during* the expected life of the project, rather than at the end. Because risks are normally greater in manufacturing and selling, businessmen expect to receive a higher rate of interest on their investments.

In summary then, the main factors to consider when assessing the worthwhileness of any investment project are:

- the initial capital outlay;
- the expected life of the project;
- the cash inflows and outflows generated by the project during its useful life;
- the expected rate of return, which will largely be related to the risk associated with the type of project being undertaken.

One pound is worth more now than in one year's time

If you were offered the alternative of being paid £1 now or £1 in one year's time, there is little doubt what your choice would be. For, apart from the risk of having to wait a year for the same sum available now, if you were to receive and invest your pound now, it would grow to £1.10 in one year at 10% interest. Thus you may possibly be indifferent between £1 now and £1.10 in a year's time, with an interest rate of 10% per annum.

Further, you would be equally indifferent between £1 now and £1.21 in two years' time, for this is the sum to which £1 grows if invested for two years at 10% compound interest. This can be calculated:

	£
Invested now	1.00
10% interest end year 1	.10
Sum at end of year 1	1.10
10% interest end year 2	.11
Compound sum at end of year 2	1.21

This can be written as an equation:

$$A = P \times (1 + i) \times (1 + i)$$

where A = the sum received at a future date, P = the amount invested now, i = the rate of interest, n = the number of years hence a sum is receivable. Or:

$$A = P(1 + i)^n$$

or:

$$\frac{A}{(1 + i)^n} = P.$$

In the example above:

$$A = 1(1 + .10) \times (1 + .10)$$
$$A = 1(1 + .10)^2$$
$$A = 1.21$$

or:

$$\frac{1.21}{(1+.10)^2} = 1.$$

From the above it can be seen that an equivalent *present value* can be calculated for any sum receivable in the future, assuming an appropriate rate of compound interest.

Activity

Given that:

$$P = \frac{A}{(1+i)^n}$$

where P = present value, A = amount receivable in n years' time, i = the rate of interest, n = the number of years hence, calculate to three places of decimals the equivalent present value of £1 receivable at the end of one, two and three years at 10% compound interest.

SOLUTION

One year	*Two years*	*Three years*
$P = \dfrac{1}{(1+.10)} = .909$	$P = \dfrac{1}{(1+.10)^2} = .826$	$P = \dfrac{1}{(1+.10)^3} = .751$

In each of the above three cases we are saying that, at 10% compound interest, the present values are the equivalent of £1 receivable at the end of one, two and three years respectively.

Activity

Show that £0.751 invested now at 10% compound interest per annum for three years amounts to £1 in three years' time.

SOLUTION

	£
Invested now	.751
10% interest end year 1	.0751
	———
Sum at end year 1	.8261
10% interest end year 2	.08261
	———

	£
Sum at end year 2	.90871
10% interest end year 3	.090871
Sum at end year 3	.999581

Note that the sum is not quite £1 at the end of year three because £0.751 is only an approximation of present value.

Tables have been constructed, giving the present value of £1 for *n* years at progressive rates of interest, and they can be a very useful aid in the evaluation of investment projects.

The present value concept applied to investment decisions

Imagine that you had recently inherited a legacy of £30,000 and had the opportunity of investing it to yield £3,000 per annum for five years. A friend of yours offers you the alternative of investing it with him, in return for which you would receive £47,000 at the end of five years. Assuming that you consider a rate of return of 10% per annum to be acceptable in both cases, which investment would you choose?

The present values of £1 in 1–5 years at 10% are given below:

Year	1	2	3	4	5
	.909	.826	.751	.683	.621

Comparison of the alternatives shows:

				Present values	
	1st	*2nd*	*PV*	*1st*	*2nd*
Year	*alternative*	*alternative*	*factor*	*alternative*	*alternative*
	£	£	£	£	£
1	3,000	—	.909	2,727	—
2	3,000	—	.826	2,478	—
3	3,000	—	.751	2,253	—
4	3,000	—	.683	2,049	—
5	33,000	47,000	.621	20,493	29,187
	45,000	47,000		30,000	29,187
	less capital invested			30,000	30,000
	Net present value			nil	(813)

Although the total cash inflow in the second alternative is greater than the first over the five-year period (£47,000 against £45,000) the former's delayed cash return results in a present value that is less than the £30,000 cash invested. This implies that it yields a return of something less than 10%, and is therefore not acceptable. On the other hand, the first alternative just 'pays its way' – returning the initial £30,000 investment, *plus 10% return on the outstanding capital* in each year.

This approach to appraising investments is known as the 'Discounted cash flow net present value' method. In summary, its results imply that where a project has a net present value (NPV) equal to or greater than zero, then it could be acceptable; but where the NPV is negative, the project should be rejected.

The approach recognizes the time value of money by applying a discounted value to future cash flows, and it is important to recognize that it is *cash flows* that are 'discounted', and not 'costs' and 'revenues' as measured and used in the profit and loss account. Thus depreciation does not feature as a cash flow, because the asset that it represents is included in investment cash flows *in the year in which it is paid*. Likewise costs such as materials are included when they are paid for not when they are incurred. Sales revenue is included when customers actually pay, and not when sales are made, which might be some time previously.

In judging what are the cash flows relevant to an investment decision, the basic rule is 'include all cash flows that result because the decision is made'. This excludes the cost of buildings already owned and occupied, or the rent if not owned. Apportionment of overhead by using a total overhead absorption rate is also inappropriate. Only *additional* overhead cash flows caused by the project are included; for example, a new supervisor appointed to specifically manage a particular project.

Inevitably, taxation will affect investment decisions. For example, the cost of machinery and plant can be set off against the profits of a business in the year in which the machinery is operational. This reduces the taxation payable by the business by an amount equal to the taxation rate payable multiplied by the value of the asset purchased. A further feature of taxation particularly important in NPV calculations is that it has a delayed impact of at least one year, because the taxation is not payable until after the year's profits are determined.

For example, the cash flows for a machine costing £1,000,

generating net cash inflows of £500 in each of three years, with a tax rate of say 50%, would be shown as follows:

Year	Cash flows £	Taxation £	Net £
1 – beginning	(1,000) – machine		(1,000)
1 – end	500		500
2	500	{ 500 (machine) (250)	750
3	500	(250)	250
4	—	(250)	(250)

Notice that the 100% allowance on the machine is delayed by one year, as is the tax payable on the net cash inflows. The tax for year 3 is properly included in year 4, as long as the business as a whole is profitable and therefore tax is payable.

Activity

The Xpres Printing Company is considering the replacement of one of its machines by a more up-to-date model which would cost £20,000. It is claimed by the manufacturers of the machine that its efficiency would save Xpres £3,000 a year for the next four years, after charging depreciation of £5,000 per annum. At the end of four years the suppliers would be prepared to allow £2,000 as a trade-in value against a further new machine.

Assume that the Corporation Tax rate is 50%, and that the machine attracts a 100% tax allowance in the year in which it is installed. The company looks for a rate of return on its investments of 16% per annum, and the appropriate present value factors of £1 are:

Year	1	2	3	4	5
	.862	.743	.641	.552	.476

(a) Should Xpres purchase the machine?
(b) What other factors would influence your decision?

SOLUTION

(a) Calculation of the NPV resulting from the purchase of the machine is as follows. Note how the purchase of the machine

is shown as a cash outflow in year 0, that is at the commencement of year 1:

Year	Machine	Cost savings	Taxation	Net cash flows	Discount factor @ 16%	Present value
	£	£	£	£	£	£
0	(20,000)			(20,000)	1.000	(20,000)
1		8,000		8,000	.862	6,896
2		8,000	10,000			
			(4,000)	14,000	.743	10,402
3		8,000	(4,000)	4,000	.641	2,564
4	2,000	8,000	(4,000)	6,000	.552	3,312
5			(1,000)			
			(4,000)	(5,000)	.476	(2,380)

Net present value   794

The machine shows a marginally positive NPV, therefore
should be purchased. Note how the high discount rate reduces
the present value of future cash flows considerably.

(b) However, other factors, some quantifiable, others more qualitative, will have to be considered before a decision is finally
taken:
  (i) Is there any uncertainty regarding the estimates used?
  (ii) What alternative machines/methods are there?
  (iii) Can the existing machine be reconditioned?
  (iv) Why does the new machine have only a four-year life?
  (v) Will there be a real need for the machine given future
       trading prospects, and technological developments?
  (vi) Has forecast inflation been reflected in cash flows?

Self-check

1 State and explain whether each of the following statements is true or false.

  (a) In discounting cash flows, present value is always
      larger than the cash flow discounted.
  (b) Depreciation is not treated as a cash flow when calcu-
      lating net present value.
  (c) Cash flows resulting from the use of all resources

engaged in an investment project should be brought into the present value calculation.

(d) Capital investment projects only differ from short-term capacity problems in relation to time.

(e) The net present value of a project is its net profit.

2 Why does taxation have to be incorporated into investment appraisal?

3 The Glendenning Hospital Board is considering the purchase of a new diagnostic machine to replace some older equipment. The new machine will cost £50,000, its useful life will be five years and it will save staff and running costs of £12,000 per annum. The old machine can be sold now for £5,000 and in five years the new machine will have a second-hand value of £3,000. Assuming an investment rate of 12% and ignoring taxation, compute whether or not the new machine should be purchased.

Present value factors at 12% are:

Year	1	2	3	4	5
	.893	.797	.712	.636	.567

ANSWERS

1 (a) False – present value is smaller than the cash flow discounted because the future worth of a present sum is greater with interest added.

(b) True – depreciation is an accounting entry only, used in the calculation of profit. It is not indicative of cash flow as the asset which it represents was probably paid for in one sum at a previous date.

(c) False – resources such as buildings might be used in an investment project. If the expenditure on them would have been incurred whether the project went ahead or not, then they are not relevant.

(d) False – that is one difference, but others include the large capital expenditure involved and the *commitment* of the firm to a major course of action.

(e) False – NPV is the surplus or deficiency arising from discounting the future *cash flows* of a project. Net profit is measured by taking account of all revenue earned in a period whether paid or not, and all the costs incurred in earning that revenue whether paid or not. Thus the two can differ substantially.

2 Taxation affects investment appraisal basically because it has an impact both on the volume and on the timing of cash flows. Taxation allowances on capital equipment can be at the rate of 100% in the year of purchase, which implies that a machine can effectively be brought into operation at a cost of 48% of its purchase price given a tax rate of 52%. On the other hand, tax will reduce the net cash flow from sales or cost savings.

3

Glendenning Hospital Board – equipment appraisal

	£	£
Capital cost of new machine	50,000	
less Sale value of old equipment	5,000	
	45,000	
less Present value of second-hand value in five years' time – £3,000 × .567	1,701	
Net present capital cost		43,299
Present value of cost savings – £12,000 × 3.605 (note: total of all individual present values)		43,260
Net present value		(39)

Having a negative NPV the machine ought not to be purchased, but this is the type of decision that will be greatly influenced by non-quantitative factors such as:

- if the quality of service is vastly improved. This is difficult to value;
- what alternative equipment doing the same function is available?
- what pressure is there on the capital budget to buy other capital assets than this equipment? It may come down to someone having to value priorities;
- if the machine is vital to the maintenance of a much-used service, then it will have to be purchased whether NPVs are positive or negative.

Extending capacity without further investment

When we were discussing the production budget in Chapter 19 it was suggested that, where machine hours limit output, overtime or shift-working could provide the additional capacity to meet demand. Indeed, it might be more sensible to adopt such measures rather than extend capacity by investing in further buildings or machinery with all their additional costs. Using existing facilities more intensively ought to be more economic.

Overtime normally refers to no more than three or four hours added to the end of a normal working day, or work completed at weekends.

In each case an additional premium payment of up to a half of the normal hourly labour rate has to be paid to those working the overtime hours. Other variable material, labour and overhead costs of production will continue, and there will be some additional fixed costs in the form of supervision, heating and lighting. Overtime has usually to be worked when additional work is intermittent, although in a number of industries it has become the norm where additional capacity is required to cope with a slightly over-full order book.

On the other hand some firms are compelled to offer overtime to attract workers who want the opportunity to add to their earnings. Whatever the reasons for working overtime, the incremental costs of doing so must pay, whether the return be in the form of additional orders or contribution from orders that would have been lost without the extra overtime.

The idea of working existing capacity more intensively is taken much further with shift-work. This also entails an extension of the normal working day, but usually by another team of employees on a more permanent basis and for longer than the average period of overtime. Hospitals would not function if staff did not work 'round the clock'. Power stations, coal mines and telecommunications all require shift-working to operate continuously.

Most manufacturing and service businesses do not have to work longer than the average working day. If they do choose to work an extra shift, the benefit must exceed the cost. There will be some additional variable and other costs, but some costs at present being incurred will not increase with the intensive working.

Activity

You are the owner of the Merrymen Chocolate Factory and, because of a large increase in orders, you are considering working two eight-hour shifts instead of the present single eight-hour day.

(a) What costs do you think will continue at the same level, even with shift working?
(b) What additional costs will be incurred?

SOLUTION

(a) These will include:
  (i) Property costs such as rent, rates, insurance and security.
  (ii) Depreciation of plant.
  (iii) General administration and selling overheads.
(b) 'Out-of-pocket' costs will include:
  (i) All variable costs of material, labour and overhead.
  (ii) Shift supervision, quality control, stores, catering, medical and other service staff costs.
  (iii) Heat, light, power, steam – the variable element only.
  (iv) An additional 'shift' premium paid to employees for working unsociable hours.
  (v) Variable selling and administration costs.

Self-check

The Phew Cosmetic PLC, a manufacturer and door-to-door distributor of a wide range of cosmetic products, had increased its turnover remarkably during the past four years. A new factory was planned to come into operation in three years' time, but it was felt that additional capacity had to be provided in the very near future, otherwise the company's growing share of the market would be lost to its competitors.

Most of its production-line staff were ladies, and it was considered impossible to obtain the necessary staff to operate a full second shift. However, there appeared to be a pool of married ladies in the district who would be glad to work on an additional evening shift of four hours.

Last year's profit and loss account showed:

	£	£
Sales		1,000,000
less Manufacturing cost:		
Direct material	250,000	
Direct labour	200,000	
Variable overhead	100,000	
Factory fixed costs	100,000	650,000
		350,000
Selling and administration cost:		
Fixed	80,000	
Variable	70,000	150,000
Net profit		200,000

It was estimated that sales would increase by £300,000 with the additional production. The relatively unskilled labour was expected to be 25% less efficient than the day workers, and they would also have to be paid a shift premium of 20% above the normal day rates. Otherwise, all variable costs would behave in the same proportion to sales as shown in the profit and loss account.

Additional supervision and other service costs will amount to £50,000.

Should Phew commence the four-hour shift?

ANSWER

			£
Forecast sales			300,000
less Manufacturing costs:			
	% of sales	£	
Direct material	25	75,000	
Direct labour	30	90,000	
Variable overhead	10	30,000	
Other incremental costs		50,000	245,000
			55,000
Selling and administration variable (7%)		21,000	
Forecast additional net revenue			34,000

Working: the direct labour cost is calculated by adding 25% to the present percentage cost of labour, for inefficiency, and a further 20% shift premium, viz:

$.20 \times 1.25 \times 1.20 = .30 \ (30\%).$

The additional shift is viable, but only just. It shows a very poor return on sales. However, it does yield a small contribution, and the operation of the shift will stave off the competition.

The big question to answer, however, is whether the additional shift will be sufficient to meet the growing demand for Phew products during the next three years.

The selling price problem

Selling price policy is at the centre of business strategic planning, and must be under constant review, to keep in tune with changing market conditions. It follows that the ultimate responsibility for pricing decisions rests with the marketing manager, who has the closest contact with, and possesses the keenest intelligence of, market behaviour.

The responsibility of the management accountant for pricing begins and ends with the provision of information, but it should be appropriate information. In Chapter 23 we saw how, in a period of under-capacity working, perhaps during a recession, a business should be prepared to accept a price for a product which just covers 'out-of-pocket' costs, plus any contribution it can get towards fixed costs and profit. Survival is probably more important than anything under these conditions. Of course, this low price policy cannot continue indefinitely, especially if it interferes with the marketing of a firm's existing output, or corrupts its general level of selling prices.

In the *long term* the aim of a business is to earn an acceptable return on the capital invested in it. To attain this aim there must be:

- a constant review of the effectiveness of capital investment, including the use of the most efficient appraisal methods, in an effort to improve the value of sales generated by each £1 of capital invested;
- a constant effort to optimize the margin between sales value and variable cost – that is, *contribution* – which itself requires decisions upon:

(i) *sales* – prices, and planned output of each product;
(ii) *costs* – product design and specification; methods of production; productivity; cost control.

Assuming that investment appraisal, production planning and cost control are efficient, it is then vitally important for the marketing manager to have pertinent information to enable him to optimize his marketing strategy, which includes the determination of selling prices. This information will come from the management accountant and should definitely include:

- the variable cost of each product;
- the amount to add to variable cost to cover fixed costs and profit;
- the selling price, cost, volume, profit characteristics of each product under current marketing policy, with forecasts of these relationships under different policy proposals.

Variable costs should present little problem in ascertainment, and their total will always represent the minimum price acceptable from customers. It is the mark-up to add to marginal cost that is more controversial.

The common approach to pricing by most firms is to calculate the 'full cost' of a product, including an amount of fixed overhead, and add a required profit margin.

For example, if the fixed overhead of a food manufacturing company totalled £500,000, and total direct labour hours forecast for next year are 500,000, then an hourly rate per hour for fixed overhead is calculated:

$$\frac{£500,000}{500,000} = £1 \text{ per hour.}$$

Further, if the company has £5 million capital invested upon which it expects a return of 20% per annum, and its total expected costs for next year are £9 million, then the addition to total product cost for profit will be:

$$\frac{1,000,000}{9,000,000} = \frac{1}{9} \text{ or } 11.11\%.$$

Applying the above recovery rates to the costs of a product:

	£ p
Variable material	1.50
Variable labour (1 hour)	1.50
Variable overhead	.50
	3.50
add Fixed overhead £1 per hour	1.00
Total cost	4.50
add Profit margin $\frac{1}{9}$	.50
Selling price	5.00

The obvious weaknesses in this method are that:

- it ignores the possibility of demand for a product varying substantially at different price levels, and
- the amount of fixed cost added will depend upon an estimate of future demand, which itself is influenced by price. A real 'chicken and egg' problem!

Information regarding sales demand at different prices is therefore far more critical to the pricing decision than 'total cost' – whatever that might be.

Activity

One of Parker Toys' products currently sells for £6. It has a variable cost of £3 and current sales demand is 5,000. Market research shows that at prices between £4 and £8 demand would be as high as 7,000 for the lower price, dropping by 1,000 for each £1 addition to the selling price.

Prepare a statement showing the contribution at each price.

Should Parker change its price?

SOLUTION

Selling price	Variable cost	Contribution	Sales demand	Total contribution
£	£	£		£
4	3	1	7,000	7,000
5	3	2	6,000	12,000
6	3	3	5,000	15,000

Selling price	Variable cost	Contribution	Sales demand	Total contribution
£	£	£		£
7	3	4	4,000	16,000
8	3	5	3,000	15,000

Parker will increase its total profit by £1,000 if it increases its price to £7. This has been brought about as follows:

	£
Loss of units sold – 1,000 at £3 (old contribution)	3,000
Gain in contribution on remaining sales – 4,000 at £1 (additional contribution)	4,000
Additional contribution	1,000

Although demand analysis is the critical pricing information, this does not imply that total cost should always be ignored in determining selling prices. For when sales demand is difficult to predict, and a firm is working to full capacity, full cost information will at least give an indication of the costs that have to be covered, if not by that product then by some other. Moreover, a full breakdown of cost into its variable and fixed elements is still needed by the marketing manager to enable him to determine that mix of products and selling prices which will opitimize total contribution.

It has also to be recognized that some contracts call for selling price to be based upon 'total cost' plus an agreed percentage for profit.

Self-check

1 'Selling price policy should aim at maximizing ....'
Which of the following completes the above statement most appropriately?

(a) total sales (d) total contribution
(b) selling prices (e) number of customers
(c) net profit (f) number of products sold

2 In what circumstances can 'full cost' be helpful in determining selling prices?

3 The Fizz Firework Company are contemplating a reduction in the price of their large selection box to £19. At present it retails at £20 and 11,800 boxes are sold. Total

cost per box is £16, including fixed costs of £2 per box. If the price was reduced, sales would increase to 15,000 boxes.

Required
Show whether the reduction in price is justified:

(a) by comparing total contribution before and after the price change;

(b) by calculating (i) what is lost by reducing price and (ii) what is gained from selling more boxes.

ANSWERS

1 (d) Total contribution.

2 'Full cost' information might be useful in setting selling prices:

(a) when a particular contract calls for selling price to be based upon 'cost plus profit';

(b) when the demand pattern for a product, for example a new one, is difficult to determine;

(c) to indicate an approximate opportunity cost, particularly if a firm is working to full capacity.

3 (a) Fixed costs are irrelevant to the analysis. Variable cost of £14 per unit is relevant:

	Per box	*Demand*	*Total contribution* £
Contribution now £20 − £14 =	£6	11,800	70,800
Contribution after price reduction £19 − £14 =	£5	15,000	75,000
Additional contribution			4,200

(b)

Loss from reducing price 11,800 × £1	=	11,800
Gain from selling more boxes (15,000 − 11,800) × £5	=	16,000
Net gain		4,200

Review

1 John Storey, who ran a double-glazing business, had asked his accountant to produce a three-year profit forecast relating to the proposed purchase of a small machine to manufacture window fittings. The cost of the machine would be £15,000. The accountant produced the following:

Year	Sales	Costs	Net profit
	£	£	£
1	16,000	12,000	4,000
2	13,000	11,000	2,000
3	10,000	10,000	nil

The costs include depreciation of £5,000 per annum.

Mr Storey noted that the average profit per annum over the three-year period was £6,000 ÷ 3 = £2,000. He related this to the £15,000 invested in the machine, and came to the conclusion that the rate of return on the whole project was:

$$\frac{2,000}{15,000} \times 100 = 13.3\%.$$

This was less than the company's minimum acceptable rate of 15%, and he therefore suggested that they should not proceed with the purchase.

The accountant then produced a discounted cash flow statement which quickly changed John Storey's mind about the profitability of the machine.

DCF factor at 15% =	Year	1	2	3
		.870	.756	.657

Required
(a) Show the workings produced by the accountant.
(b) Advise Mr Storey.

2 The Cubic Rude Company is examining the possibility of reducing the price of product A, with a view to stimulating demand for it. The following analysis is produced:

| | *Present price* | | *Proposed prices* | |
	£	£	£	£
Selling price	10	9	8.50	8
Variable cost	6	6	6	6
Contribution	4	3	2.50	2
Fixed costs	2	2	2	2
Net profit	2	1	.50	0
Demand	5,000	7,000	9,000	9,500
Net profit	£10,000	£7,000	£4,500	nil

The managing director is disappointed that the forecast does not show an increase even with the additional demand, and suggests that the present price of £10 be held.

Required
What advice would you give to the managing director?

1 (a)

Year	*Net profit*	*Add back depreciation*	*Net cash flow*	*DCF factor @ 15%*	*Present value*
	£	£	£	£	£
1	4,000	5,000	9,000	.870	7,830
2	2,000	5,000	7,000	.756	5,292
3	—	5,000	5,000	.657	3,285
					16,407
less Capital investment					15,000
Net present value					1,407

(b) After adding depreciation back to net profit, the project meets the 15% return criteria. Indeed, its NPV of £1,407 indicates that the actual rate of return is nearer to 20%. The major reasons for the difference between the profit and loss and the DCF methods of appraising the project are:
(i) adding depreciation back increases the cash flows;
(ii) because the greater proportion of cash flows are re-

ceived in the first two years, they have a relatively high present value.

2 Revised contribution statement:

	£	£	£	£
Selling prices	10	9	8.50	8
Contribution	4	3	2.50	2
Demand	5,000	7,000	9,000	9,500
Total contribution	£20,000	£21,000	£22,500	£19,000

The above analysis reveals that a reduction in price to £8.50 would increase contribution, and thus net profit, by £2,500. This appears to be the optimum selling price for product A.

The full cost statement is misleading because it assumes that the £2 fixed cost addition applies to all additional units. Relatively speaking, fixed cost *per unit* will decrease as output increases.

It is presumed that capacity is available to produce the additional quantity demanded. If capacity has to be transferred from some other product, the contribution per limiting factor on A must be shown to be higher than that currently being realized on the product to be displaced.

Index